1

A special thanks, in no particular order to Zachariah, Edward, Cyril, Austin, Gavin, Dalis, Alexandra, Nick, Kevin, George, Rigel, Yoni, Bruno, Chris L, Will, Bishop, Campaign, Devil Dogs, Armin Van Buuren, Sagar, Tu, Skyler, Alvaro, Schuyler, Biren, Jorge, Abena, Shelby, Hanif, Sir Robert Bryson Hall II (Logic), Marcus, Ryan, Amie, Monck, Ethan & The Family, Sammi, Karen, Corbin & Brian, Bobby, Grant & Elena, PBD, Kaleigh, Jeff, Dagmar, Andre, Kris, Fatima, Andi, Taghi, Serbal, Clara, Bobby Thompson, Cynthia, Vivian, all members of the justice system and J. Thanks to all of you, I have never again attempted suicide and was able to craft this work.

Based on the true story of two fraternity brothers Ace & Luthor who successfully pulled off a non-violent 6 figure ($$$,$$$) bank heist in hopes of paying off their student loans. They were later caught and one was sentenced to prison. The other fled to Europe with only $250 in his pocket and after a brief struggle, rebuilt his identity and became a multi-millionaire in the cannabis industry.

How to read this book:

Sex scenes do not occur until after page 30. Keep it in your pants. If you struggle with tens thousands of dollars in student debt, read my story. If you hate one or both of your parents for whatever reason, read this book. If you are frustrated with your sex life, or wish it was better, read on. If you had religion forced on you and it consumed thousands of hours of your life against your will, I feel you. Live vicariously through me and vent all of your anger towards the system. My frustrations started in early childhood and just like you I fought with my parents, especially about money. The story begins in my childhood and continues to the present day. Although the first half of the book might seem a bit bland, understand my life's adventure is not linear, but exponential. Problems and hatred within families often takes years to develop and lifetimes, to forget.

This will not be an easy read. It is written at roughly a 5ᵗʰ grade level, but at times I can be quite the potty mouth. Or even, 8-ball, stank hooker, vomit burn, mouth. I remember my first time in New Orleans. Yet, infused just as chocolate chips in fermenting cookie dough, you will find literary elements and some sentences that quite frankly, do not make any sense. Bitch please, I took the LSAT and scored well enough to qualify for the United States Armed Forces JAG program. Do you want to read a book that confuses the fuck out of you, or one that you actually enjoy? A majority of this book was written sober. Please read the entirety of the book and all loose strings will hopefully tie at the end. Everything in the book is connected, be patient. Read each chapter and note the quotes and when prompted listen to the soundtrack. Authors that inspired my attempt at producing a literary work include, Steinbeck, Faulkner, Vonnegut, Hemingway, Melville, Jules Verne and James Joyce. Authors who inspired me to write include Grant Cardone, Patrick Bet David, Ray Kurzweil, Dale Carnegie, David Barry, Malcolm Gladwell and Tim Allen. By no means is this book written at a difficult level, but stream of consciousness and time distortion can often be hard to follow.

I am a reflection of all those who have looked into my eyes. Drug addicts, a neurosurgeon, prostitutes, teachers, prisoners, doctors, professional athletes, bankers, convicted felons, engineers, translators, exotic dancers, pastors and clergy, programmers, organized gang members, lawyers and entrepreneurs represent only the tip of my iceberg. If you or a friend you know consumes cannabis, psychedelics, or MDMA, pass this work onto them. The use of these substances combined with my global experiences shapes my reasoning. I encourage debate over everything depicted.

The way you need to read this book is imagine that I am one of your lifelong friends. We have been through it all, we can talk about anything. When I bitch about my family, it will probably remind you of a 'scenario' that occurs in your own. I'm letting out some steam and you know exactly what I am thinking and how I feel. While reading this book, understand that the story is not over, but only beginning. Tangents may lead to nowhere, but nowhere is not the destination. We are friends until the end, get ready. Take the time to enjoy the pictures, quotes and soundtrack. Everything in my book happened. Names, dates, locations and gender might have changed, or maybe, they did not.

Do not read more than 1 chapter per day. Reading should be something that you look forward too, but you shouldn't overdo it, like dessert. As children, reading was more fun due to pictures and shorter paragraphs. This is not the type of book filled with vivid imagery, lengthy descriptions or saturated by literary elements. Use your own imagination. This book is designed to make you think, while reading only a few pages at a time. Education in the 21st century is much different than those prior. Society must embrace the technological revolution and you will find 'enhancements' throughout the book to fill in the gaps, or establish a mentality. Music, quotes and illustrations can accomplish the same as thousands of lines of text. I am not here to bore you and show you how 'sophisticated' I can appear on paper. My wish for you is to remember every line when it first appears and recall the information later in the story. Remember, all loose strings tie at the end.

When I tell you to listen to a song, you should do it. I would describe this work as an 'interactive' novel. Treat each chapter of this work as an episode in a series, hopefully consuming 15-45 minutes of your time, including the music. Every great series has music. If it takes longer than that, your reading speed has dropped and could use some improvement.

Best of luck,

Ace Thielmann Loathing

Other Works by Ace Loathing:

Beaches, Bedrooms & Barcelona: An Erotic Novel

How to Make Money Without Defrauding a Financial Institution

How I Made My First Million in the Cannabis Industry

Tau Iota Tau: Tales From Fraternity Life

Going Out of Business: The Circuit City Boys

Chapter 1

"Too many kings can ruin an army" - Homer

Intro music
"Drive" by Incubus

As my mother looked out from her front window, she noticed that I was playing in the leaves. I however, was holding an object in my hand and for the first time in my life I decided to voice my opinion. "Stick!" I proclaimed with excitement while looking to my mother for confirmation. My first word, stick, I guess you can call me a natural.

The first two years of my life I lived in the great state of Colorado. Yet, seeking to avoid the pestilence known as family, my parents decided to pack their bags and head to the hot, sweaty state of California. I do not recall any instance in Colorado during my first two years of life. I have some faint memories of our first rental in Los Angeles. The entirety of my childhood and formal education was spent sleeping the hollows of 2180 Oceanside Drive. I shared a room with my brother and we slept in the same bunk bed our entire lives. My journey begins from here.

I have always been at the top of my class, not near the top, but at the top. When I was at the top throughout grade school a few of us shared the #1 spot, but at a young age it is tough to distinguish distinct differences. At age 8 I scored a 129 on my IQ test but was one point short of being classified as "gifted". The school then asked my parents if it would be okay to place me in the gifted program, they opted yes.

Aines

Normandy, France

"Beaches, Bedrooms and Barcelona" by Ace Loathing

Starting in 4th grade, I left my original primary school and took the bus to the "Omega program" on the other side of town. After just one year in the gifted program, I excelled to the top and led the entire group of gifted students. (I guess IQ does not matter). Outside of school, everyday of my life was saturated with "our lord and savior" the man, the myth and the legend, Jesus Christ. The religion of Christianity was forced upon myself and my other siblings. Just as many of those fear the "radical" forms of Islam, I would classify my parents as "radical" Christians. Brainwashing is merely an understatement.

I digress... My mother is the daughter of both a man and woman who met in the Navy, fell in love and then gave birth to two daughters, the youngest of which was my mother. My grandmother underwent experimentation (electroshock therapy) during her time in the United States Navy, before giving birth to both my aunt and mother. Grandma always displayed signs of bipolar, schizophrenia and manic depressive disorders. To combat these disorders she went through all types of drug administrations and electroshock therapy both before and after giving birth to my mother. As it turns out, the treatments only enhanced her disorders to the point that the United States Military discharged her. My grandfather later divorced her and then never paid child support. My grandfather disappeared when my mother was young and she did not hear from him for close to a decade.

My mother then spent her whole life in orphanages, foster care and at the hands of the state. Periodically throughout her life, her mother would be cleared by the State. During these times, my mother and her sister would be in the hands of a schizophrenic maniac. My grandmother would frequently commit crime and land herself in jail, meanwhile leaving her two children at home for days, even weeks at a time without food or supervision. My mother never had a stable environment, bearing or understanding of love, connection, family, or security. Nearing the age of 16 and after suffering a lifetime of yearning she turned to the church and was "saved" from her horrible life. My mother brought it upon herself to get a job since her own mother was not reliable enough to support her.

At age 16 my mother worked at McDonald's. My aunt had already graduated high school and had a full ride scholarship to a university. Therefore at the age of 16 my mother was paying her own rent, food and clothing all while attending high school. Due to the unreliable nature of my grandmother, my mother almost failed out of high school while working full time and walking 5 miles home each day from school. From what I recall, my mother said the school bus would pick her up in the morning and take her to school, but by 3rd or 4th period she would have to go to work. She would walk to work which was several miles away and then after finishing her shift, walk nearly 5 miles home to save money more than four nights a week.

She saved money for a bike, which was quickly stolen. She paid the bills that my grandmother was unable to pay and has supported herself through everything. My mother, grew up between Colorado and California and spent a majority of her teenage years in the slums of Denver. I can understand why turning to the church seemed like such a blessing and the "answer" to her horrible life. What I do not understand is why she forced it on her children to the point that all three of them ran away from home and all three of them attempted suicide.

After graduating high school, my mother in her 20's moved back to Aspen, Colorado. A small portion of my family settled in Aspen, during the 19th Century and my mom wanted to be with the normal part of her family. She waited tables, worked miscellaneous jobs and of all places, met my father.

My father stands roughly 180 centimeters tall, sporting blue eyes, red hair and a pencil thin figure. He moved to Aspen after flunking out of university. At the age of twenty he bought a motorcycle and then decided to live where the billionaires reside. My father made friends, ran a business in Aspen with his business partner and countless celebrities know him by name. The real name of my father is Terry but in Aspen during the 80's, he was known as T-BONE. My father and his business partner ran the ONLY gas station in Aspen during the 80's.

11

My father claims to have almost killed Arnold Schwarzenegger while shoveling snow. He frequently shot the shit with Jack Nicholson and "Mr. October" was a regular, every holiday season. My father is a jack of all trades, a master of none, and a really good "bro" but not a good father. He now teaches 5th grade and just like most 5th graders, he claims to know everything. A "functioning alcoholic" he never spent time with his own 3 children. Once off the clock, he always viewed children as "work". He drank my whole life and the few times I spent with him outside of our home, I truly enjoyed. It is amazing how honest people are when they drink. I wish that he had actually wanted to spend time with us as children. This would have made my brother, sister, and I hate him exponentially less.

The only time he spent with us whilst sober, was when he made us perform excruciating amounts of construction work against our will, without pay. These were not small construction projects, we built docks, installed irrigation systems, laid tile, removed fully grown trees, poured concrete, xeriscaped a majority of our property and countless other projects. Almost all of the projects were performed illegally without acquiring permits and other paperwork from the county office. At the age of sixteen I learned that all the new additions would increase the annual property taxes. Yet, since none of them were registered, he never had to pay. To stop the slavery, I threatened my father that I would go to the county office and rat him out. He never asked me to do anything besides mow the lawn, ever again. I do not have a good relationship with my father, I never have and I never will. Parents should not neglect, abuse and steal from their children even if they verbally regret birthing them, while simultaneously donating tens of thousands of dollars every year to the church.

Back to my "gifted" expenditure. I was always at the top, first chair in band, perfect marks, citizenship award winner and all the other superfluous bullshit they present to children at the end of the year. My teachers loved me and in the classroom I received nothing but praise, I was a model student.

In my home however, it was another story. I was never rewarded for my good behavior growing up, it was always expected. My father always preached that children should be seen and not heard. Yet, we were not allowed to close the doors because the house suffered from poor circulation and my father always had an obsession with control. Since age five my father always screamed at us that we lived in "his house" and it was not "our house". Despite having three children, my parents believed that we would never have a reason to fight. Thankfully the world we lived in always separates into groups of three ever so easily.

It was simple, first come, first serve. Oh, you want an off brand pop tart? First come first serve, motherfucker! Those bad boys come in packs of 4. Window seat? Your mother. Set of two, and the list goes on and on and on. Whenever one of my siblings or I failed to achieve perfection, we were severely punished and beaten, usually to the point where it broke the skin and my father would stop only because we were bleeding. (the joys of alcohol). The main reason we were beat until we bled, was so we could 'experience' what the supposed 'Jesus Christ' figure 'experienced' as he bled and died for our sins on the cross. My father or mother would recite scripture after our beatings. On top of being 100% brainwashed by Jesus, forced to pray multiple times per day, listening to Christian music and going to church 2-5 times a week, I began to have very strange doubts in my mind about what and who to believe. I was only age 5 and whenever I would ask my parents about science they always put up the Jesus answer "you are in the world, but you are not of the world" and said that I do not need to believe what is taught in school in regards to science. I had taken a rather large liking to the stars and all I could think about was astronomy. I decided that I could continue my passion for astronomy through books at the library. My parents at an early age made me dismiss science and view it as Satanic. I was very confused about the subject of science, especially since my father taught science in his class, to all of his elementary school students. He was a 5th grade teacher for a public school, whereas I was a student in the 5th grade.

13

Hopefully by now you can imagine my dilemma. I am arguably the smartest kid in my entire county (the leader of the gifted program) but I am told to not believe and retain any of my education due to my ingrained religious indoctrination. I would consistently receive the best grades, scores and marks, but I was constantly told from scripture "you are in the world, but not of the world". Whatever I learned went in one ear and out the other. Christianity like all religions are meant to control those with weak minds and highly susceptible emotions.

The gifted program at my school also received special funding from the county including computers in the classroom and many other advantages that other children did not have access to. One activity, called "the invention convention" was an expo of fifth grade students regardless of "gifted" labeling, who each posited a dilemma and then made an invention to solve it. Most were fictional inventions and quite childish, but for those of us that actually made a decent attempt, I believe we warranted quite an impressive achievement.

At this point in my life, my grandfather was dying of amyotrophic lateral sclerosis (ALS) and confined to a wheelchair. My invention was a set of stairs that folded up into a ramp, allowing him to use his wheelchair. I made a model door frame with scraps of wood from my father, scaled down and used a few hinges, pulleys and ropes that allowed for someone in a wheelchair to turn the stairs into a ramp. Very simple I know, but it could simply lay over a step, so new construction would need to take place, keeping costs low. My father then decided to copy the "invention convention" idea and has used it every year at his school, they host it at the end of the year. He even keeps my model door frame as the original "invention" in his classroom.

My school also had the "mathlete" mathematics competition. All year long, we had a weekly contest where you took a math test. About half of the participants were from the gifted program and the others were from the general population. I won almost half of the weeks throughout the year and ended up winning the entire thing at the end of the year. Further feeding my hubris, I had a documented intelligence quotient lower than all the gifted kids in my program. Booyah.

After a grueling year of academic enlightenment, the end of year drew near. My family started attending a new church and I was becoming more and more depressed as the days went on. It was always a nightmare to go home and face my alcoholic father day after day. The constant mental and sometimes physical abuse was not pleasant. I was becoming suicidal at age 10 and I really needed help. Near the end of the year, my teacher, Ms. Moore, had all of us write down on a sheet of paper "our secret" that only she would know. We were all leaving for middle school the following year and I think she wanted something to remember us by. After we all wrote down our secrets, she called us back, one by one and read it to herself, silently. It was one of the last days of school in which she gave us a hug and said goodbye. I decided that it was time to come clean and tell her how I was feeling. I was after all, her model student, mathlete and one of, if not, the leader of the gifted Omega Program. I wrote down something along the lines, of "I hate my life, everything I do to impress my family, fails. I am a failure, I want to die" and submitted my paper.

We went back to doing some assignment and Ms. Moore started to call us back one by one. The assignment was not serious, a majority of us talked in groups. I was one of the last people called and Ms. Moore had a huge smile on her face. I meanwhile, was holding back a fountain of tears as I walked to the back of the room. She smiled, gave me a big hug, I sat down right in front of her and she opened my paper. The look of joy quickly disappeared and she gazed at me with with her mouth open and was virtually speechless. She uttered and stuttered "A.. Ac....Ace..." and repeated verbally what I wrote with a dying, whimpering, stuttering voice. It was at this point my eyes were gushing with tears and the bell rang for lunch. I said in a crying sobbing voice with tears rushing down my face "I need to use the bathroom" and walked away from Ms. Moore. Just before I closed the door, I made eye contact with Jeff (now married) and he asked if I was okay. I lied and said "yes" with tears all over my face and closed the door to the bathroom.

At the end of the year is the 5th grade graduation awards ceremony. My father, who taught 5th grade in the same county told me that he could not take off a day of work to come watch me receive my awards. At this point I was beginning to feel like an utter failure. All I ever did was succeed to be the number one in my class and try to be the model citizen and not be one of his kids that he had to "deal with" at work on a daily basis. Still to my father, I was a nothing. No matter what I did, I never made him happy, I only cost him money and he kept drinking and beating my brother, sister and I.

The next day after the awards ceremony, I came to school with a water bottle full of bleach and drank it during lunch time. (to date, the worst tasting thing I have ever put in my mouth) I had the sole intention of killing myself at age 10 because I had amounted to everything that my society asked of me, but I still had no recognition from my father. I also wrote down that I wanted to die in a note and gave it to my 5th grade teacher and she was deeply troubled for me but I could not stop crying to explain to her why.   Children   committing suicide is quite rare. Between 5-8 children annually in the United States commit suicide at age 10. You must have some serious problems, or life must really be bad for a child to rationally take their own life, as the only way out. The way I looked at it was that my 10th birthday officially made me an adult. I was finally at a double digit number, no more single digit age. 10,18,35,65 all of them were double digit numbers. In my eyes I was the same age as many adults. I was already reading books at a high school level and I understood mathematics and science beyond my level as well. Age was just a number. Being forced to go to church, being forced to pray, being forced to feel guilty for committing sins against god, being beating until my father broke our skin all the while being called "shit for brains" and "fucking retard" since I could remember, was too much.

When I was age 5 my mother cooked a horrible dinner and burned everything, my father forced us to eat it and I commented that it tasted horrible after the first bite. He made me stand up, slapped me across the face and sent me to my room without dinner. I went to bed hungry. My father does not understand the difference between punishment and torture. A punishment is something that, if performed once, causes an inconvenience, then results in a lesson learned. If this punishment is performed multiple times, it will continue to create the same level of inconvenience. Telling a child to go stand in the corner and stare at the wall for 15 minutes for example, is a form of a punishment. Torture on the other hand, when repeated, will cause sickness, injury or death. Repeatedly withholding nutrition from a child will cause them to die. Repeatedly beating a child until they bleed will also cause them to die. I do not know of any other parents who claim to be 'educated' that beat or starved their children as a form of punishment.

The bible says honor your father and mother and even though I was at the pinnacle of accomplishment from math, to science, band, role model and leader of all the "gifted" kids I still was not good enough for my father to say "good job". My younger brother, sister and I suffered from years of domestic violence, constant verbal abuse and what I like to call domestic financial abuse. Even though in the gifted program, I was constantly beaten and verbally assaulted, being called "shit for brains" and "fucking retard" by my father. I faced a constant state of enigma. All of us lived in this enigma. My sister was a natural at sports more so than both my brother and I, but she was never good enough for my father to invest some money into her pursuits. My brother received letters of invitation to recite the national anthem for public proceedings. Yet, our father mocked him and continually insulted him for wanting to pursue a career in music.

A few words about the gifted program. I entered at age 9 and exited at age 14. From 4th grade through 8th grade, I was with, roughly, the same 50 kids. Since all of us were classified as the "smartest" in the county we all had to have the same classes and basically the same curriculum. A majority, as nerds, decided to stay in concert band for all those years. The group was split roughly down the middle when it came to gender. At age 8-9 the opposite sex is not really a main focus of attention. At age 13-14, coupled with puberty, it most definitely is.

17

From my unprofessional opinion I was able to deduct the following logic that leads to the personality type that describes most of the students/friends/peers that I spent crucial years "developing" with. Because we were in the gifted program, the teachers always had more work for us to do, most of it was repetitious busy work, but at least some of it was challenging. If we weren't working, we had books to read, to continually fill our minds. We always remained focused on our school work, constantly improving our Intelligence Quotient (IQ). We never spent crucial years developing our Emotional Quotient (EQ) and learning how to interact with other people, flirt, and understand emotions. I am speaking mainly about the males in the class because I am one. Women are usually more social and have an easier time conversing.

My core group of friends at this point, consisted of Schuyler, Skyler, Silva, David, Austin, Jeff, Chaz, Deacon, Sam Reynolds and the newest of the gang Rigel. All of us played video games and that was our main source of entertainment, not girls, but video games. I, however, was not allowed to have video games at home, because my parents thought they were evil and tools of Satan. My father also made it well known, that the stupidest kids in his class, played video games and we were "stupid shit-for-brains retards" if we also had video games. Until the age of 15, the only video game experiences I had were, at the houses of my friends.

My father also did not believe that we needed a computer at home, let alone one with internet access. I failed multiple school assignments and my life was fucking miserable. I was living like it was 1960... no joke. It was 2005 and there was no computer in the house connected to the internet. People called me "Amish" in school and my parents did not understand. The real world was much different from the "Jesus land" that my parents constructed. I played cards and boards games like those in a retirement home. It was very difficult to level with those my age. Having a limited amount of access to new people in the classroom and literally growing up with the same females in the same classes, day in and day out, the "sexual feelings" that I assume normal children begin to develop at young ages, never developed with a majority of my friends, including myself. The only thing that we all discovered was masturbation. Since the girls we sat next to in class were working just as hard on their school work as we were, nobody ever flirted, and if we did, it was an utter failure and rejection that deterred us from attempting again.

At age 12 I always had two classes that would not require my full attention early in the morning. One was band, and the other, was some bullshit class that I had to choose because my school system did not have other options for the "gifted" kids. I remember one morning I was sick and went to the medicine cabinet and took the wrong type of allergy medication. My mom always said, "take two" but I was feeling extra sick that day so I decided to take 6, because I obviously was a "gifted kid" and more medicine obviously makes you feel better. Not only did I take six, I also took the wrong type, which had symptoms of drowsiness.

After about a half hour into school, I was on cloud 9. From this point, and still to this day, I do not know why I began abusing over the counter medication. I think maybe it was because I saw all the other children at school when I would change classes, interacting, kissing, and I guess "growing up" like I saw on television or movies. I desired to feel something, since I never had the opportunity to talk to girls. I also wore glasses and was classified as one of the "nerdy" kids in school. I always knew that being good to the books would pay off, but at the same I wanted to feel something and I guess over the counter medication was my temporary solution. I abused prescription drugs for almost the entirety of 7th grade until I turned 13 and discovered a new way to intoxicate myself. Alcohol.

My best friend since 1st grade, Chaz (now a bar certified attorney) decided that we should be adventurous and try this magical substance known as beer. We stole a few from his parents fridge, and we drank a few sips and decided it tasted horrible. We mixed it with Sprite, which made it taste even worse. Anyway, after getting through 1 beer each, we started to feel something. This perpetuated my abuse of substances well into my adult life. It had nothing to do with Chaz, but the fact that I discovered an entirely new way to "feel" something. When you are in middle school, there are always those times of the year when the police come and talk to you about drug use and what it does to you. They went through many different drugs from cannabis to PCP and told us all the negatives in an attempt to scare us away from using them.

I however, was an experienced user of over the counter medicine and had gotten drunk a few times, I didn't believe they were telling the truth. In 8th grade, the most attractive girl in class Ali asked me "are you going to try weed?" (meaning cannabis) while we waited for the bell to ring. For the first time in my life in a "flirtatious" manner I said "Eh, probably" (she smiled). +1 for the nerds. Drugs couldn't be that bad, I was still hesitant to try anything that was illegal, but I always knew I would experiment eventually. Jesus was always telling me no, and I always had a constant battle with religion, but I knew that I only had a few more years of appeasing my parents then it would all pass and I could do what I wanted.

Outro Music
blink-182 by blink-182 (2003 Album Version - Entire album)

Chapter 2

"Of all human powers operating on the affairs of mankind, none is greater than competition." - Henry Clay

Intro Music
Can't be touched (feat. Mr. Magic & Trouble) by Roy Jones Jr.

It was the year 2005 and FINALLY after 5 years of having the same children in the SAME classes for 6 periods a day, there were new people in almost all of my classes. I still had about half of the same kids from the OMEGA Program, but we were mixed in with others from different schools around the district. The first day of school, my emotions and everything else went haywire. Still a nerd, and trying to find my identity behind my super polite christian self, I struggled to talk to girls, let alone know what to do if they said, "hello" back to me.

The first day of 9th grade I was so excited to see new females walking around. There were sophomores, juniors and seniors, who might as well have been supermodels. All day long, I could not stop gawking at the amazing girls and I was finally beginning to think "I could get use to this". The entire day went by and I was continually impressed in each of my classes knowing that I would spend the rest of the year with these new people. My final class of the day was English, it was sixth period and I made my way to Ms. Zanno's room.

Ava

Vancouver, Canada

"Beaches, Bedrooms & Barcelona" by Ace Loathing

My mother was an English teacher at my high school. Every teacher already knew who I was at the 2000 person school. Ms. Zanno was one of her good friends, let alone her colleague, I had to be top notch at all times.

I walked into Ms. Zanno's room and I noticed that about ten people were there, all of whom are girls. There were about 35 chairs in the room and I looked at the seating chart and took my assigned seat. The girls were already talking and people were walking in every few seconds so I just took my seat and took out the syllabus. As the chairs started to fill up, I noticed that only 2 other guys were in the class, the rest were women. I think it ended up being 4 guys in the class with about 27 girls. Not a bad ratio. But just before the bell rang, I swear I felt something coming up the steps of the classroom. The door opened and I saw the most beautiful girl of my life. She walked all the way across the room and sat down as far away from me as possible. I later found out her name was Monica, and I would never forget it.

That Friday after all of my friends finished class, we met up at someones house and started playing video games, just as we did back in middle school. All of us were talking about everything we discovered at high school, the common theme was "did you see that girl _____ she was so hot!" Imagine all the nerds playing video games and not even looking at each other as these conversations ensued. We continued conversation all night, but for some reason, we all had one common factor of who was in fact the hottest. Monica.

All of us were so overwhelmed at this new experience of real social dynamics that we mainly just smiled, kept our mouths shut and observed. After all, we were still nerds that love to hit the books, perform well in school and make sure we at least had a chance of getting into the IVY leagues. After a few weeks of school we noticed that people started dating, some girls were dating in their grade, others were dating a sophomore. Monica however, happened to be dating the captain of the varsity soccer team.

The next Friday, all of us nerds are again, playing video games at someones house, still, without looking at each other and going "WHAT THE FUCK bro, why is a junior dating a freshman, are there other options for him?" "Is she really that hot?" etc. All of us then started rating the hottest girls in our classes, but understand that we still had honors classes and not regular classes. I'm not saying anything about the hottest girls in school, but they usually weren't exactly the brightest. We only had interaction with the honors girls and limited interaction with the rest of the general population. Just like middle school we suffered from the same syndrome that we faced in the Omega program. Monica was in the honors classes which made the torment even harder to swallow. After we all compiled our lists we narrowed it down to the 10 hottest girls to choose from.

It seemed almost like clockwork that as every single one of us made an attempt to talk to the 'Top 10' she was scooped up by someone older than us. I'm not sure if you know, but nerds not only have high standards for their educational experience, but also their women. I would argue that many nerds have an all or nothing mentality. If you are going to do something, why waste your time? You should really try and do things correctly the first time, every time. Brutally honest, all of us were horrible at talking to girls and it was utterly frustrating to face constant rejection. You have to understand the mentality that "being book smart, does not make you people smart" and things that come so easy for some, are the complete opposite for others. All of us started trying out for sports or finding something that we could excel at and maybe we would meet girls there.

Sam Reynolds took to football, track and field, ultimate Frisbee and eventually weightlifting. He pursued these all throughout university and is now a monster among men. He works as a computer programmer. A very calm and collected man, women view him as husband material.

Jeff started working at Circuit City and eventually hired me on to work with him. Later the company went out of business in 2009. He works in the pharmaceutical industry, has a great career and is married to a beautiful woman.

Chaz went to the opposite high school on the other side of the Harbor and took to mock trial debate team and is now a bar certified attorney in California. He had girlfriends all throughout high school and college and is dating a mamacita from Colombia right now out in Los Angeles.

Austin was always a social hermit, he played soccer for a few years, was first chair saxophone in band, ran cross country and spent a few years of high school on the Model United Nations Team. Austin had the best mom named Cynthia who really lived for her children. He lives back in our hometown.

Deacon took to the stage and started playing guitar, dancing and acting. He now lives in New York and is trying to make it in the big Apple. He went to the same school as Chaz and all of us are still friends today. He loves everybody.

Rigel was a state qualifying cross country runner, percussionist in the marching band, a highly successful member of Model United Nations debate team and even had girl friends from time to time. He now attends law school at University of California.

Skyler joined ROTC where he quickly found a girlfriend and started having sex and actually enjoying his life. His family is also incredible, a much more loving culture and virtually no christian brainwash influences on his life. He is now married and serving in the NAVY.

Schuyler started smoking weed. She acquired a job at GameStop the video game store and still smokes weed to this day. She has lots of sex and loves her life. Her mother Viv is a beautiful woman that helped us all grow up. Thank you Viv. Schuyler now lives in Germany.

Silva joined the swim team and broke some school records. He lost his father when we were younger to cancer. With the help of a new mustang and personal development, Silva, started having girlfriends in high school and university. He is now Bar Certified in California. We even dated the same woman, except years apart. Eskimo Brothers. She has a kid now. IT COULD HAVE BEEN US BRO. DODGED A BULLET.

A precursor to the Model United Nations Academic Debate Team. All over the country universities such as Harvard, Yale, and Georgetown hold conferences of up to 3000 high school students to simulate a United Nations session. Our delegation would dress up in shirt, tie and jacket and research for months, our country, their policies and the topics at hand to make sure we were the best prepared for debate. These conferences lasted anywhere from 2-5 days and ran from 8am until late at night and sometimes had surprise sessions in the early morning. Please understand that the schools I competed against from 2006-2009 were not schools from my county, district or state. They were schools from all over the world. These are also not public schools, but the top private schools and academies on planet earth.

A few examples would include the Dalton school, Horace Mann and the University of Chicago Lab school. If you didn't know, Chicago lab is where President Obama's children attended school. These are the most elite programs that money can buy. If you can also imagine, the schools that attended internationally were not public schools, but private. I met the children of the people who control the world that we live in. The prime minister of Pakistan, the CFO of Starbucks and members of congress were only a handful of the competitors I faced, well, their children at least.

My public school however, was not funded AT ALL by the state and we had to acquire the funds to attend these conferences, pay for flights, hotels, let alone hundreds of dollars for conference fees and admissions. We also had large fundraisers, but please understand that I worked almost all fundraisers, and a part time job at Circuit City to get by. I saved all of my money for Model UN because I knew in the terms of professional character development, this program was worth my time and my money.

My parents however did not understand that I was member of a team that was preparing me for University and the professional world. Our program was consistently ranked in the top 3 of all schools participating in the United States. Numerous team members attended Harvard, Georgetown, Vanderbilt, Columbia, Brown, Cornell and other prestigious Universities as a direct correlation of their performance on our Model UN team. I had very high hopes of attending a quality university. I asked my parents for money to attend a conference and they said no, which was fine, I worked a job and did numerous fundraisers. However, a majority of the parents paid for their children to attend conferences, thus giving more time for their children to study and perform well both at conferences and in the classroom. They understood that spending a relatively small amount of money would provide their children with the time necessary to gain acceptance to an Ivy League.

Basic economic principles such as opportunity cost, demand, scarcity, etc, do not ring a bell with my comparatively uneducated parents. Let me explain with a brief example.

Let's say your child is smart enough to go to Yale. Including room and board the price is roughly $66,445 annually or $265,780 for an undergraduate degree. But when you graduate you earn an average starting salary of $66,800 which increase 6.88% annually and by the end of your first decade you continually earn more than $130,000 annually. This means you would have to invest (-$265,780) the first 4 years, but you would earn $980,859 over the next 10 years. Profit = $715,079.

Let's say your child is smart enough to go to a normal State University. Including room and board this might cost around $25,000 annually or roughly $100,000 for an undergraduate degree. A big difference right? $165,780. But what about the average graduating salary? If you are lucky $55,000 with an annual increase of 3%. You would need to invest (-$100,000) the first 4 years but then you would earn $649,334 over the next 10 years. Profit = $549,334.

By the end of a 'career' the difference was more than a $1,000,000 without extra returns from investments! I tried to explain this to my parents since I was age 8. They thought I was just a kid using my imagination and this argument continued until I graduated high school. My father was always drunk and he thought I was insulting his intelligence by explaining this to him. My mother blindly agreed with my father because the bible told her so.

This was just the money to pay for school, acceptance to the school was a much different story. Acceptance into University revolved around 3 elements, grade point average & course difficulty, SAT/ACT scores and extra curricular activities. I was already in the top 8 of my 421 person class (top 1.9%) and I took more classes than anyone else, putting me in the top 2, only behind Rigel. For extra curriculars, I was a State qualifying Cross Country Athlete and a decorated award winner on the Model United Nations team, I was set to go to a great school. However, I did not have the time nor the money to pay $549 for an SAT prep class that took place on Saturday's. Rigel did not work a part time job and his family paid for the class. When we got our test scores back he only did 20 points better than me on the math, but his reading was roughly 200 points better, putting him in the percentile to go to a top university. I wonder if that class helped at all? Hmm.

The battle to get into a great university is not only between students. It is a combination of the parents helping the students (Time = Money) as they combat the other Parent/Student teams for few elite college entrance positions. I however was fighting these Parent/Student teams, by myself without the help from my family.

"In man's struggle against the world, bet on the world."

- Franz Kafka

The main reason my parents never gave me any money is because my brother sister and I were sexual mistakes. My father and mother do not understand the concept of raising children very well. When you decide to have children, or accidentally have children, your life and your life goals shift. You no longer have the freedoms that you once did, nor can you lead the lifestyle that you did while in your 20's. It took my father a few years to realize that being a father would mean that he could no longer maintain his adventurous, reckless and intoxicated lifestyle, at least not to the levels he was accustomed too. A father should take the money that he earns and invest it into the future and well being of his family.

My father bought a Porsche 911 and his wife a BMW 328i instead. Way to go dad.

When we were younger in order to reconcile his mistakes, my father decided to enroll all of us in the California Prepaid college program. After careful budgeting, my father was able to calculate that paying for this program, was the easiest way to justify that he was a great father. He never had to invest a second of his time, only a very small portion of his money. A majority of my educated friends parents participated in the program and under peer pressure so did my father. My father literally equated all of his children into his budget, so we would not slow down his life. We were given less than a dollar a day for all forms employment for his ridiculously posh lifestyle. My father spends more money on beer every day then he did, giving money for his children to advance, grow and eat lunch. I will break down the example.

Each one of us began this program when we turned age 13. My father paid a small amount every month and by the time we graduated we would have our 4 years of university education at a state school 'paid off'. My father paid that fee every month and NEVER paid for anything else. I was NEVER given money to do anything, let alone advance myself. If I needed cleats for cross country, food for lunch, clothes or shoes since I was GROWING, ANYTHING he NEVER paid for it. I worked since 2004 (age 13) and bought clothes at goodwill, as a minor. School lunch is what really made me angry. The moment I started working, I finally started to eat well and eventually moved from underweight to a normal healthy lifestyle.

Age 15-18 is not when a high school student should be buying their own food, while their father drives a Porsche 911 and owns two homes. For Christ sake, he gives over $10,000 annually to the church, but all of three of his children are underweight? Insanity.

My father literally looked at the development of his children as an "expense" that classified as the California prepaid program. I even paid for my own application fees when I applied to universities. My father is a horribly brainwashed man. I can only imagine if he actually treated his children as an investment, just as the parents of my friends did, whose children are now doctors, lawyers and high net worth individuals.

I never received physical, tangible, cash, from my father. He was so brainwashed by the church and society that he believed I was going to buy drugs with it. He said "get a job" so I did. At age 13 in 2004 I began as a referee for the YMCA for youth sporting events. This was quite a lucrative job I earned nearly $15 a game and would earn roughly $60 per week. I started saving this money along with mowing lawns in my neighborhood. Needless to say I always had very busy Saturdays. I saved roughly $200 a month for a 3 month season and I kept all of my money in the bank. I came to high school with about $500 saved.

The other main problem with Model United Nations was my advisor, let's call him J. A former US AIR FORCE Officer, J was a liberal minded and very successful citizen, father and educator. To both of my parents, including my mother who taught at the same high school as J, he was some crazy devil minded liberal that did not believe in the god almighty and was taking me away on these conferences to turn me against the will of god. One of the factors that set off both of my parents was that one of the conferences was going to be Thursday to Sunday late evening. "Will you be able to go to church? You can't miss church! Ace, this is the devil tempting you, you can't let him win!" We would fight and fight and FIGHT. Eventually I was able to attend the conference, a long hard fought road. I never thought it would be this difficult to go to a great school. I was fighting not only the parent/student teams, but my own parents as well.

This conference was at California Tech University and it was considered a big conference because they gave out individual awards. J however, had faith in me. The conference went really well, I won the first place best delegate gavel. I was also against 2 other people from my own school and my friend Schuyler won third place. Imagine that the greatest competition is not the other school, but your own! J was really happy, the team was really welcoming and understood that I was going to succeed and bring great fame to our program. I called my parents after I won first place and they were upset that I missed church. I made the argument, "Would you punish me for joining a sports team and I won first place?" It is tough to reason with people that believe the earth was created in 6 days. I was not punished for attending the conference, but tensions were always high and I constantly fought with my parents and I still do until this day. Organized religion is a plague that dooms this earth.

I remember that J had so much faith in me after meeting me only a few times, that he decided to pay out of his own teachers salary, my first conference as a freshmen. It was roughly 150 bucks, but at the time I had barely $500 to my name, I was greatly thankful and really surprised. I went to the conference and I learned from the one of the best seniors on the team, Kristen. She showed me how to debate, work the room, write resolutions, and develop the professional skills necessary to become literally, a world class delegate. Kristen was the older sister of one of my classmates, Lindsey. Kristen and Lindsey both had a mother, not just any mom, a MILF. She was the manager of cosmetics at Dillard's and always looked like a supermodel. Lindsey, whom I had known since 4th grade, never really stuck out as being an uber attractive classmate, but all of that went away when I discovered her sister, Kristen. To put it lightly, Kristen was a Hooters Girl. Literally, she worked at Hooters. She was 18, getting ready to graduate, been on the Model UN team for years and had everything down to an art. Not only was she academically intimidating, she was sexually intimidating and that combination was pretty hard to beat. She won many first place gavels and is in our hall of fame.

J thought that I should shadow her and have her teach me all her tricks since it was her last conference and my first. Remember, I'm still a NERD, beyond nerd, I've never even seen a woman like her before. Not only was she gorgeous, but she was wearing a suit and acting super sophisticated and debating difficult topics. A NERD GRAND SLAM. I was in heaven.

My first conference, was a very small setting, maybe 15 people the entire time and I had plenty of opportunities to begin

practicing my speeches. The next few days I had the chance to learn from one of the best in the business and Kristen always performed. Now, I must say, it was quite difficult to not gawk at her beauty let alone watch her go from 0-100 since she was a champion at many large conferences across the United States. This was a small conference in the state of California and her last as a senior. She had a small case of senioritis and was not going 100%. The last day of the conference we had a break to enjoy the evening and we all went to the movies. We watched V for Vendetta. Please remember that my ignorant christian mentality was against seeing such a movie, Kristen even sat next to me in the theater, it was the closest thing to a girlfriend that I had ever had. I was 15 years old and had never been to an R rated movie, it was quite the experience. I felt like a badass. Kristen sat on my right mainly because she asked to switched seats, her ex, Scott, sat on my left with other members of the team.

Kristen was a million times hotter than Monica, mainly because she was older, fully developed and was not afraid of anyone, mentally or physically. The rest of the conference, Kristen fell sick and I followed her around like a little pet trying to take care of her. It was awesome, even though I was doing everything wrong she was still talking to me, apparently being genuinely honest is attractive. Lets just say the few days I spent with Kristen, coupled with the fact that I did not have to attend church and the fact that I discovered a new passion in the area of global debate manifested itself into a "spiritual experience", Model UN had me hooked.

We watched V for vendetta and I was very naive and did not really understand it at all. It was also really hard to focus with a beautiful woman on my right. We all went back home on the bus and had roughly two months of school left until the summer began. One of the weeks following the conference, Kristen was in the lunchroom and pulled aside Rigel and told him "If Ace wasn't a freshman, I would be dating him" still until this day, I am not sure why this happened. Maybe she was disappointed with one of her current boyfriends or realized that there was something special about me. I will never know, we have not spoken in years. Rigel immediately told all of us the following Friday night. All of us were taken back and to be honest, I think we labeled her as crazy.

Thank you Kristen for everything you taught me, you are not crazy and I hope life is rewarding you with many blessings.

I finished out my first year of high school as a physical failure. Academically I found my place within the Model United

Nations team, but sports were not my strong point. I was an utter failure at Track and Field. Remember Monica? She was a freshman on the varsity women's soccer team and was also on the varsity Track and Field team. The district meet was approaching and my school had won the district meet the year prior, needless to say there was hype. Rigel and I were both on the track team, but were not the best. When the time came for the district meet, only certain people got to attend, those who were best in their respective events. Rigel and I were not good compared to the upperclassmen, but we were characters on the team and everyone cheered us on.

Since my mother taught at the high school everyone knew who I was and the upperclassmen all liked my mother as a teacher so they respected me in turn. The head coach filled up all the slots for the district meet but he had a few empty slots for events that I had never trained for, the triple jump and 300m hurdles. With one week left until the district meet, Rigel and I began training for these events without prior experience. Coach Coffer wanted us at the meet and said that we were a part of the team. We were delighted to go. Our performance was quite the spectacle, we were both so slow at the triple jump that when we ran and gained speed, it was not enough to make us land into the sand and we were disqualified. With most track meets, they have prelims and finals. Rigel and I along with one other guy had our own heat in the 300m hurdles because we had documented times that were so slow, they couldn't put us with other racers. Going back to Monica, she was quick and was also in the 300m hurdles, but actually competing at the district meet. When Rigel and I finished the race, we looked up and saw our times. Monica beat both of us. Not only were we unable to attract or talk to women in school, the hottest girl in our grade beat us in a foot race. Monica 1 - Nerds 0.

My sophomore year began and I mainly spent the summer running cross country preparing for fall season. I was really beginning to like cross country, Rigel had run it the year before and it was a smaller team so we were able to create more of a brotherhood.

Now comes a comical chapter of my sophomore year, the first race of the cross country season. I was in pretty good shape, I ran the first half of the race really well, but then I hurt my leg and bitched out the rest of the way and had to walk the last mile. I was currently the third best guy on the team and only the top 5 placed. I felt that I had finally found my new sport, the injury put me back a few weeks, but I still had a good season. As I walked the last mile, I saw two of my teammates run past me, but Rigel should have been ahead of them. I screamed "Where is Rigel?" and one of them said "Rigel shit his pants!" I was a little puzzled by what he meant, and thought nothing of it. About 4 min later Rigel came running by and had a lot of mud in shorts, but at the end of the race, I found out it was not mud. One of my best friends had actually shit his pants in the middle of a cross country race.

I have always been a practical joker, but I was also in pain from my leg and was not really in a joking mood. I had an extra pair of underwear and shorts in my bag and I extended them to Rigel so he could have something clean to wear. I remember everyone else on the team laughing at him, but you should only laugh with your friends, not at them. The worst part about all of this were Rigel's parents. Rigel comes from a somewhat wealthy family lineage, but more importantly a very high academic lineage, his grandfather, mother, and father are all doctors that attended medical schools in the United States. His mother was currently a pathologist and was able to take off a day of work to come and watch Rigel in this first race of the season. Rigel's father did not work but was a medical genius nonetheless. While Rigel was changing in the bathroom, I experienced for the first time in my life the personal side of his mother. As she thanked me for helping out Rigel, she had a look of confusion, and the universal WHAT THE F^%! look that we all face from time to time. While sitting on a picnic bench she said something I will never forget "well... I guess this is when the shit hits the fan" And to this day, we joke about what happened.

While all of this was going on, the junior varsity race was underway. We had two members on the team that were not there because they were athletes but because their best friends were on the varsity team. I now introduce Curly and Trevor. Trevor did the morning announcements and everyone in school loved him. He was a short fat Jewish kid that understood how to make everyone laugh. He ran cross country because his main group of friends were a year older than us and were on the varsity team with Rigel and I. Then there was Curly, he had a slight physical deformity and could not run efficiently, a typical class clown and character nonetheless. Both Curly and Trevor had a battle every time to not be the last to finish. Now, I do not mean the last to finish for the team, well, that would be obvious, they were always competing to not be the last out of ALL the schools which was usually the case.

The race was almost over, but the two of them were still not done. The officials were taking down the clock and packing up everything and Trevor and Curly were nowhere in sight. The varsity team decided to go looking for them and bring them in. The 5km course went through a few small rivers and bridges and we assumed that a few of them were lost in the trails. As all of us ran to the edge of the river, we heard something approaching from the other side. One of us yells out "Curly is that you!?!?" and through the bushes we heard "Yep". Trevor beat curly that race only because curly had gotten lost. He ran the wrong way up the river. I guess you could say he was up shit creek.

Whenever someone set a new personal record (PR) we always celebrated. Trevor was the only person in Cross Country history to set a PR every race, the entire season. Our junior year, we were really strong on the varsity team and we had just won the county race.

Since it was a smaller race they ran the JV and Varsity at the same time. Trevor was coming up to the finish line about set a new PR for himself by several minutes. As he crossed the finish line, we took one of the large Gatorade coolers of ice water and dumped it on his head, just as they do to coaches. The local newspaper captured the shot and he made the newspaper! The slowest runner in the race made the paper and as a team, we could not have been more excited. When the sports section interviewed him, and asked why he did not play other sports he said something along the lines of "football

36

was too easy" even out of breath he was still the comedic genius. He also worked at Fantastic Franks and one time, he had to swipe a credit card for a woman and her children. Her last name was Stifler, just like in American Pie. Trevor met Stifler's mom.

After winning the county meet the team went on to tackle the district meet and hopefully move on to the regional qualifier. I was not the fastest on the team and we struggled to produce a solid 5 guys with competitive times. We had a really good top 4, but the final 3, including myself, were significantly slower than the others. The scores were based on the top 5 guys and we were always lacking that 5th guy to make the significant difference. The district race came around and our top 4 killed it so we were allowed to move onto the regional meet, something we had failed to do the year prior.

We all kept training for the regional meet and the day of the race, I had a horrible race. I started feeling tired and ran two minutes slower than I ever had before and thankfully the other guys on the team picked up the slack and we still qualified for the state meet. As a member of the cross country team I was not as popular as the football players, the basketballers, the soccer team, none of them, but I was much more successful which I guess is what mattered to me the most. I was amazed that after only a year of training and two summers of work, I was going to represent my school in the California State championships. A state larger than many countries and I could say that my team ranked among the best. I thought to myself "I will surely get a girlfriend after all this," which didn't happen, but there was always the dream.

A year prior when my team lost the district race, we all went home with a feeling of defeat and I remember going to my room and taking out a piece of paper and writing "next year, states" and left it on my dresser so I saw it every single day. The next year, we went to the state meet and I recorded the quickest race of my life, even placing 4th on the team.

Between running cross country, participating in Model UN, working at Circuit City, studying for school, attending church twice a week, and dealing with my brainwashed christian parents, I was always busy, even suicidal. Every year

37

for Model UN we attended the same conference in California, and that is when I met my newest of friends, Scott. He was eldest son of a powerful attorney in our city. He began drinking, smoking cigarettes and using drugs at a young age. Even those with all the riches in the world still handled their stress with substances.

On the opposite side of that mentality, Scott was nice, friendly polite and quite sophisticated. He will remain my friend until the end of time. The first time I went to California Tech and won first place, Scott and I and a few others left the hotel to go and get groceries from a market a few blocks away. Being a brainwashed christian kid, I saw nothing wrong with it, since I was learning from my elders. We went and got some groceries and came back, and I didn't have to eat at restaurants since I couldn't afford it. Scott was always so giving and I cannot thank him enough for teaching me many things that helped developed my character. I never had a big brother, but Scott was a few years older than me and use to sleep with Kristen rouse, who was older than him! I am still impressed until this day. He always told me I was smart and he was a super wealthy and highly successful academic so it was nice to have support from someone from another walk of life that I could trust, instead of being brainwashed by my parents who called me names and labeled me as an idiot.

The next year at the conference, Scott went off to college and I was now a junior. The first night, I rounded up a group of people that wanted to go to the grocery store, and about 13 of us went out into the city, at night. If you can imagine the nightmare for J, he was the advisor of the most successful project to ever emerge from our school. California Tech was the biggest conference because the entire team attended. Model UN was almost as popular as football. The MUN team was about 50 people. In the evening, I took about 13 children out of the hotel, for an "evening stroll" to go get some groceries. It took about an hour and a half and we came back without any problems. The only problem however was that one of the new members of the team went and told everyone what we were doing and the next morning at breakfast all of us were in the deepest of trouble.

J took all of us aside before the conference and gave us a stern lecture, before he finished I stepped forward and said "All of this is my doing, let everyone else go, I was the man behind the madness" J really respected me after this and that evening after conference sessions we had a very long talk. He asked me what I was thinking and I really did not have an answer. Deep down I really did not feel as though I had done anything wrong, but the child inside of me quickly hushed. The night before the conference, J lost a close friend of his. His friend was leaning back in a chair and fell over, knocked his head and died instantly. The next day, J had to embark with 50 kids with whom he was responsible for and hope to god that nothing would happen. Not even 24 hours later, I walked out of the hotel with 12 of his responsibilities, without telling anyone. I am surprised he did not have a heart attack.

Rewind back a few months to may of that year, the team voted to attend Mcgill University conference in Montreal, Canada the upcoming fall. I was already emerging as one of the key players on the team, J told me that I needed to buy a passport so I could attend the conference in the fall. I paid the money and had my passport made over the summer to be ready for the fall. As J and I talked in the hotel lobby he asked me what would happen if he told my parents what occurred in California. I assumed that they would kick me off the team and possibly even withdraw me from his world history course that I was currently in. He looked at me with a serious glare along with hint of sympathy and empathy. After a few seconds he said

"It's going to cost you Montreal, but you need to be here, deal with your parents and tell them that you need a break and that Montreal was too much on your plate."

I was expecting to be kicked off the team, and have the course of my life changed forever, but the grace, discernment, wisdom and to be honest, fatherly nature of J allowed me to continue.

Back to cross country. Leading up to the state meet, they finally announced when it was. Rigel was also highly successful at MUN and was going to Montreal. But, the

Conference in Montreal was also the same day as the State Meet for Cross Country. If you can imagine, both J and my cross country coach were not happy. Rigel told our coach that he had too much invested in Model United Nations and could not run in the state meet. Rigel ran the race of his life for the regional meet and ended up giving us enough points to attend the state meet. It is amazing how much mental motivation can really lead to success. Any great runner will tell you mind over body, every time.

I was not able to attend Montreal as my punishment, someone had to be that 4th runner on the team of 5 for cross country and I rose to the occasion. After running horribly weeks prior, all of us stayed in a hotel the night before the meet and we said that if we made it to states that we would all shave our heads. I am always a man of my word so one of the other team members, said he would cut my hair. He had never cut hair before in his life and gave me the worst haircut I ever experienced. Fucking prick. He also had long blonde hair and bailed on shaving it off. Only two of us shaved our heads, the rest were cowards. When we got to the race course it was an old horse track with huge sloping hills, something that we were not used to. It was also freezing cold, roughly 40 F when the race started. I had never run a race like that before in my life and with so much motivation it was hard to not feel 100%. BANG. The gun went off and I start at my pace, most people flew past me. I knew that I would finish in the last half of the pack but I did not imagine that I would be this slow. All I could think about was Rigel in Montreal going to the conference that I could not attend, while simultaneously running the race he could not.

I kept thinking back to the time we both ran the hurdles a few years ago and lost to Monica and now after years of training, a few nerds had amounted to a greater physical accomplishment than any other athletes in our school. No other sports team went to the state meet that year with the exception of a few female weightlifters. I was a nerd at the top of a physical accomplishment running the greatest race of my life in freezing cold weather with someone over a thousand miles away doing something that I equally wanted to enjoy.

40

The first mile came by at 5:58! Too fast, but I kept on going and by the time the two mile mark came around I slowed down to 12:22. I needed to pick up the pace for the last 1.15 miles. I chased down every person that was in front of me to the point of utter exhaustion and I ended up finishing 145/190. I had already let the MUN team down, I could not do the same with cross country. With Rigel as my motivation I finished 4th on our team, I could not let him down like that. Not only did I finish 4th for the team, which, I had never done before, I also set my best PR of 18:53 for a 5k. I ran the greatest race of my life and finally proved to myself that if you put your mind to it, you can do anything.

As they announced the awards for the Montreal Conference, Rigel was Awarded a first place gavel. The school who wins the conference receives a helmet worn by a UN peacekeeping troop. My school has multiple helmets, enough that we constructed a pyramid.

Chapter 3

"If you're not cheating, you're not trying" - Eddie Guerrero

Intro Music

"Scotty Doesn't Know" by Lustra

Scott had a car and I was not even old enough for my learners permit. One of the seniors on the MUN team, Olivia, invited me to a Christmas party. There was alcohol at the party, and it was hosted by some University students home for the winter break. Olivia picked me up dressed to the 9's and I wore jeans and t-shirt. At the party I barely drank anything, I was hesitant as to what could happen. I played beer pong for the first time, but did not really remember the party all too well. Scott showed up at the party already a little messed up and I told him that I was drunk and if I went home my parents might kill me. As the party died down, he said I could crash at his place. I hesitated about getting into a car with a drunk driver because this is not what my parents had taught me. I mustered up the courage and decided to go with Scott back to his house. His house however, was on the other side of town almost to another city. I thought we were never going to get there.

We arrived to a gate at the end of a street and I noticed very few houses around. Scott beeped us in and the gate opened to a gravel road. I soon learned that this gate was his driveway.

"Here we are on Cochran lane,"

We drove across his estate and in the distance appeared an enormous house.

"Welcome home" Scott said.

We walked up to his room, I crashed on his floor and we woke up the following morning to his father, nurturing mother and 3 younger siblings along with numerous pets. What a loving home. After breakfast he decided to drive me another 30 minutes back to my house. I was super scared coming home because Scott smoked cigarettes and my family would instantly notice. Cigarettes were not something that god would not approve of.

The end of the year for my 16th birthday I was getting a little sentimental and I was talking to Scott about the frustrations of my family. I was forced to attend church, they never bought me necessary things like lunch or clothing and that I was never going to attract girls if I was this loser. Note, this is my sophomore year, the year my team lost at districts and did not advance to states in cross country. I told Scott that I tried to kill myself when I was younger and that I was really thinking about it again because I hated going home to my brainwashed parents and their ideology that was ruining my life. Scott told me "don't ever say that again, you are not going to kill yourself, you are going to smoke some weed and never think like that again."

That year on April 20th, 420, I smoked weed for the first time and did not think about suicide until after college. I was really happy and since then I am a supporter of cannabis consumption. I turned into a stoner in college, but while in high school, we still burned like timber. After Ali in 8th grade asked me "are you going to try weed?" I could finally answer her and say "yeah". After Scott left, Schuyler and I burned down the house junior and especially senior year. I was a secret stoner, smoking weed was more fun than drinking alcohol and you didn't feel like shit the next day.

My junior year of high school was the most stressful year of my life. When you apply to college early, senior year, the only thing that matters are your grades leading up to that point. I and many other individuals understood that the junior year was the deal breaker. We put everything on our plates and had to make it the best year of our lives. I will try and do my best to give you a Monday to Sunday schedule.

Monday:
7:30 Wake up
8:15 School Starts
15:05 School ends
15:15 XC practice
17:30 XC ends
18:15 Work at Circuit City
22:30 End work and drive home
22:45 Arrive home, eat
23:30 Sleep

Tuesday:
5:00 Wake up
5:15 Drive to Cross Country Practice
5:45 XC Practice
7:30 Shower and eat at school
8:15 Class Starts
15:05 School ends
15:15 MUN Conference Prep
19:00 MUN ends
18:15 I leave MUN early for work
18:30 Work
22:30 End work drive home
23:00 Arrive home eat
23:30 Sleep

Wednesday
7:30 Wake up
8:15 School Starts
15:05 School ends
15:15 XC practice
17:30 XC ends
18:15 Work at Circuit City
22:30 End work and drive home

22:45 Arrive home, eat
23:30 Sleep

Thursday
5:00 Wake up
5:15 Drive to XC Practice
5:45 XC Practice
7:30 Shower and eat at school
8:15 Class Starts
15:05 School ends
15:15 MUN Conference Prep
19:00 MUN ends
18:15 I leave MUN early for work
18:30 Work
22:30 End work drive home
23:00 Arrive home eat
23:30 Sleep

Friday
7:30 Wake up
8:15 School Starts
15:05 School ends
15:15 XC practice
17:30 XC ends
18:15 Work at Circuit City (Not during the cross country season)
22:30 End work and drive home
23:00 Arrive home, eat
23:30 Sleep

Saturday
05:00 Wake up
05:15 Drive to school
05:30 Get on the bus and go to XC meets
08:00 Run meet
12:00 Finish meet
12:30 Get on bus and come home

14:00 Arrive back at school, drive home
14:30 Arrive home, shower and get ready for work
15:00 Drive to work
15:30 Work at circuit city
22:30 Finish work
22:45 Drive home
23:15 Arrive home, eat
23:45 Sleep

Sunday
7:30 Wake up
8:00 Drive to church (my church was two cities away)
9:15 Church Starts
11:00 Church ends
11:15 Sunday school starts
13:00 Sunday school ends
13:15 Drive to some christian potluck with people I did not know
16:00 Finish potluck
16:15 Drive home
17:00 Arrive home
17:15 Prepare for the next week, school, chores, etc.
20:00 Sleep

Repeat.

This was my first semester of junior year. Some mornings I had to arrive early to school for meetings, whether it was Honor Society, a special meeting we had for MUN, or I had to meet with a teacher to make up an assignment that I missed because I was traveling on MUN trips. I am pretty sure I was the only student kicked out of honor society because of attendance. Ever. I remember the teacher in charge of the program delivering me a letter from the "National Honor Society" with letterhead and everything. *** fart noise ***

Please understand that MUN was a serious endeavor. I would miss anywhere from 10-15 days per semester and be completely absent from the classroom. More likely than not, I would be in another state, completely engulfed in debates, molding the world we all share. I could care less about what was going on in the classroom. I was never there and I was still getting really good grades so I did not care. When you are at the top you feel like no one can challenge you. I have learned multiple times from hubris and I have a feeling hubris will haunt me until the end of my days.

I took as many advanced placement courses as possible, no fun electives and worked and worked and worked. I also continually fought with my parents because they believed that model UN was the work of the devil and that me missing school or church was Satan and his plan to corrupt my perfect upbringing. I was super stressed and on Friday nights before cross country races, I would smoke weed to relax. This habit grew exponentially more common by my senior year.

A final curveball to completely change the course of my life forever, took place the second semester of my junior year. All great students have a secret, some study hard, some work in groups, while others, CHEAT. Yes, I will openly admit that I cheated, starting from 8th grade up through senior year and even through university. I'm not talking about peeking over and copying exam answers, that was only necessary for random occasions. I am talking about entire classes. I had chosen my junior year to enroll in a series of online classes even though I had no computer at home. My plan was to do the classes during my free time, or during other classes when I had access to a computer. I was busy taking all of my Advanced Placement classes (AP) or Dual University enrollment courses during school hours and knew it would be a challenge.

Simple math.

6 periods in a day each worth 1 credit and one period was a double period so it counted as 2. At the end of the year you earned 7 credits. You needed 24 credits to graduate and most graduated with 24-28 credits, a few classes were

electives. I was not trying to be average. I wanted to go to Yale, or somewhere big and I knew that if I worked hard enough all of it would pay off. I saw students grades ahead of me work really hard and get into big schools I thought I was destined for greatness, but boy was I wrong.

I graduated with 31 or 32 credits. I do not remember. If you do the math, I took almost an entire year extra, of school. The only person in my class to attempt more credits than me was Rigel and he had 33. But he also had a computer... at home... which is kind of necessary to take online classes.

I went to the students before me and asked them for their answers to the assignments. The only class I was having a real problem with was honors physics. I never had time to learn the lessons and when I copied and pasted some answers from a fellow student's work, even though it was years later, the online class caught me. I had never been good with computers, but I guess that I slipped up so bad that they determined me a cheater for the rest of my life. There were many of us cheating and swapping answers, unfortunately I was the only one who got caught.

The entire University system blackballed me. I was instantly placed on a list of cheaters and it was sent to every university in the United States. Needless to say, my life was ruined. Every college application has a box that you check if you are labeled as a cheater and I had to fill in this box. This is very similar to the felony box on a job application. My online virtual teachers called my parents and said that they were removing me from the course and I got a big fat (double) FF for my file.

Instead of letting my future college acceptance be punishment enough, my parents went a step further. After I raised over $400 to attend a MUN conference and paid that money to the team, my parents came to a meeting (the only meeting they ever attended) and told J and the other team members that I was a cheater and should be ashamed of myself. This is 5 days before the conference which I had prepared months for, let alone spent hundreds of hard earned dollars on.

My parents then said "Ace will not be attending the conference, he needs to learn from his mistakes".

I had to give my spot to one of my teammates. He studied for 5 days and ended up getting a second place Outstanding Delegate Award. Great work Jon. I am very mad at my parents because getting kicked out of the class was already punishment enough. I had an FF on my record and I know what I did was wrong, but they had to once again, be radical. They forced me to let my team down. National titles were at stake along with the reputation of my high school, my parents could care less. I do not think anyone listened to the rules more than my parents. Are you not supposed to help your kids get into college, grow up and succeed? Everyone makes mistakes, but to further damage a teenagers chance of getting into a good University, is utter madness. They also took the my car keys almost costing me to lose my job. Brainwashed Christian Alcoholics.

My sophomore year of high school when I was on the MUN team I had to do countless fundraisers, mow lawns and whatever side jobs I could to earn enough money to stay on the team. My father meanwhile was having a midlife crisis. He bought a Porsche 911 and my mother a BMW328i. He never paid for our school lunches, bought us clothes that fit, or helped us advance in school. He drove a fucking Porsche while his children were malnourished and underweight, just to prove to us that we were mistakes. He also made it clear that once we turned 18 we were no longer welcome in his home.

Do not think for a second my parents did not have money. Teachers do not make astronomical amounts of money, but they have a lot of time off while making upwards of $95,000 combined salary every year. My parents paid off their 20 year mortgage in 7 years. When I was around 13 years old they owned their first home. Depending on the year, my father always owned more than 1 car, sometimes as many as 6. Along with cars, he owned multiple boats and had loads of savings. My father controlled all of the income earned by himself and his wife.

His children were "justified" by the $200 he paid to the California prepaid college program every month from age 13-

17. Great job dad, you invested $12,000 in each of your children and look how they turned out. You sold your Porsche for more than that. You and your wife earned $95,000 dollars a year since I was 13. Why was I not worth the $70 application fee to a University? I could only afford to apply to 3 schools when all the applications where due, further limiting my chances to attend University.

Let's do a little math. Excuse the variables, I will try and make this as simple as possible.

(TIME = the total number of years my brother sister and I were in the Prepaid college program. 5 years for me and then 4 more years for my brother and sister to complete the program total of 9)

TIME = 9 years
COLLEGE = 3 kids * $12,000 = $36,000
SALARY = $95,000
MORTGAGE = $0
TITHE = $10,000
EARNINGS = SALARY * TIME = $855,000
CHURCH = TITHE * TIME = $90,000
COLLEGE/EARNINGS = 4.2% = 1.4% PER CHILD
CHURCH/EARNINGS = 10.5%

My father invested a total of 1.4% of our household income on my development.

If you cut it in half, because my mother earned half the money, I am not even worth 1% to my father.

He gave over 10% of our household income to the church, without question.

"It's my money, not your money, why do I need to spend it on you?" - My Father

You should want to spend money on your children because you love them and you want them to succeed in whatever they love. A $500 SAT course is actually worth millions. I moved on Dad, but I will never forget. Keep driving those fast cars, but be careful, they might kill you one day.

When I attended an MUN conference against the richest aristocrats in our society, I was wearing a $7 suit that was second hand from Goodwill that I paid for, myself. It was all the much sweeter to win a conference, Harvard for example, after taking a flight and staying in a hotel that I paid for, myself. Hate for your parents, that serves as motivation is not healthy, nor necessary. As the icing on the cake and continual neglect of his children, my final year of high school, my father, dropped $50,000 on a second home, the likes of which, I have never even seen.

Outro Music

"That was a crazy game of Poker" by O.A.R.

Chapter 4

"A lion runs the fastest when he is hungry." - Salman Khan

Intro Music

"Go" by blink-182

The summer between my sophomore and junior year, my family decided to take a "vacation" for nearly 35 days. If you can imagine, my frugal parents, made vacation even worse than living at home. My father thought it would be a great idea to purchase a pop-up camper. We were going camping, which is fine, but my parents were often too scared to let us go off by ourselves, even when at the campsite. It was mainly my family crammed into an SUV for thousands and thousands of miles. My father used this opportunity to visit properties that he considered purchasing. It was a real estate trip.

Since we were not allowed to have technology, my brother sister and I brought books with us. My parents however, always listed to music, which made reading extremely difficult. Most of the time we decided to look out the window at the interstate. This pattern repeated for thousands and thousands of miles. My parents bought the pop-up camper in horrible moldy condition. My brother, sister and I cleaned, resurfaced and repaired the inside, which took several weeks during our summer vacation. My father wanted to buy it cheap, fix it, use it and then sell it. Hopefully the difference would end up making the entire vacation free, for him and his wife. We were paid nothing for countless weeks of work. It was a great idea, but exploiting your children and requiring them to do labor on something that they will not gain any monetary value from, is horrible. Again, why would I would ever be paid for work, I am expected to "honor my father and mother" just as the bible says.

We either cleaned the camper, or my father beat us until we cleaned the camper. I found it strange that my father physically abused his children until they were age 15. I assume it was his way of displaying dominance. One of our stops on this "vacation" was Washington DC. After a couple of days in Washington, I was so fed up (no pun intended) with my father that I wanted to kill him. We would walk around DC all day in the summer heat but he would not buy us food. He always said, "We will have a big supper tonight when we get home" and always in a high pitched toddler accent. We would walk miles every day and only drink water. One day when my father went into his fanny pack, he pulled out almonds and snacks for HIMSELF. When we asked him for some he replied "you will be fine, just wait until supper" My father literally viewed his children as prisoners, I was just another "shit for brains" student that he taught in class all day and he assigned me a number like I was sitting in a cell.

We walked all morning and all afternoon and after several hours of complaining, my father finally caved and bought us lunch, as if it was a new concept. He paid a few dollars for something all of us could share and puffed out air like a child as he placed it down on the table. For whatever reason (maybe it was the christian brainwashing, attempted suicides, or the fact that my father did not believe his children needed food) I finally snapped.

I backed away from the table and started screaming "Fuck you Dad you don't want to feed your family, we have been walking all day in the heat". At this point I had attracted a rather large presence and people were watching this malnourished white family have problems in the middle of the Washington Mall. I then looked around at the people watching me as I screamed "This man beats me, he beats my brother, and my sister!" I then turned around and ran away.

Remember how I was training for the state finals in cross country? I could run miles and miles without stopping, let alone at a decent pace, there was no way they were going to catch me. As I ran I remember hearing footsteps and voices screaming "Ace come back! stop Ace!" but I just kept running towards capital hill. I kept running behind the capital until I knew that no one was chasing after me. I had just turned 16 years old a month prior. This happened on Sunday and for the first time in my life I was free.

Absolutely free.

I had no obligations, no one to tell me what to do. I decided to start walking around and check out DC for myself. I had no money, no cell phone, and quite frankly my dear, I didn't give a damn.

I began wandering around and trying to find food, I was very shy and a little scared and I always had problems talking to people, just to make conversation. I was good to the books and they were always good to me. I wandered around for a while and since I was use to not eating all day, I was perfectly fine. My mind and eyes were searching for ways to start my new life. I thought about going to fraternity houses because college kids were always open minded (at least that's what I saw on television). I found a map of the city and started heading into the Georgetown University area. After walking around awhile and realizing that everything was closing early due to Sunday I mustered up some courage to talk to a few girls that were studying the MCAT in a coffee shop. I went up and talked to these college girls, and I honestly think that was the smartest thing I ever did in my life. I interrupted their studying and quickly explained my situation and said that my family was not feeding me and I was always getting beat and I had to run away from home. They were really amazed and they told me a few hostels to stay at, but because it was Sunday, everything was closed.

I have always been really hard on myself and some point during the conversation, I said

"I don't want to stay with you or for you to get in trouble"

I would assume these girls would have taken care of me for a while, but they did something else that changed my life forever. One of the girls said that just a few streets away there was a Starbucks that's open 24 hours and she knew one of the baristas. They drew me a map of how to get to Starbucks and I walked away almost in tears by the generosity of complete strangers.

Walking down the block I heard "HEY YOU!" I didn't turn around because I didn't think it was for me. Then again a little closer this time I heard "hey you!" I turned around and one of the girls ran after me and said "hey, I forgot your name, sorry, but you said you didn't have any money, so, here" and she handed me a $20 bill. I told her thank you and wished her the best of luck on becoming a doctor.

I put the $20 in my pocket and was in tears and just so thankful for the blessing that life was giving me. I once heard a saying that "god helps those who help themselves" and for once I was helping myself and not serving a god that made my life miserable. I made it to Starbucks talked to the person working and took a nap on the couch. This only lasted for a few hours until a security guard came and woke me up saying that I had to go outside or she would call the police. I was however, able to take lots of free food from Starbucks. Apparently they throw out all food and make it fresh daily. I had sandwiches, parfaits and all types of food. I think it was my first time ever eating Starbucks.

After a full stomach, I again, began wandering around. I had 20 dollars in my pocket and figured out I might as well see the sights. I headed over towards the White House, which was on my to do list. I'm strolling, drinking free water from somewhere and as I turned the corner, a man on a bicycle stopped me and says "don't move!" then two more appear men out of nowhere and said "freeze!" To be honest, I almost shit my pants, but thankfully I had not eaten much and had nothing to shit out. The police officers then held out a photocopy of my driving license blown up on an 8.5×11 sheet of printer paper. They said, "Are you Ace Loathing?" I responded as a jackass and said "ya caught me". They then responded by saying I needed to wait in this area for my parents to come get me and I needed to talk to some other officers.

I noticed that the police looked a little different, and all of them had ear pieces and were not wearing cop uniforms. I asked who was arresting/detaining me and one of them answered "We are the secret service, your proximity to the white house, makes you our jurisdiction" I stood up a little straighter and thought "holy shit I am being arrested by the secret service... COOL!" obviously not cool, but again, an interesting story. I was detained on the corner of Pennsylvania and 17th right next to the White House. I was so close but never even saw the damn building. How un-American.

I waited for close to an hour only wondering what was going to happen to me. I quickly remembered that I knew someone attending Georgetown, a former MUN team member. When a very intimidating officer started questioning me the who/what/when/where/why of the situation. I said I went and spent the night with a friend that attended University here in DC.

I've always been more scared of my parents than the police. You can ask anybody that comes from poverty and they will tell you the same damn thing. I told the officer while holding back tears of fear "I went and stayed with a friend, he attends university here"

"Which one, What is his name?" the officer asked

"Does it matter? He is not involved in the case" I said with confidence as tears built behind my eyes.

"Did you tell your parents? were you planning on telling your parents? ..."

At this point my father emerges from his SUV looking pale as a ghost and hugs me. I stood there and did not hug back. I was disappointed that I was caught. Afterwards the officer asked for my SSN# and then let my father and I go. The ride back to the campsite was rather silent.

After arriving I saw my siblings pale as ghosts and my mother looked like she aged a few years. I was exhausted and slept the rest of the day. The next few days I didn't really remember, my family was pretty quiet and they tried to explain what had happened while I was away, but they were so hurt and afraid for my life that it was difficult for them to communicate.

Apparently after I had left, my parents took my brother and sister and waited until sundown exactly from where I had left. They sat on a park bench because they thought I was coming back. My father told me later, that he learned in all of his child psychology classes that whenever a child runs away you are supposed to stay where you are because the child eventually becomes afraid and returns the point of origin. I was not scared. I was happy that Jesus was not ruining my life anymore and could care less about what happened to me.

Once it became dark my parents called the police. Apparently it took 5-6 hours of not having their son, for my parents to call the police. One would think, that they would want to call immediately after I ran away to isolate the situation. I could run upwards of 7 miles an hour and was a varsity cross country athlete. I was even training every day, at our campground, running in the mountains!

Whatever.

I honestly think it was because my parents are brainwashed into believing that they were always right and that their solutions would always come true. Apparently my mother started praying that I would return. Its funny that it took the secret service to track me down when "the god above" could not find me. Remember how the secret service men held out a photocopy of my driving license? Apparently when a child runs away in Washington DC they become a top security threat to the entire national capital. Here is why. If a child runs away and somehow, someway, ends up dead on vacation, Washington never hears the end of it. The national capital will be splattered with headlines such as "children not safe in Washington" "Young boy, murdered in national capital" and tourism will literally suffer by millions or potentially billions of dollars.

In the best interest of my parents and the economy, the authorities had to find me and make sure I was returned safely to my parents. The first thing the FBI asked my parents for was my cell phone number. My father told them that I was not allowed to have one. They said that this was not good. Apparently what the FBI does is Geo locate you based on your cell phone. Remember this is the year 2007 and I did not have a phone. It was pretty crazy, they also told my parents that if I had a phone they could turn it on via satellite if I had it turned off and then find me. Edward Snowden would have been proud of what I had discovered.

The government has a great amount of power. Privacy is meaningless. I used my mothers phone a few days a week during cross country practice and it had a few numbers of my friends in it as well. The police went through the entire phone and asked about each number. They asked if I had a girlfriend and even called the few friends I had in my phone to ask personal details about me. I remembered that they called Chaz and he had a conversation with the F.B.I. This next part is the real kicker to show how fucked up my family is. My father had my wallet, which had my driving license and a few other miscellaneous things. He was so possessive about items that we were not allowed to hold our own wallets on vacation. He did not trust us in public spaces with items of value. I was 16 years old at this point and he would not let me hold my own wallet in public when I was with him.

They asked my parents for a photo so they could send an image out to all the police of every department in the area and find me. My mother had her purse, and my father his wallet and fanny pack. Neither one of them had a photo of any of their children. The only photo of me available, was my driving license. How embarrassing is that? Parents that don't even have a recent photo of their children. They really could care less about us. If I would have had my wallet with me when I ran away, who knows where I would be right now. The police would be looking for a white teenage male. They cannot stop every white teenage male and ask to see his identification, I might have actually gotten away.

My father decided to keep in contact with the officers and stay inside the city, but the FBI drove my mother, brother and sister back to the campsite in a large black SUV like you see in the movies. They were crying the whole time thinking I was going to die. Apparently the police eventually found some video of me at the train station and started to trace me, but since I did not have a cell phone, they had no idea where I was. They still had people on the street, it was only a matter of time before I was found. The secret service found me the next morning and returned me to my parents. I did not even make it a full 24 hours on my own. I guess I made it a bit easier for them since I walked in front of the white house. [insert a very boring summer full of chores and strict punishments, no car, no traveling anywhere] I then began my junior year of school as posted above.

At the end of my sophomore year, my MUN advisor J, was also the one who organized the euro trip for the school and had been doing so for the last decade. The trip this year, was Spain, Italy, Greece and Turkey. J is a very well traveled man and gets paid to travel by different companies, one of which called EF (education first) tours.

He only had trips every two years so it gave people enough time to prepare and this trip would take place the summer before my senior year. I asked my parents if I could go since I had already begun the process to apply for my passport for the Montreal trip. They said no. I asked for a reason and they said "When you are 18 you can do what you want, until then we are your parents and we know what is best for you". I was infuriated, thankfully Scott introduced me to cannabis and all was well after that. I continued to work at Circuit City while almost all of my friends spent a month in Europe. They bought me back a flask filled with absinthe and gave it to me as a present my senior year. Thanks everybody that chipped in for that. Good times, with good people. The first time I ever left the country, was coming to Spain. 6 years later in 2013

I was an ass to my family. But I never meant to hurt my brother nor my sister and quite frankly, not even my mother. Humans only do as they are taught which is why we have so many problems on the earth today. It is one thing to look and defend your own argument, but another to confuse opinion with facts. Being an ass gets you nowhere.

Chapter 5

"The art of acceptance is the art of making someone who has just done you a small favor wish that he might have done you a greater one." - Martin Luther King Jr.

Since I would file my college applications during the first months of school, I knew I could take it easy and actually enjoy my senior year of high school. I opted for OJT (on the job training) for the last classes of the day. It allowed students who have jobs, to leave school early because they had to go to work. All we had to do was bring in our pay stubs and we could leave the last few periods of the day. After getting caught cheating, my motivation to perform well in school, evaporated.

My super crazy busy life came to a screeching halt. I finished school everyday at 1pm instead of 3pm. I had time to relax, goof off, and hopefully work towards something I had never attempted before, a girlfriend. I still ran XC and I still did model UN but I did not stress about school as compared to years prior. It was the greatest year of my life. I finally started dating a girl that ran XC with me. My sister was also on the XC team and helped me out. It did not happen until after the season, but I finally landed my first girlfriend, Brittany.

It was not until February my senior year that I had a girlfriend, let alone kissed a girl. I was 17 and just beginning to learn emotional intelligence. Brittany was smart, sometimes. She took honors classes and one AP class. When it boiled down to taking tests, she was not the best. Her body made up for every missed test question. Blonde. Tall. Curvy and constantly playing soccer. I wasn't complaining.

Now, I do not mean this in any negative way at all, but compared to my "Jesus Land" conservative upbringing, Brittany was wild. I lost my virginity in the backseat of my

Saturn sedan. I had this car through college and sold it before coming to Europe. It will always and forever be named after my first girlfriend Brittany. Brittany also had a crazy ex-boyfriend and fucked him while I was away on MUN trips. I learned this years later. The first time we had sex, I didn't wear a condom and I came inside her. This is also right around my 18th birthday as I was graduating my senior year.

For about 6 weeks, she did not have her period and I thought I was going to become a father. This was also around the time of AP examinations. Of all possible dates! She called me one night as I was away on grad night trip in San Diego and she told me that the tests came back negative and we were not having a baby. #alwayswearacondom. We stayed together through the summer, but I was laid off by Circuit City in March and since I was 17 years old I was not eligible for unemployment. I spent a lot of time and money on her before I went off to University. We separated only weeks into my University experience. I never looked back. Silva ended up having a relationship with her a few years later. Eskimo brothers. After I saw all the new women walking around campus, I realized that the world had plenty to offer. Brittany came and visited a few times and we finally had undisturbed sex in my dorm room.

Remember how I was caught cheating? Every school I applied to put me on the waiting list. All of my other friends had applied to college and were accepted, but I wasn't going anywhere. My entire life was ruined and I felt sick and weak for about two months. In the same week that Circuit city filed bankruptcy, I also received my final letter of rejection from my dream school the University of California. After learning that I was going to lose my job and I was not accepted into a university, my mind began to unravel.

I went and smoked weed for about 5 days straight. I showed up late for everything, school, work and was literally falling apart. This was also the time I was trying to get Brittany to be my girlfriend. A few more days went by and I checked my admissions status at the University of Southern California, they changed my admission status from "pending" to "accepted" and my heart filled with joy. I immediately went to the school website and paid all the admissions deposits and copied the receipts, in case my 'accepted' status was a mistake. The end of the same week, I asked Brittany to be my girlfriend and she said yes. My life went from 0 to 100, real quick. I started working out and gaining a bit of muscle after I got laid off. I always knew that if I could get one girl to like me, then I could definitely get more girls to like me if I had muscles. (What horrible logic)

Leah

Innsbruck, Austria

"Beaches, Bedrooms and Barcelona" by Ace Loathing

I moved into my dorm room with one of my best friends at the time, Austin. Complete opposites, extrovert and introvert, we were a great match and enjoyed living together. We were both the same omega nerds we always were, but I really wanted to get out and explore the university. I joined a fraternity and he stayed in the dorm room. I didn't just join any fraternity, I joined Tau Iota Tau or TIT for short. This was also the fraternity that my father was in and when I told him about it, he said I should give it a shot. It changed my life forever. TIT was an Alpha Male group, but compared to the guys in it, I was a nerdy young man with comparably poor social skills.

Recruitment season was tough, you were invited to the first night and if they liked you, they ask you back for the following nights. This was also the year following the economic crisis of 08. They accepted almost everyone my year, the economy was that bad.

The first night was a night of hanging out at the house, getting to know the guys and watching some sporting events. I connected with a few people and they invited me back for the second night which was speed dating with sorority women. I was always a confident speaker, but when it came to talking with girls, I was always nervous. The hottest girls in greek life sat in a room with clipboards and asked us strange questions. I went around the room and at the end of the night, I thought I was going to get kicked out. No respect from my father and no fraternity life. Turns out, all the girls liked me, I was very professional and very well spoken so I guess all those years of MUN paid off. The brothers invited me to the traditions dinner and then later gave me a bid to join.

Most fraternities had an 8 week pledge process. You are a bitch, they make fun of you, treat you like a slave and then haze you for a weekend and allow you into the fraternity. Mine was similar, but instead of lasting 8 weeks, it lasts two semesters. TIT was the largest fraternity on campus, it had the student body vice president, football players, conductor of the marching band and many student leaders in both medicine and law. We didn't fuck around. We had the highest GPA of all fraternities on campus and still threw huge crazy parties. There a was a reputation to maintain.

64

I worked like a slave the whole time and was elected to the executive board while still in my pledge process. There were 7 exec members and I was one of them as a pledge. After we finished the final weekend of hazing, I was selected to go through 2nd out of 9 even though I thought I deserved to go first. My big brother in the fraternity was the student body vice president and he said that there was a reason I went through second. I think it's because he wanted to teach me that now matter how hard you work, you do not always deserve what you think you deserve. Take failure with a grain of salt and always know that you can improve and do better next time. This has always motivated me to keep trying. The words smart and liar remain separated by a very thin line.

The next year, I opted to be in charge of the frat house since it was on campus and this meant that I got to live inside for free. Some of the brothers nominated me to be the president of the fraternity, but I denied, fear got the best of me. I am glad that I did not become the president because my life would be much different than it is today. Living in a fraternity house is quite the experience, National Lampoon's Animal house was no exaggeration. I was stressed beyond belief and could face expulsion from school because underage drinking was occurring at the house and I was responsible.

I started smoking a lot of weed and I used my money from my scholarships to pay for my alcohol and cannabis habits. I was resorting back to my 8th grade days because I wanted to feel something. I tried talking with girls, but the girls in greek never found me to be the macho figure that the other guys were. Having a lack of self confidence and big lack of sexual experience made me feel insecure. I still felt guilty every time I thought about sex and my christian brainwashing was still present. Was there a god? Was I sinning? All I know is that I was always feeling guilty and confused and I wanted to have sex, but could not figure it out.

I finally broke free from this chain once coming to Europe and I will forever despise the church for brainwashing me into believing that natural instincts such as sexual behavior are wrong and that eternal death is the ultimate sin for going against the ways of god. After going through the final hazing

65

ceremony my nickname given to me by my big brother was El Cristo, or "The Christ" in Portuguese.

After living in a Fraternity house for two summers and two regular semesters, I was burned out. I was only 19 years old and I was responsible for an entire Fraternity. A single case of underage drinking in the house would result in termination of my job and the possibility of expulsion, from university.

Almost no one understood the dire consequences of what would happen if someone was caught underage drinking, or even worse, if someone needed medical assistance because they consumed too much at a party. The consequence was that the fraternity was kicked off campus and we would no longer have a house. The house is the heart and soul of the fraternity. Where do you have your meetings? Rituals? Parties? Socializing? EVERYTHING?

I was in charge and the older and younger people in the fraternity simply would not listen, including the current president. Those ignorant fucking hypocrites did not understand the laws of the University. My JOB was to understand the laws and make sure we stayed out of trouble, which we did, the entire time I was in charge of the house. We never had an issue with the police. Yet, because of the hierarchy within the fraternity, they thought that their little 'executive board' was the law. You stupid fucks should be grateful that I lied every day at work, to my boss, University Officials and sometimes even the Police just so a few of you could drink underage. Children.

God knows, how many hundreds, even thousands of people I met over the those summers and semesters. To get caught smoking weed in the house, legally, would result in the individual member being removed from campus housing, but the fraternity was safe from expulsion. Yet, If any individual was caught underage drinking on the premises, legally, the entire fraternity was kicked off campus and house was lost.

Only the stoners of the fraternity understood this concept. 3 of which, were my closest friends. James Monroe, Gibrarian and Luthor. With the exception of the other stoners, many of the others were idiots and didn't understand that some illegalities outweighed others. They in fact, believed the opposite and thought that underage drinking was a less punishable crime. James and Gibrarian are both model citizens, James is now bar certified in two states and Gibrarian is in the middle of his residency. I am happy to say I invested my time with both of them. Confucius once said "Life's rewards are good friends and great conversation".

Gibrarian, James and I consumed an earthly amount of cannabis, quite frequently. Gibrarian was the bank, providing everything and was beyond giving. James was very similar to me, aspirations for law school, long distance runner, came from a middle class family and always worked really hard. These guys are both very intelligent and had better opportunities in High school because they were offered International Baccalaureate (IB) instead of Advanced Placement tests. Out of the three of us, we all had our strengths, mine was public speaking, James was longevity and Gibrarian, was the doctor. We shared many adventures, one of which occurred every few weeks, acquiring cannabis.

Back in the days of illegal weed consumption, you always had to find the best dealers, price and overall, the safest bang for your buck. James was always super scared and quite frankly, offered money and never wanted to go, all with perfect sane logical reasoning. Gibrarian, had the blanket of wealth to cover him. His reasoning, while driving a BMW, dressing somewhat business casual and living in a rich neighborhood made him virtually invisible to the police. Needless to say, we always used the BMW to go and "pick up". I was the oddball. I had already been arrested for underage drinking at a tailgate (2010) which started my weed smoking phase. My sense of adventure always took over and I was never scared.

After being in the fraternity, a new pledge class arrived and one of the newest members was named Luthor. To gain entrance into the fraternity we held interviews, but these were not normal interviews. The 'interviewers' were usually intoxicated but still wearing suits. You were however, completely sober and had to answer very strange questions while trying to be professional. I remember my interview. The three gentleman all had on business attire and we began the interview. I sat in a chair roughly 10 feet away from the table at which they were all sitting. We began with the basic questions, aspirations for University, familiarity with Greek Life, etc. But then, one member stood up and walked towards the trophy case to begin his soliloquy about TIT's reputation. It was then I realized that he was not wearing pants, but only Santa Claus boxers, accompanied by black socks and brown dress shoes. Nearly a minute passed and he returned to his seat. The interview died from there and at the end they asked me if I had any questions. I had none and I walked across the room to the table to shake all of their hands. While shaking the hand of the brother only wearing underwear, I said "You know, black socks with brown shoes is bad luck". All 4 of us smirked at the comment and I left the interview feeling confident.

If they could think quickly and wisely on their feet we wanted them to become a part of our brotherhood. Luthor grew up in a military family and was well traveled. Most of his teenage years he lived in Los Angeles and was half African and half Caucasian. He always smoked weed and because of a security guard wanting to toot his horn at the age of 13, he was arrested for a petty crime. One thing led to another and eventually, he was selling coke with a gun at age 15.

"Open Fire" by Tupac Shakur

He bought a car and had $7,000 in his pocket at all times, while carrying a TEC-9. He was by all means a career criminal and after being caught with many different substances, he ended up going to juvy. If you do not understand, juvy is where they send kids who have committed adult crimes if they are under the age of 18. Luthor applied to USC at age 17 and ended up getting caught and sent to juvy while his application was processed. He was admitted to the University of Southern California even though he was a career criminal before the age of 18.

Inside juvy, it is exactly the same as prison. Once inside, you had the baddest of the bad swapping stories, learning strategies and literally making a school for the criminal masterminds that the world faces today. After attending juvy he then wanted to get his life together and have a fresh start at the University. He enrolled in the college of engineering and began going to school. His third year of school, a fellow fraternity member brought him in for an interview and he came clean. He told us about his criminal history, he use to be addicted to coke, and all of his other questionable habits. He said "I'm trying to change" and Luthor, to my knowledge has never committed a crime that was against another person, only against property, or sold drugs. I will defend him to the grave as a person, that society has warped into being evil, but at the core, is someone who is just as good/bad as everybody else.

We felt the genuine honesty of Luthor was worth giving him a shot into the fraternity, he worked his ass off and was a leader. With all that being said, Luthor liked to consume drugs, a weak point in his character. He was very smart, and had an electrical engineering degree, but at the end of the day, he continued to do drugs, drive drunk, sell drugs and eventually with the help of a certain someone, land himself in prison. When I had trouble finding a place to live between the fraternity house and my new apartment, I lived with Luthor for a few days. Those who had a hustler/coming up spirit, connected within the fraternity. Luthor and I always had a connection.

Anyway, after 2 years in the fraternity, I finally quit and took more of a loner path. I realized that I needed to get my life together, stop smoking weed and get away from rich assholes that did not understand the law. They were making me stressed beyond belief. I moved into a studio apartment, a 15 minute drive away from campus. It was in a horrible neighborhood with lots of crime. Within the first two weeks of living there, my mailbox was broken into. On Christmas week, a few people with loaded shotguns, killed the postman and stole the van with all the presents inside. My apartment always had cockroaches and I never brought a woman back there because I was too embarrassed.

I went from having a private suite in a fraternity house, to a rough studio apartment. I worked 20-30 hours per week and went to school full time. drive over an hour everyday to get to and from work at 5:15 in the morning. I also decided that this was the final year that I would try and get into law school. I didn't have the best of grades because I was partying so much and never went to class. I went to military recruiting stations and decided to join the US MARINE CORPS reserve. My recruiter told me that I could join the reserves for 2 years, go off to boot camp during the summer and then when I graduated university apply for officer candidate school (OCS) and join the JAG (Judge Advocate General) Program.

Starting in October. I began the busiest school year of my life. I will break it down into 2 semesters. My Junior Year of University was very similar to my Junior year of High School, very stressful. A few key factors that people really do not understand is how fucking difficult my life was my junior year and I never asked for help, my parents were not there to give me any money so I was always kicking my own ass and once you land in a negative mindset, it is quite easy to stay that way.

1. I lived by myself in a studio apartment
2. I had no laptop or computer or smartphone (2011)
3. I could not afford internet at my studio apartment
4. I had to drive over an hour, almost every day between work and school. (time lost)
5. I had to cook all my own meals, could not afford to eat out. Ever.
6. I am still very shy when it comes to personal relationships and did not confide with any friends until later the following year. I had no sexual activity during this time.
7. James and Gibrarian were still in the fraternity, but were in their senior year of school and I had left the fraternity to get away from all the people I could not stand. I had virtually no friends.
8. I still felt guilty about topics such as sex and having a girlfriend, It has always been difficult for me to completely forget my deeply ingrained christian dogma.

Here was my schedule Fall semester. The following numbers below represent the limits of my schedule. Understand, during the late evenings, I often sacrificed hours in the Library for hours asleep in the bed that my parents miraculously brought me. I moved the few things I had into my new apartment in a horrible neighborhood. I was there one, and only one, night and had even budgeted my time and money to purchase a bed the next day via Craigslist. My parents showed up out of nowhere. I really do not remember the event that well, a strange turn of events. Apparently the church was having a yard sale and my parents bought a bunch of things for a very cheap price. They called me and said they were coming up tomorrow, we found some things for cheap to get you started. They brought me a bed, table, chairs and some kitchen amenities.

I was grateful. After neglecting me for over two years while I supported myself at University. I guess $100 worth of furniture was fair, while they drove sports cars and owned multiple homes. Thank you for giving me something to get me started.

Monday:
4:30 Wake up - Shower - Cook Breakfast
5:00 Drive to work (15 Min No traffic)
5:30 Start work - Catering Business
11:30 Load vehicles and drive to Catering Location
13:00 Finish work and drive to School - Go to Library and Use Computer - No computer at home
15:30 Class Starts - Small break - Library - LSAT Prep
18:30 Evening Class
21:45 Evening Class finished - Library until exhaustion
23:00 Drive home
23:15 Arrive home and cook Dinner
00:00 Sleep

Tuesday
4:30 Wake up - Shower - Cook Breakfast
5:00 Drive to work (15 Min No traffic)
5:30 Start work Catering Business
11:30 Load vehicles and drive to Catering Location
13:00 Finish work and drive to School - Go to Library and Use Computer - No computer at home
16:30 Class Ends - Drive to Poolee US MARINE CORPS Physical Training

19:30 Finish Poolee training - Drive Poverty Poole's Home (recruits that did not have cars)
20:30 Arrive Home - Shower - Cook - Drive to Library to use computer - LSAT Prep
23:00 Drive home from school
23:15 Arrive home and Sleep

Wednesday
4:30 Wake up - Shower - Cook Breakfast
5:00 Drive to work (15 Min No traffic)
5:30 Start work Catering Business
11:30 Load vehicles and drive to Catering Location
13:00 Finish work and drive to School - Go to Library and Use Computer - No computer at home
15:30 Class Starts - Small break - Library - LSAT prep
18:30 Evening Class
21:45 Evening Class finished - Library until exhaustion - LSAT Prep
23:00 Drive home
23:15 Arrive home and cook Dinner
00:00 Sleep

Thursday
4:30 Wake up - Shower - Cook Breakfast
5:00 Drive to work (15 Min No traffic)
5:30 Start work Catering Business
11:30 Load vehicles and drive to Catering Location
13:00 Finish work and drive to School - Go to Library and Use Computer - No computer at home
16:30 Class Ends - Drive to Poolee US MARINE CORPS Physical Training
19:30 Finish Poolee training - Drive Poverty Poole's Home (recruits that did not have cars)
20:30 Arrive Home - Shower - Cook - Drive to Library to use computer - LSAT Prep

23:00 Drive home from school
23:15 Arrive home and Sleep

Friday (Sometimes no work, I would sleep in)
4:30 Wake up - Shower - Cook Breakfast
5:00 Drive to work (15 Min No traffic)
5:30 Start work Catering Business
11:30 Load vehicles and drive to Catering Location
13:00 Laundry - Library - Possibly take a nap
18:30 Class Starts
21:45 Class Ends
22:00 Drive home
22:30 Cook - Sleep

Saturday
6:30 Wake up - Eat - Hydrate
7:15 US MARINE CORP POOLEE PHYSICAL FITNESS
10:30 Finish - Drive Poverty Marines Home
11:30 Arrive at home
12:00 Combination - Attend Home Football Game - Library - FULL LSAT - Visit Friends
20:00 - Library - Eat - Relax
22:00 Sleep - Party - University Related Fun

Sunday
Sleep in
15:00 - Library - Full LSAT - CHORES - Laundry
22:00 Sleep

Lather, Rinse, Repeat.
GPA with 16 Credit hours. Above 3.0
Thankfully I had the weekends free to catch up on sleep. I was averaging 5 hours or less, 4-5 nights a week. It was a tough schedule, but Spring was even more difficult.

Chapter 6

"Our only real hope for democracy is that we get the money out of politics entirely and establish a system of publicly funded elections." - Noam Chomsky

"Sleep Now in the Fire" by Rage Against the Machine

Watch the Music Video

A prelude to my spring semester. After learning that the Student Body president was a paid position, I made plans to run for office my junior year. The student body president is paid roughly $15,000 and gets a seat on the board of directors of the University. A seat on the Board of Directors means that a student, roughly the age of 20 gets to help manage and direct a multi Billion Dollar University System. USC is worth roughly $1.5 billion with an annual economic impact of $3.7 billion. In the fraternity, my mentor Bruno was the student body vice president during my freshman year.

Bruno, was a charismatic man from Brazil and the son of a very wealthy man who started from nothing and turned into a success story. He is by all means a very influential figure in my life and I respect him greatly for the lessons and few experiences we shared. He was a ladies man, and quite charismatic. He also ran for student body vice president with a large financial backing from his father. In my opinion, he was aware of the wealth of his family, but did not realize the extent, power and ultimately the influence that money can have on every aspect of the human experience. In politics, usually the candidate that spends the most money, wins. Unfortunately for me, I ran in the most difficult race in USC campaign history with the smallest budget, using my own personal funds. Let me break down how the campaign worked for many, many years at USC.

My election was year 2012. In 2011 two candidates ran against each other, one of which was running for the second time and stayed in school an extra year and had his parents pay for everything so he could win because he was aware of how powerful the position of student body president really was. He was also in the same fraternity as I was and I always had a good time partying with him. He came from wealth and one time, I was outside the frat house and he had to do a naked lap because somebody beat him at beer pong and I saw him run through the neighborhood holding his balls looking like a monkey. Good times. The same individual went behind my back and talked shit about me to the other individuals in the fraternity when I ran for student body president. A majority of people booed him and he eventually separated from the fraternity. Talk shit, get split.

In 2012 when I ran, it was not 1 or 2 people running against each other, but 6. It was Obama's re-election year and I guess everybody had the fever.

I no longer had the support of the fraternity, I was literally on my own. A man from my high school named Elias attended USC with me. We hardly ever hung out in high school, but we smoked a lot of weed together in college and are still good friends to this day. I prefer the personality types of stoners to those that consume alcohol. Both prove themselves to be entertaining, but the ones that consumed cannabis always made me think and in my opinion, those are the friends that you should keep. I ran the idea by Elias that he should be the student Vice President and go in with me on the campaign. He had no idea the bearing that I was placing on the event and he had a girlfriend, with whom he had been dating for about 5 years. One day Elias called me up and said, "let's run" and the underdog story began.

Our strategy was a little bit different than others, since we had a very small budget $1500 we tried to break down how we were going to get the attention of 50,000 people on campus in just 2 weeks time. The rules of the campaign were very strict and we could only campaign on certain days. We had lots of rules, so many rules that quite frankly it ruined my campaign strategy because I wanted to expose the corruption of the school and show how the University President Trudy Ballshaft was wasting school money and stealing from her own students. My original Platform went as follows:

#1 Build a Football Stadium

USC was the 9th largest University in the United States and did not have a football stadium. We lived in the same City as the Los Angeles Rams so we rented their stadium on Saturdays and played inside. However, the stadium is more than 20 minutes away by car and you have to pay $15 to park. Another large factor was that a majority of undergraduate students were not 21 years old. Since they could not consume alcohol legally, they would have to sneak alcohol into the parking areas and "tailgate" illegally. City, County and State Undercover police officers walked around and found reasons to arrest and quite frankly RUIN the lives of young, educated adults that wanted to consume a beer.

In 2010, I was arrested for Underage Drinking. Fuck DA Police! Students were afraid of getting caught and it deterred them from attending. They would also have to buy food, or buy things to cook and leave the comfort of their apartments or dorm rooms to consume food. Most large college campuses have a stadium, directly on the campus. Students tailgate and party on campus, the campus police tolerate underage drinking and do not go around arresting people. They realize that these are the future leaders of society and are there to make sure no one gets in fights or incites riots.

Most students at other large universities lived within walking distance of the stadium. They could easily wander over to the stadium drunk, and go home, drunk, without any fear of a DUI. My proposal was to knock down the GREEK Village (High Liability Cash crop for the University) and build a Stadium in Its place. This would all be done over a plan of 15 years, raising funds for the stadium and allowing the greek system to raise money through their alumni associations to build proper Greek houses off campus and not have them live in dorms that were under strict regulation from the University policies. This would also give them the chance to have greek systems like other Universities all over the United States.

#2 Campus Parking

USC is a commuter campus and almost everyone had a car. USC is one mile, by 1.5 mile plot in a city grid system. It's huge. Traffic and parking whether coming or going from campus was always a nightmare. Students are always on a budget so they can only afford certain types of luxuries. At my school we had the "S" pass and the "Y" pass. The "S" pass was for STUDENT parking. Most people bought this pass and all over campus there were several floors of parking garages dedicated to students. At the busiest times of the day, every parking space was occupied. There were however, random parking lots with small allocations of "S" passes all over campus but in areas literally a mile away from your class. This led to many problems across campus. A brief example.

Class starts at 1:45. You have work afterwards, therefore, you must drive to class. Most students had jobs. You live 10 min away from campus by car, with traffic you should budget 15 min. The nearest garage is 200 meters away from your classroom. You should budget 20 minutes in total to account for driving and walking. Upon arrival to campus you cannot find a parking space. You drive to the next closest garage and it's also full. Class starts in 5 minutes and you are still in your car, you finally snag a spot but it's on the OTHER side of campus, 1200 meters away from your classroom. You are now 5 min late to class with 1200m to go. You decide to hop on the 'Trojan Horse' a shuttle, provided by the university, that takes you around campus. The shuttle only comes every 12 minutes. Congrats, you just missed the shuttle because you had to run all the way from your car across the massive parking garage and down 3 flights of stairs. You arrive roughly 20 min late to your 80 min class. Depending teacher, some would lock the door when class starts and you, therefore miss the class because you were not there on time.

I chose the "Y" pass because it was only valid on the far side of campus and it was the cheapest pass available. Almost everyone at school called the Y pass the "Poverty Pass" Real shit. With the Y pass you were almost guaranteed a place to park, but you were on the far east side of campus, separated by a forest and all of the athletic stadiums, parking lots and practice facilities. It was a good 600 meters before you arrived at any significant classroom. I chose the pass because I did not have the money, but I had the time. The bull runner came by every 10-15 minutes and It would take about 7 minutes once I was on the bull runner to get to my classroom or the library. I was a long way from class and at night I would have to walk back because it would stop running, but at least I wouldn't be late to class. Good thing it only cost $105 per year.

The last option for students presuming they didn't live on campus was the FU1 pass also known as "golden zone". This pass was literally twice as expensive as the S pass and I think 4 times as much as a Y pass. $400 dollars a year. I forget the exact numbers but students on a budget that are already scraping by to make ends meet cannot afford this pass. Another thing that made this pass even worse is that they didn't really advertise it, people didn't understand what they would get. the FU1 pass was for the first two levels of all parking garages so you could pull right up and park, it was pretty much VIP parking.

Violet

Perth, Australia

"Beaches, Bedrooms & Barcelona" by Ace Loathing

The office of transportation on campus has a certain number of spaces and sold parking permits based upon availability. Legally and technically, they under and oversold the passes because they wanted the money. The University had their own police, parking facilities, they could do whatever they wanted. Universities literally are their own universe. Since no one wanted to, or could, pay twice as much for the FU1 pass, they didn't sell several hundred of them all over campus. When students were late to class and had to drive up and down all the floors of the parking garages, they would see rows and rows of empty spaces, but did not have permission to park there. It was separation of classes. I proposed that we eliminated the FU1 pass and opened up hundreds of more places for students to park. Another problem with the FU1 pass was that if you wanted to upgrade from an "S" or "Y" pass they wouldn't transfer your credit, you had to buy an entirely new pass. University system, their rules, their jurisdiction. People couldn't afford to upgrade and missed critical time in the classroom. What the fuck you greedy pigs!?

#3 Free Printing

"On campus printing" was a fairly new concept. It costs $.11 per page to print in black in white and the printing situation was HORRIBLE. In a school of 50,000 individuals there were less than 15 printers on campus. The university, included in our "tuition fees" a budget of $2.50 every day so we could print. You could always add more money on your account, and it would stay there. Most students would print a few pages a day, to make the most of their budget, assuming they had the time.

Example of the printing nightmare. After arriving late to the library because you could not find a place to park, you would need to print some papers before class. The 15 printers were located in exactly 2 labs on campus. They were also connected to roughly 150 computers and you could only print from those specific computers. You might have well as gone to Disney World on a Saturday if you wanted to wait in these types of lines. It would take upwards of an hour to print a piece of paper. Sometimes the computers would fuck up and you wait in line to print for something that never came. Even worse, you were a few cents short and they canceled your print job because you did not have extra money in your

81

account. Oh and you have to pay by card, from one of those 150 specific computers.

After clicking print, respectfully, people would log out of the computer and then go wait in the line, that formed roughly 50-100 people deep during peak hours. After waiting in line for 20min...30min... even 1 hour to print, you had to swipe your ID card into the printer. Presuming the system did not crash, lose your information or just say "fuck you have a nice day" you would be able to select which items you wanted to print. The system frequently crashed. I would assume by now, you are already late for class. Students would frequently curse at the printers. I have even seen people crying, fearing they would fail a class due to a printing scenario.

I got to thinking that there has to be a better way. If you take $2.50 and multiply it by 180 semester days it equals $450. This amount is almost enough to buy an Ipad. As it turns out, the school was scheming the students out of their money. I never printed $450 worth of documents, where did my money go? I know where it went, exactly into the hands of our dictator, I mean, president, Trudy Ballshaft.

#4 Trudy Ballshaft

Trudy and her family owned a meat packaging company among many other businesses. School lunches have to come from somewhere right? What about prison slop? The Ballshaft family through generations of control, are one of the families that makes billions annually because of your taxes. True aristocrats. Trudy will more than likely be a figure for politics in the coming years. She made $833,559 in 2011 as her salary from USC. Obama only made $400,000. Trudy was supposed to live on the USC campus. Years ago, USC built a 12,000 square foot mansion, in which the University President was supposed to reside. President Ballshaft and her family decided that they would rather live in a gated community and closer to the private schools of their children. The University still included in the annual budget a $40,000 'property maintenance' allocation, which of course, was paid for from our tuition. This cost occurred annually. By the time I graduated,

82

over $160,000 was spent taking care of a house, that no one lived in. The Ballshaft family also owned companies directly related to the University. When it came time to 'contract out' jobs, our tuition and fees would directly enter her pocket, or at least the 'the family' who coincidentally owned these companies.

"114th Annual Ballshaft Reunion"

I was going to expose all the evil things Ballshaft was doing and provide a solution for the on campus mansion that costs USC 40k per year. My idea was that since nobody lived there, we should allow the student body president, vice president and maybe a few members of the cabinet live there. Who would not want to live in a cocaine drug mansion? Instead of giving us salaries and paying us as a job, allocate the money towards our parking pass, university meal plan, pay all of our books and provide us housing and help with the cost of tuition. I even went as far to suggest that Elias and I would donate our Salaries and use the money leftover to buy a Green and Gold Cadillac CTS. We would donate it to the University so the Student Body President would have a car to drive for years to come. President Obama rides around in a Caddy and President Ballshaft makes more than him, why not have the student body president stunt like Obama.

#5 University Lecture Series Budget.

The university lecture series was a program that took student allocated funds and spent them on events like motivational speakers, authors and political figures. The University booked these people to visit campus and hopefully inspire, motivate and ultimately influence the student body. The way they spent the money however, was ridiculous and not effective.

All events were poorly attended and some quite frankly, just wasted our money. The University had no idea how to promote, they always under/overbooked and it made them look silly. It felt like Vegas. One time they paid over $10,000 for a motivational speaker and booked him for the middle of the day. Less than 100 people showed up making it cost over $100 a person. I could have gone to a nice steak dinner and visited Veronica's strip club for that price. My problem with the program was that they were holding lots of little events instead of just one big one. It is easier to advertise a big name ($50k Music Artist) then a bunch of small names that nobody gives a fuck about. Go watch YouTube if you need motivation, don't waste my tuition on this bullshit. I wrote on our campaign website that I wanted to allocate the funds and put them towards a big concert like the rapper who was exploding at the time. Wiz Khalifa. This was my platform and I wrote all of this in 2011 going into 2012. Voting was Feb 27 to March 3, 2012. Wiz Khalifa performed at my School the following year.

Vice President Elias Redding

Elias and I were total opposites, I was always moving at light speed while Elias moved about reasonably. I would come up with a crazy idea, which he toned it down. I never had a girlfriend, and he had a relationship with a beautiful woman and an amazing sex life. We did however share many common views. We cared about other people, we went to high school together, we identified problems on campus and wanted to be true politicians "men, of the people". We also liked to party.

Elias came up with some money and I budgeted just over $1200. I promised Elias that no matter what he put down, I would pay him back eventually. We knew that we were going against teams of people, most of whom had their parents money or other student organizations backing them. I was a great public speaker and Elias was a great conversationalist. He had the patience with the people and I had power to shut down our opponents arguments in front of a crowd. We did however have one huge problem. We didn't have a team.

The people that wrote the school newspaper worked for the student government. They wrote the paper catering to the people already in the student government, running for student body president. Jimmy Mudford was mentioned first in the articles and he was already a member of student government. Guess where his money came from? His parents. The article written about the candidates even declared Elias's major incorrectly, out of spite.

Let me break down the competitors:

1. Javier Rodriguez - A member of an all Latino fraternity who had a really good heart and the fraternity helping him the entire way. They held signs, talked to people, and helped him with the election. He was a real honest

guy trying to make an impact. He wasn't corrupt enough for politics.

2. Jasmine Jones - She was the most powerful African woman on campus. Every student organization knew her by name. Super smart, studied Economics and was sexy. She knew her stuff and had a plan to empower the students. She also had every African organization on her side. I honestly thought she was going to win. It is a damn shame that she did not.

3. Rutherford Wimsley Jr. - A masters student trying to earn a degree in "public administration" whatever the fuck that means. He was significantly older and significantly fatter than all the other candidates. He tried running in 2009 and lost. He stayed at USC for extra years just so he could prepare and run again. He understood the power of politics that came from USC and how powerful the position of student body president truly was. He was a horrible liar and I felt that he was only there to gain for his own personal advancement, whether it be wealth or power. I am also amazed as to how he was affording all of his degrees, I assume he was an adult spending his parents money.

4. Helga Spamoni – She was one of the leaders of all the resident assistants (RA) on campus. The RA's controlled all of the dorms on campus. Helga, already had a team working on her campaign. She had many connections and had her cabinet chosen. Everyone working for her would get a job if they won. Availability and resources gave her a huge edge against people that were working on the campaign with very few people. She had an army.

5. Jimmy Mudford - The typical rich frat boy, with skin whiter than a sheet of paper. He was from one of the fraternities on campus that was NOT popular with women, the Chi Chi Chi's or XXX or short. All they did was play video games and watch porn. Greek was not very popular at my school, but almost all of the Greeks voted because they were the ones involved in student government. Out of 50,000 students about 5,000 were

greek. If you won the greek vote you had the election. Less than 7,000 people voted my year. Mudford had money and an entire fraternity backing him.
6. Elias and I - It was just us. Elias had his sister and her boyfriend Jimmy help us out a few times, and I had a friend of mine, Sammi, help out once, but at the end of the day it was just us going around, campaigning and making it all happen. We also had a cameraman, Trevor who helped us make a video, but it was a painful process and the video was done late and we fucked ourselves. He really tried, but it was too late.

The strategy. Elias and I decided in November that we were going to run, this was also the same month I solidified my signing with the Marine Corps. During late November the university allowed us to choose our classes for the next semester. Elias had a very busy schedule and did his best to schedule time off in the evenings. Classes were simply not available and he had very few hours to dedicate to the campaign. Elias also had a relationship with his girlfriend and I had no idea what that was like. At times I became a bit frustrated and thought I was working harder than he was, but he had a girlfriend, which is a responsibility, equally as important. It was going to be tough.

One strategy that I realized helped candidates win the year prior, was that they expanded and campaigned to the other campuses of the University. USC had 4 campuses, spread over the greater Los Angeles area. The next closest campus was an hour drive, but it would be untouched by other candidates. My plan was to budget an entire day of classes at the satellite campus. After I finished work I would drive 45 min to the other campus, spend the whole day there and talk with students. I had two block classes of 3 hours and during my free time I talked to people in the library. I found a day that worked out perfect, Thursday. I booked two classes and was getting ready to win this election. I also had work almost every week-day morning, military training every weekend and a full schedule of 18 credits, while continually preparing for the LSAT. Talk about stress!

I knew I wouldn't have any drug tests until I went to boot camp. During this time I was introduced to another substance that was apparently supposed to keep you awake and help you focus. Not adderall or Ritalin, but the almighty white powder. Cocaine.

When I was in high school, all of my siblings explicitly remember our drunk father at the dinner table one night. We were actually getting along and laughing and he was talking about when he lived in Aspen. One of my siblings asked where all of his money went because he made a lot with his business partner. We all know how drunk people are honest and my father was buzzing quite hard. He said something like "well, rent was around $15,000 a month split between my roommates and when you are doing coke, or taking trips all the time it adds up, we would go and play golf blah blah blah blah" when my siblings and I heard the coke part all of us locked eyes and our father was still rambling on, but for the first time, it all added up. My parents lived in Aspen in the late 70's through the 80's while they were in the 20's so I'm sure they were doing more than just a few lines.

My mother use to say, "the only reason they tipped hundreds was because there weren't bigger bills" my mother was a waitress at a restaurant and worked at the ski station. My father owned a Jeep, truck, and a few motorcycles. He went to Vegas once a month and frequently visited the Caribbean. He said one time a man in a truck came flying around the corner and crashed into my father's jeep, but just barely. Apparently he was driving too fast or just lost control and the truck slid and scratched the entire side of the jeep. There were already scratches all over the jeep, it's not like it made it look any worse. A man wearing a big cowboy hat got out of the truck. This man walked over to my father, pulling out rolls of hundred dollar bills. He peeled off a bunch of them and handed them to my father while saying "I think that should take care of it". My father counted the money and had enough that he went and bought a new truck. Crazy rich people.

I always heard rumors that politicians used coke, Elias and I decided to try it and see what it was like. We did it at a party before, and decided it would fuel us the rest of the campaign. Included in our budget we bought a couple 8 balls and a few victory cigars. The weeks leading up to the campaign and the campaign itself would be very stressful and we would be tired. We had to stay focused. I definitely consumed more than Elias did, but every morning as soon as I would hear my alarm go off, I would do a line to wake up, cook my food, shower, do a line right before work, work my shift and by that point I would usually be fine for a majority of the day. If I was ever dozing off, I would simply do another small line. I did very small amounts and I am honestly impressed by what manufactured cocaine is and how it really provided assistance for the majority of my campaign. We weren't doing it to get high. We treated it like a prescription and only used it when we needed it. I would use it for 3 days, and stop for a few if I didn't need it. Neither of us ever felt addicted nor craved more.

I now understand why politicians and lots people consume manufactured cocaine. I honestly believe that the leaves should be available and we should experiment with the natural benefits that this plant can bring. In true form, before every debate, we would get dressed in our top hats and bow ties and do lines. I did a line minutes before appearing on stage, with hundreds of people watching, it was great. We also had special guests cheering us on. Monica. I think my public speeches made her proud, maybe even wet. Who knows.

Now a brief digression about the pinnacle crush of my adolescence. In 10th grade my world history class was taught by my MUN advisor and he was a finalist for teacher of the year in the state of California. He gave me some of the most challenging course work of my life, even compared to University. I can honestly say he was a major influence of the man that I am today. His class had two sessions, one in the morning and one in the afternoon. Students were assigned to only one of the sessions. I was given the period after lunch, and Monica, the period before.

At the end of the year, we had two different presentations, one, was a group presentation about global issues and the other, was a final speech on whatever we wanted. I specifically remember (call me crazy) that students were allowed to ask their teachers if they could skip their class, to watch the other groups present their projects. Each presentation was roughly 45 minutes about complicated global issues and foreign policy. If the teacher said yes, the students could come and watch our presentations. Monica was in the 3rd period meaning she had to ask for 5th period off. She did, but only on the day that I presented and I noticed her sitting in the back of the auditorium.

My group, was the only group to go that day and she was not friends with any of the people in my group. I wondered. A few weeks later, we had our speeches on the final exam days of school. We all drew numbers out of a hat and that was the order in which we had to give our 3-5 min speech. I drew the last slot by chance. I was the last person to go, on the last period of school on the last day of school. Most people want to begin their summer as soon as possible. We always dressed up in suit and tie so we could practice our professionalism. When the bell rang for the end of school, about ten of us still had to present. Those who wanted to leave, left, but as I stood up to give my speech with only a few people left, I noticed a girl sitting and listening at the back of the library. Monica.

Summer passed, I ran away in Washington DC. and came back to school to start my junior year. I finally had a truck and this was the first year I could drive both myself and my younger sister to school. Insert my crazy schedule for Junior year. Between 5th and 6th period I would always hang out in the back of one class that all of my friends were in, we would talk until the bell rang. I would leave and go to my research class, which is where I used the computer to do my online classes. Besides having almost all of my friends in that class for 6th hour, Monica was also in that class. It was a shame I had some cheating to do.

During that year, people started to sign up for the Euro Trip that would occur the following summer. People had to start making payments, acquire their passports and prepare. My parents would not sign the trip form, so I was not allowed to go. At the same time, I worked at Circuit City. Monica asked me one day in class if I could help her find a camera. The bell rang and I had to leave, but she kept talking to me and when Monica talks to you, you listen. She then asked for MY NUMBER in a very mature, sophisticated and classy, voice. Mama Mia.

Her voice was not normally like this, she was a little girly and cute. Maybe I was still very intimidated or imagining things, whatever, but it still happened. Here is one of the best/worst moments of my life. Because my parents were radical Christians and it takes them a rather long time to understand the necessities required to succeed in the developed world, they were told by their preacher at church that children should not have cell phones. Even though I had money, I was not allowed to have a cell phone. This is also the time (2007) where SMS, not whatsapp, Facebook, snapchat or anything else was used, but texting, good old fashioned texting. I didn't even have a phone. The nerd dream of the century. I finally have my own automobile, I have a job, I'm making money, doing well in school, and the hottest girl in school just asked for my number. Yet, I didn't have a phone.

I think I even said "I'm not allowed to have a phone" which at first glance is kinda "James bond/ dangerous / flirting/ playful" But it wasn't, I was dead fucking serious. When I explained that my parents would not allow me to have a phone the smile/sexy hypnotism face faded away and turned to Monica's beady eyes of "Wow, he isn't kidding, that's weird, but I still feel sorry," face. I took down her number and said I would call her. I left the room feeling stronger than ever. Thank you Monica.

I was super busy, and quite honestly on a spiritual high. The first time I got a number, EVER, was the number of the hottest girl in school, whom I had a crush for. I waited two days and I called her to tell her my work schedule, hoping we could meet. Camera's were not my department at all, so I waited two days to call her because I went and learned everything about cameras in those two days hoping to impress her. I called her, it rang a few times and went to voicemail.

FUCK!!!! WHAT DO I SAY IN A VOICEMAIL? I WASN'T PREPARED FOR THIS.

Maybe she didn't want to pick up, but after the way Monica asked for my number, I thought the stars had aligned. My emotional intelligence was non existent and the Christian Dogma was still deeply ingrained within my thought process. I was told to ignore and suppress all of these feelings of attraction and eventually I turned pretty robotic. I left the shortest voicemail that I could and hoped that she would get back to me. She never called back and I didn't have a phone or texting so it fizzled from there. I went on an MUN trip or something later that week and did not see her for a while. When I asked about the camera again in school she said. "It's okay, I already bought one".

I overthink, everything. I have very little experience with my "feels" and this makes all of my friendships, relationships, and interactions very difficult. The junior year ends, everyone, including Monica went off on the Europe Trip and I stayed at home and worked at Circuit City saving money for senior year. After a month passed, everyone came home, showed me all the pictures, shared all the stories and I was quite jealous of their experience.

My senior year started and if you remember Trevor, the class clown from the cross country team? He passed away just a few days before the homecoming football game. The entire school was in shock, it even made me tear a little bit. It took almost a full day for me to cry. For the first time in my life I was knew there was nothing I could do. Trevor was gone. He was a figure in the school, over 1,500 people came to his funeral. A few of us decided to carpool to the funeral, the driver was my friend Monica from 3rd grade, my friend Eric who now attends law school, Matt from Canada, and Jenna.

Normally I didn't hang out with all of these people, but we all went to school together and shared all the advanced classes and we knew each other's personalities. Jenna was also one of the more attractive girls in school and was a good friend of Monica. I sat in the middle between Jenna and Eric and we found parking among the thousands of people attending Trevor's funeral. Everyone had gotten out of the car and I was waiting for Jenna to leave because Eric stepped in mud when he got out on his side.

As everyone was out of the car except Jenna and I. I swear turned to me and uttered "Now, I probably know this isn't the best time to say this" (In my mind I can only think about the death of my friend and teammate as we arrive to his funeral)

"But I was talking with Monica the other day"

and I said "Monica who?"

Jenna said "Reid"

At this point in time the mix of emotions that overcame my brain were almost too much. I just lost a friend, I'm at his funeral and the girl next to me is about to tell me something about the girl I'm crazy about, without talking to her in 6 months.

Jenna then says "We were talking about getting serious the other day and who we would choose if we wanted to be with somebody (dramatic pause, no joke) Monica said she would choose you".

My jaw dropped to the ground. I sat for about 5 seconds in shock and then Jenna in a giddy childish voice said "Sorry, I closed the door on your" To be honest, once the funeral started, I forgot everything that Jenna had said and it was really hard to take in everything that was going on. After the funeral ended we dropped everybody off at home. What an experience.

My senior year was really relaxed, but since I had so many commitments at school, I was almost always there. Running XC, preparing for MUN conferences, or working at Circuit City consumed all of my time. Monica enrolled at the community college on the other side of town and took what were called Dual Credit courses and was almost never at school. She vanished from my life. Meanwhile, I started hanging out with a different crowd, influenced by my sister and eventually in February of 2009 I kissed a girl and eventually she took my virginity.

It only took 17 years for me to begin my emotional intelligence. Thank you Brittany. After I joined the fraternity, and was going through my pledge process, we had an event where we invited a sorority to dinner. Our idea, was to go to the top of the highest parking garage, set up tables and have a sunset dinner of Italian food and get to know the new girls in the pledge process. Please understand that this is a great concept, but not for the pledges.

The pledges do all the work and act like slaves, while the "full brothers" of the fraternity got to enjoy all the pleasures and have a nice dinner with the girls. There were about 10 pledges, getting everything ready for a dinner of 150 people. Cooking food, driving people everywhere, buying materials, etc etc. After we set up everything, we quickly showered and changed into nice clothes and those of us that had cars, had to go pick up the girls at their sorority house and drive them across campus to the event. I would have to make 5 or so trips because I had a good car. All of the waves of people went by as I kept introducing myself to BEAUTIFUL women and drove them across campus. I would drop them off and say, "enjoy, see you later, blah blah" I was completely baffled by their beauty and was trying to do the least amount of talking as possible. The final time I came to pick up ladies, I pulled up to the rotunda and only a group of girls remained. I heard my passenger door open and a woman stepped inside.

Monica.

My mind began to race. She looked like a painting and smelled like a bouquet of flowers. Her eyes always had this tint of blue that was tough to recreate in nature. Was it the sky? The sea? A gem? All I know is that it was hard to look away. My brain retracted to Ms. Zanno's room recalling the energy of Monica coming up the steps. Nearly 4 years had passed and she still blew me away. I don't know why I viewed her as angel, but something inside of her was different.

I AM AT UNIVERSITY!?!? or High School?

What the fuck is she doing here?!? She goes to University with me?!? She is in my car? Alone?

Am I dreaming?

Don't crash the car!

It's okay, you put it in park.

What on earth is going on?

What do I say?

How do I sound cool?

Calm down, remember to breathe! HOLY FUCK.

Don't worry, you will know exactly what to say.

Just be yourself Ace. You go this.

"hi" I said

"hi" she said

I started to pull away, both of us were in shock and she started to talk to me in, as if she was trying to hypnotize me. I guess that all beautiful women sound this way, a feeling I always enjoy. We talked for a few minutes and then for some reason, rushing and overthinking things like I always do, I asked her (with the most confidence it has ever taken me to do anything emotional in my life) to the fraternity formal, which was in the coming weeks.

"My formal is on November first, would you like to go with me?,"

I always overthink everything, and I can never be honest because I am always thinking that the other person will judge me, or I think I'm smart enough to predict what they were going to say. Monica was always a sought after item, I would assume that men hit on her everyday of her life. She is beautiful at first glance and has the brains to match. Her response blew mind after a few seconds of what felt like eternal silence.

"Was that difficult for you to say?" said Monica

At this point while I was driving, we stopped at a red light. I am not sure what was going on, but both of us had locked eyes and I swear that I started visually hallucinating and the only thing I saw was her eyes, everything else started to swirl and it was if I was on a mushroom trip. I have never felt connection or had an experience with a female like that ever again. Maybe I felt or experienced, love, I still have no idea what that was. To date, I have never experienced anything like that moment. We both continued to gaze at each other and I said something that I regret and will continue to regret until the day that I die.

"Nothing is difficult for me to say"

(WHY THE FUCK DID I JUST SAY THAT, SHE WAS LOOKING FOR YOU TO BE WEAK AND ADMIT THAT YOU LIKE HER, FUCK FUCK FUCK YOU ARE AN IDIOT, WHY ARE YOU ACTING TOUGH WHEN YOU ARE NOT)

All of the hallucination retracted and I popped back into reality and she looked away and I saw a genuine sad expression. Then she said "I'm seeing somebody right now" and the conversation died from there. The rest of the ride was pretty silent.

I drove all the way to the top of the parking garage and then opened her door and started walking to the tables. I was hungry and I really wanted to eat. As I sat Monica down in her chair, with the sun setting in the background overlooking the entire Los Angeles Horizon I then made my way to my seat. I was about to sit down next to her and possibly rekindle any opportunity that might exists. The moment I sat down one of the elder brothers said 'LOATHING, GO TO WALMART AND BUY MORE SOLO CUPS AND NAPKINS".

Give me a break. I grabbed my keys and went to buy some solo cups. By the time I got back 45 minutes had passed, there was miserable traffic and the first wave of girls and guys were ready to go back to the house to continue fraternizing and getting ready for the night. I got into my car and started shuttling back everybody. I saw all the older brothers connecting with girls and all I heard was "LOATHING, PUT SOME MUSIC ON! DRIVE FASTER. etc etc" After another few waves of people everybody was gone except a few older brothers and all the pledges breaking down the tables and chairs. I asked "where is the food" and everybody else said "We at it all". Besides working like slave, realizing that the girl I had a crush for 4 years now attended my University, ruining my first impression with her in a very long time AND not being able to eat the food that I prepared, I was exhausted. I didn't even get a bite of lasagna.

About two months later in the middle of the fall semester of my freshman year of college, it was my turn to be a Sober Tau. Between the hours of 10pm and 5am I had to be on-call to drive drunk fraternity brothers home. This was one of the worst parts of my hazing. I had to spend lots of time and money driving these people around and they would be hammered drunk and even vomit in my car. I would also see all of these guys getting tons of girls and I just couldn't figure out how to even talk to women. One night I was trying to enjoy a night at Trojans Club. It was a sleazy college bar that was busted multiple times by the ATF. Everybody was drunk, having fun and I was sober as a bird waiting for older brothers to come and say "drive me home pledge".

I'm at the bar trying to talk to people, but it's very difficult to talk as a sober person to a drunk person. I had plenty of confidence, just not in social settings. After about an hour, Guess who comes stumbling over to me? Monica. A few of my fraternity brothers were sitting at the bar and talking. Monica saw my face and mouthed "ACE!". While looking left, she slaps all of my fraternity brothers on the back of the head, grabs me by the collar of my shirt and starts making out with me. All of my fraternity brothers started cheering and chanting my last name. I'm still completely amazed at what the fuck happened. This is the first time I have a kissed a girl since I dumped my girlfriend AND this is the first woman I've kissed in college. I have kissed two girls in my life up to this point. Unbelievable.

She then, with her eyes half open and quite drunk, says "fuck you guys!" to all of my fraternity brothers and drags me out to the dance floor, continually kissing me and trying to teach me how to dance. I was really bad at dancing. I am also very sober and she was quite drunk, a great time nonetheless. One of her sorority sisters found her on the dance floor and wanted to go back to the house. I was sober and had my car, I offered to drive. As we were walked to the parking lot, one of them vomited outside my car. One of Monica's sisters, Jacquelyn, really had to pee. She pulled up her skirt, squatted down and took a piss right behind my Saturn. Classy. After finishing she looked at me and muttered with eyes half open "You saw nothing!" The other girls all got in my car and passed out. It looked like I administered drugs to all the girls because they were passed out on top of each other. I finally got them back to their house and even carried one of them into the living room and set her on the couch. I fetched her a glass of water and made sure she was okay. By this time, I don't even think Monica would have remembered her own name, let alone mine. She vanished into the sorority house. I returned to pick up more brothers until the early hours of the morning. At least I got to say to all of my friends that I made out with Monica. Legend.

Two years later and while running for student body president, Monica again, appears in my life. Elias had a girlfriend of many years named Cindy. Elias, Cindy and Monica had all been friends since high school and continued to be friends through college. When we started getting ready to run for office, I only had a few spectators at the debates, one of which was Monica. She brought her current boyfriend along, every time. I always knew that being a good public speaker would pay off, apparently it's rather attractive. Now back to the campaign.

My plan was quickly sabotaged during January, weeks before the campaign. School was already in session and I was driving to other campus once a week. Before campaigning, there were a few meetings to explain the rules. Fraternity fuck boy Jimmy Mudford was already on the student government. He had all the connections, power and influence with those on the board that oversaw the campaign. Corruption was present, even at the collegiate level. A few things came up in discussion that pretty much ruined our campaign strategy and I was almost left for broke and very discouraged about what to do. Roughly 1 week before the campaign:

1. I was not allowed to use Trudy Ballshaft in ANY material of my campaign or else I was disqualified.
2. The other Campuses, including the one I was driving to every week for class (ONE HOUR each way to attend) were "no longer voting this year".
3. I wanted to include the Scarface cocaine mansion in my campaign, which was also against University Policies.
4. You can only have 3 strikes against your campaign otherwise you will be disqualified.
5. All campaign material must be purchased during the campaign
6. No early campaigning
7. Cannot campaign within certain distances of Student centers, libraries or dormitories

I was royally fucked and could not say what I wanted to say about the University. I was wasting my time driving to another campus once a week, I was really discouraged and had to modify my campaign strategy. My schedule for the spring semester was very similar to my fall schedule except I had to cram in the campaign in every single second of space that I could.

At the end of the campaign, we ended up not only losing, but getting last place, out of the entire school. There were a few contributing factors to our loss, but I learned more in those few than anyone could have learned in the classroom. I ended up in last place with 434 votes. The first place winner spent the most money per vote. The last place winner, spent the least amount of money per vote. Rich people won. Poor people lost. Micro and Macro economically, it was the same game as real politics. It is disgusting that this was true at the University level.

I finished the semester, with a 3.5 GPA and it was my best semester of college. I learned a lot about a good friend of mine, Elias. I learned a lot about how the world functions and I could not have asked for a greater experience. Many more details obviously filled the campaign, but I think it could be a movie in and of itself. I would like to thank Austin and Elias roommate Ryan who were key factors in developing a massive top hat that strapped onto my car and paraded around campus. We wore top hats to every debate. Not many people can say they made 434 friends and had them vote for them in just under two weeks, but Elias and I can. We had the message, but not the delivery. Dollar spent, per vote, was the lowest out of everybody. Even though we earned last place, it was one hell of an experience.

Chapter 7

"If you're afraid - don't do it, - if you're
doing it - don't be afraid!"
— Genghis Khan

Elias and I lost the campaign but
continued to work hard and finish out our
semesters. Boot camp was about 2 months away
and I needed to be physically and mentally
ready. I spent the next two months working and
exercising, relentlessly. 12 weeks of pure
hell, during the hottest part of the summer,
San Diego California.

I never got my deposit back from my
landlord. She was quite the crazy lady. Her
husband died a long time ago, I felt sorry for
her. She had 3 studio apartments built on her
property, practically, in her front yard. I
was very happy to get out of that
neighborhood. They murdered the mailman! It
was not the nicest of places. People even had
"fuck the police" spray painted on the outside
of their homes.

I turned 21 years old the day I left for
San Diego and experienced United States Marine
Corps Recruit Training. Watch the first half
of Full Metal Jacket if you have not seen the
film. Close the Book and watch the film.
Please. Boot camp, besides my childhood, was
the most intense experience of my life.

Less than 1% of the United States
Military ever enters combat. I had a combat
job. MOS 1833 AMTRAK. I drove amphibious

assault vehicles and manned a mk-19. However, my reserve unit was far removed from current obligations making it very unlikely that I would ever see combat. For some reason, I wanted the experience of a lifetime and to literally be on the front lines, changing the course of history.

The main reason I chose the Marines was because all the other members of my family served in the NAVY or Coast Guard. Both of my grandfathers and one of my grandmother's served in the NAVY while my uncle currently serves as an officer in the Coast Guard. I joined the Marines because they had the toughest physical requirements, the most intense training and the most respect all over the world. The Marines are the first boots on the ground after congress declares war. The President even has permission to call on the Marines before congress makes a decision. The Marines do the initial damage, seize, and conquer and the ARMY picks up the leftovers. We have the best weapons training on earth. Every soldier in the ARMY is certified at 200 yards with a M16A2 rifle shooting .556 full metal jacket.

The Marines are certified at 500 yards. 2.5 times further than those in the ARMY. NAVY and (CH)AIR FORCE do not even apply in this category. They do not have proper weapons training. They play with guns a few days during basic training, but they do not spend every second of training with their rifle. We even slept with ours.

The Marines physical fitness test included the following:

Pull-ups - 20 - Perfect score
Crunches - 120 in 2 minutes - Perfect score
3 mile run - 18 min or less - Perfect score

No other branch of the military does pull-ups, nor are they required to run over 3 miles. The Marines are the best and most respected all over the world for a reason and I wanted to be part of that reason. The white hat really sticks out.

Boot camp is not a pleasant place, you have no freedoms. Some actions by other branches of the military allowing tobacco consumption, phone calls and being allowed to leave if you cannot complete training. The ARMY, NAVY AND (CH)AIR FORCE give their staff more liberties during training. Depending on the branch, they could consume tobacco, make phone calls and even give up and go home if they could not complete training. When you sign your contract for the Marines, you are never allowed to use the phone or consume tobacco. If you cannot complete a section of your training, they hold you back and move you to another platoon until you can. If you injure yourself, you stay on there until you are better and can complete training. As my recruiter explicitly told me "The only way you leave the Recruit Depot San Diego is by graduating, or in a body bag"

My year, multiple recruits left Recruit Depot San Diego in a body bag.

The term "basic training" or "boot camp" applies to all branches of the military. Here are the duration's starting with the easiest:

Navy - (Ch)Air Force - Coast Guard - 8 Weeks
Army/National guard - 10 weeks
Marines - 12 Weeks - wake up at 4am every day

Marine Corps Drill instructors never stop yelling, whether inside or outside. We would have this intensity all day, everyday, for 90 days. We would be naked in the shower and have them yelling at us wearing a poncho. Eating our food, in the cafeteria with drill instructors yelling in our faces. "Chew faster, you fat worthless slob, my grandmother with no teeth chews faster than you! Disgusting!" The only time we were not yelled at was in the classroom, learning history. Also, during the two weeks on the rifle range, our range instructor would talk to us while learning about rifles. But as soon as we were not learning about rifles, it was back to yelling.

If you have ever seen the movie 300 depicting Spartan warriors, there is a scene that will describe the USMC compared to other branches, perfectly. "SPARTANS, WHAT IS YOUR PROFESSION? AHHH UUUU AHHH UUU AHHH UUU!"

One of the other reasons that I decided to join was because of two Fraternity Brothers. Yogi and Freddy. Yogi is one of the best role models life could have given me. The ladies loved him, he always had his shit together, and above all, the genuine character and vibe he emitted drastically changed the way I interpreted social settings. We only hung out a few times, but I can honestly say I learned from him every time we spoke. He became a Marine in 2009 and when I joined the fraternity, he was in charge of hazing my pledge class. The first meeting with the new pledge class, the older brothers came and watched. Yogi, with a mouth full of Dip, gave us the most difficult workout I had ever experienced. Some people threw up, while others simply gave up. He stood there with a smile on his face the whole time and I could not believe the intensity. Jeff was with me, he remembers. The fraternity gave me many lessons in life but one with Yogi I distinctly remember.

Around 20 of us decided to go to Tijuana for spring break. I was a pledge, therefore I had to drive. I also had a test on Friday and could not go until the late afternoon. My crew was the last to hit the road. Brandon, T-Dog & Hanna. After I drove 7 hours through spring break traffic and made it to Tijuana it was already past midnight. We slept in a hotel with 10 other fraternity brothers and Hanna. We planned to sleep on the beach and just rough it for the entire break. Spring break was always adventure time. One of the girls named Jessie was pretty much one of the bro's, she was always saying stupid things, got along with us really well and lived just next to Tijuana, one village over. We would have a combination of partying at her place, partying in the street and partying at the beach. It was party city.

A few people were also in hotels and one of the nights, we all pre-gamed and got ready inside someone's hotel. Jessica and a few girls were still getting ready while the rest of us talked and consumed alcohol. One of the drinking games that evening was named 'cannonball'. The instructions for cannonball were rather simple. You were required to hold a handle of rum and boast "Cannonball!!!!" as if you were about to jump into the pool, every time you drank. You would then pass the 'cannonball' to someone else, who would then continue the pattern. There was always this vibe between Yogi and Jessie and everybody knew that they liked each other, but both of them always denied it. As we were getting ready to leave, no one was drunk yet, Yogi said something that really defined his character among all the animal house antics. "Do you guys find it strange that the only purpose some of these guys go to bars is to sleep with the girls? I mean, I know we are on vacation, but can't people just talk and have a good time, and if it happens, it happens?" As a pledge and as the oldest member of all my siblings, I realized that Yogi was a man of character and I had joined the right fraternity. Looking back on it now, if there was ever a time to impress Jessie or all of her close friends, in the intimacy of spring break vacation, he picked the perfect cue. A few years later, they married each other, good work Yogi.

Yogi actually went away to war. I enlisted while he was away and when he returned home we had a welcoming party for his tour in Afghanistan. It took almost an hour into the party for him to notice I was there, but we talked for a few minutes and I told him I enlisted and that I was shipping off for Boot camp in a few months.

The face that someone's gives you when you have their respect, I earned from a true Marine. Yogi returned home because the truck he drove ran over an IED (Improvised Explosive

Device) Yogi suffered mild injuries, but is physically fine, mentally I hope you are doing okay. Respect for you until the day I die. More on that later, now going back to Boot camp.

Most Drill instructors (Marine with the smokey the bear hat who yells) never went to combat, had a combat job, did anything dangerous or were shot at. Less than 1% of the military see's combat. Being a drill instructor is usually what Marines have to do to move up the ranks. If they get past their 6th or 8th year it usually means they are going to be a Marine as a career and to be in for that long and not get axed, one of the paths was usually becoming a drill instructor.

The guy that started out as a chef on a 2 year contract, then worked in a warehouse for another 4 years had the option of being a drill instructor to help their marks and hopefully advance their ranks. My drill instructors were a bit more, how do you say, authentic, Marines. Salty dogs indeed.

My senior drill instructor SSGT SMITH served multiple tours in Iraq and Afghanistan and was a SGT in charge of an entire combat platoon in the infantry division. After serving his tours he decided to become a drill instructor and has done so for almost a decade. I do not at all support war, but SSGT SMITH is arguably the most patriotic man I have ever met. He told us a few war stories and was a great example as a leader of men. The Marines made him into exactly what they desired. One of the recruits asked SSGT SMITH if he ever killed anybody. The entire platoon gasped, yet calm as a dove SSGT SMITH looked at him and said

"I did what I had to".

All of my other Drill instructors had combat/field positions as well. SGT GOOBER was a pyrotechnic and explosives Marine. SGT PRICK was field satellite communications he carried the radio during combat. The most intense was SGT ASS who had to wear a radioactive suit in 105 degree weather and go into very dangerous situations and make sure the area was all clear. I literally had a team of killers instructing me.

Now, I'm not saying the other drill instructors in the other platoons were soft, or easier, as a matter of fact, I think my platoon had it the easiest. None of the other drill instructors were from combat positions and I think they were "acting" tough, while all of mine actually "were" tough.

I went into boot camp thinking that I would be smarter/better than everybody else, but I always knew I had room for improvement. I mean, that is the point of our lives right? Continually grow, improve and hopefully leave the world in a better place than how we found it? I find it very difficult to describe Boot camp. It truly was something that you have to experience. Watching movies cannot bring justice to what actually occurs on base.

Originally I was chosen as the guide, which is the one who leads the rest of the group. I lost my title of guide after I messed up some basic things the first few weeks of training. Originally, I had no idea what the guide was supposed to do and I remember the senior drill instructor saying "You are thinking too much, you only have to listen and react." I assume that because I experimented with Psychedelics prior to joining the Marines, it was rather hard to brainwash me into the Marine that they wanted me to become.

It was clear that I was supposed to be the leader of the group, and the drill instructors kept giving me all these chances, but I just couldn't hack it.

SSGT SMITH pulled me aside and said something along the lines of "You are too smart for this, we need a dog we can train". I guess I was supposed to just shut up and take orders. I was finally removed from the position and sent back into the general population.

After months and months of training, we had our final test, the crucible. I will be honest, it was no easy task but I cannot help but feel that it was watered down compared to what my drill instructors did many years before me. The final 54 hour test used all of our skills we learned in the field. The toughest part was not performing physical tasks, but not losing your nerve due to the lack of sleep. Since I was one of the leaders the drill instructors put me to the test. Normally we had 8 hours of sleep interrupted by a 1 hour shift of Firewatch, which could be at any time during our sleeping period.

Ex. I slept every day from 20:00 - 04:00. Somewhere during that time period I would have a 1 hour shift where I was required to get fully suited up, and take over the post and make sure all weapons and recruits inside, were safe. Let's say we went to sleep at 20:00 and my shift was from 21:00-22:00. I would be woken up at 20:45, get dressed and then take over the post at 21:00 and then leave the post at 22:00 and finally be undressed and ready to go back to sleep at 22:15 . If you do the math, let alone the REM cycles, I was getting 6.5 hours total of non consecutive, every day, for 90 days. We performed the crucible the final two weeks before we graduated.

The shifts were always on rotation. Some shifts were better than others, but try and imagine for 92 days, not getting a full 8 hours of sleep and ALWAYS having your sleep pattern interrupted, or broken into segments of 1 then 6 or 2 hours and 5 hours or 3 hours and then 4 hours. I, along with everyone else was going insane.

Nika

Skopje, Macedonia

"Beaches, Bedrooms & Barcelona" by Ace Loathing

When it came down to the crucible, I was a leader in the platoon, my drill instructors, put me on fire watch both nights. I never slept. During the crucible, we received less than 4 hours of sleep per night. We also faced the hardest physical challenges of our training. I walked roughly 40 km in a 54 hour period with a backpack weighing 25 kg, M-16, and full gear, Kevlar helmet and other supplies that were were required to carry weighing up to 20kg. All in the final week of July in 95+ degree weather.

On the final night of the crucible, all of us were getting dressed and yelled at to organize our things. Recruits were required to stand at the position of attention and could not look around. While I was screaming and responding to commands, one of the drill instructors apparently came up behind me and took one of my boots and walked away. It was a chaotic situation and the dialog went something like this as I searched for my missing boot.

Drill instructor SGT ASS: "Only a STUPID recruit like you could lose a BOOT, How the hell did you lose your boot!"

Me - "THIS RECRUIT DOES NOT KNOW SIR"

DI - SGT Ass "FIND IT"

Me - "AYE SIR"

I start frantically searching for my boot, I ripped apart my gear, looking everywhere, but during this time, everyone is still standing at the position of attention, silent.

SGT Ass "WELL?!?!?! WHERE IS IT LOATHING"
voice escalating even louder

me - "THIS RECRUIT DOES NOT KNOW SIR" my voice
also escalating louder with anger

SGT Ass "FIND YOUR BOOT LOATHING, STUPID
RECRUIT" voice is still escalating

me really full of anger "AYE SIR!!!!"
escalating

SGT ASS "Where is your boot LOATHING???!?!?!?!
TURD BRAIN" escalating

It was at this moment, that I snapped. My
father always called me "shit for brains" and
anything directly insulting my intelligence
always struck me quite hard. I could not find
my boot, I had no idea where it was and I
finally, with all the drill instructors
watching, and every recruit in my platoon
listening, I bellowed out a response with all
my frustration.

"THIS RECRUIT HAS NO FUCKING IDEA… SIR!" with
sweat dripping down my face.

Swearing was forbidden and highly punishable.
The drill instructors would always threaten to
move us back and keep us here for another few
weeks if we ever disrespected them and swore.
Nobody had sworn at a drill instructor yet and

112

we were two weeks away from graduating. All of the recruits were in awe and trying not to laugh, because at this point, nothing made us scared anymore, we only had frustration and at times, all you can do, is laugh. Senior drill instructor SSGT Smith bellowed back at me from the entrance to the tent.

"LOOOOAAAAATTTTTHHHHIINNNNNNGGGG,   WATCH IT!"

It was at this moment, that another drill instructor came up behind me and put my boot next to my other one.

SGT Ass looked at me said "Lace your boots, recruit!"

A few days later as we were enjoying our rest days before the awards ceremony, different recruits continually approached me "Loathing, you are a hero, I wanted to curse so bad this entire time, but you did it man, you are a legend." People would come up to me in groups when we had a few minutes free time "Loathing, you are the man, we were all trying so hard not to laugh, thanks bro". I am so glad that I earned some respect in the platoon.

When I lost the title of "guide" during the first few weeks one of the other recruits asked why the fuck I was even here, he said I should go be a surgeon or something. "Surgeon Loathing, it sounds right" I wish I remember that recruits name.

After we survived the 54 hour crucible (The crucible killed two people in my battalion that summer) we marched all the way back with our gear roughly 10 km to the base, had a ceremony and then the crucible was over. It was also 9 in the morning and we had inspections in the coming days. Until 20:00 that evening, we were all awake cleaning our weapons, fixing our uniforms and trying to not fall asleep after all we had experienced. At the end of the day, I earned less than 6 hours of sleep in a 65 hour period, while performing physically demanding tasks in scorching hot weather. I slept like a baby that night.

I was woken up 3 hours later at 23:00 for my shift for firewatch. Some people just never get a break. As we say in the Marine Corps "Pain is weakness leaving the body". I graduated a few weeks later and then started my final year of undergraduate studies back in California at the University of Southern California and this is where the story really begins.

I was then 21 years old. A Marine with prospects of going to Law school and a small amount of savings to my name, the only thing I was missing was a girlfriend. Maybe this school year would be the year I finally have a real relationship with a woman and actually have the courage to pursue sexual relations without feeling all this confusion and guilt that my crazy christian indoctrination brought upon me. Maybe I had finally found my path and was ready to begin MY LIFE and not one that other people had brainwashed me into believing.

Maybe...

The first day of school, since I had worked so hard my years prior, I lived right next to campus in an apartment with one of my best friends from childhood, Austin. Austin already had two roommates. Topher, who also went to high school with us and was in ROTC training to become an (CH)Air force Officer. His other roommate was named Jamal. He was first member of his family to go to college and lived in section 8 housing in the slums of Miami (Where Rick Ross comes from) and his father was from Haiti. All three of them loved the internet and had good senses of humor. I was a bit more extroverted and social than the rest, but we all got along pretty well, the first semester at least.

Now, the reason they had an extra room for rent was because the 4th roommate, Dante, was moving to another apartment on the same floor and wanted his own bathroom. The room I was moving into shared a bathroom with Topher. I had just returned from having people yell at me while I washed my balls and taking a 5 minute shower. Did I mention that it was 4 people to a shower? and 5 people to a sink while we shaved… I was happy to share a bathroom with Topher.

When I first met Dante, I didn't like him. Austin told me that he had a child when he was 18 and his parents and family back home were taking care of her. He dressed like a goon, cared a lot about his physical appearance and I thought he was just a wanna be. While Dante was frequently bringing girls back to the apartment, I was still planning on waiting until marriage or at least until I was dating a girl until I pursued anything more with her. When I ran for student body president, I asked him to help me and he gave me this look like "Do I even know you?" He got a me more than a few votes though and by the end of the campaign we had finally started to call each other friends.

School had just begun and once per month I was required to go to my Marine Corps station which was about 30 min drive from where I lived. For that entire weekend, I fulfilled my reserve obligation for the United States Marine Corps. The Marines along with every other branch of the Armed Forces have a strict, No Drug Use Policy. I gave up consuming cannabis before I went in, but since I knew exactly when I would have drug tests, or the possibility of drug tests, I went right back to consuming.

Marine Corps Drug tests occur as follows, if we have training on Saturday and Sunday, usually less than 10% of the population is randomly selected for drug testing. The test was usually on Saturday and once the test was conducted they did not test the rest of the weekend. I was also in very good physical shape and I understood (to the best of my knowledge) how the test was conducted and what they looked for. I can confidently say I consumed cannabis almost everyday while in the Marine Corps Reserve and when I was tested 3 times, I beat each test.

Here is how.

All tests are run through a Mass spectrometer which breaks down the individual Urine Samples and checks them for a few key traits.
    1. Water concentration - If the amount of water in your Urine was too high, they suspected you of drinking too much and

flushing your system so you would be required to take the test again.

2. Drug and Alcohol concentration - A mass spectrometer breaks down urine samples to the smallest detectable increments identifying all different properties inside your Urine. It was based on concentration. If you tested positive for any type of narcotic, you had a very strict chance of a dishonorable discharge.

3. Creatine - Every time you pee, your body secretes creatine. If you drink a lot of water, your body dilutes the levels of creatine in your urine and then your result comes back flagged and you are suspected of flushing your system and you have to test again.

These were the 3 main things that the Marines were looking for and depending on the levels of lipids (fats) in your body, and your metabolism, it was pretty hard to beat these tests. Millions (possibly billions) of dollars of research and development went into these tests, and I can only assume how many doctors and engineers worked at the drug testing center of the armed forces.

I understood that cannabinoids stayed in the lipid (fat) cells for certain lengths and the lower the lipid concentration, the less likely they were to remain inside of my fat cells. Simple science, fat people have more fat, meaning they can hold more cannabinoids inside them. People with less fat have less ability to hold cannabinoids. Now what really matters is the concentration and frequency of cannabinoids in the system. I was always working out and keeping my body fat low, I was not really worried about that part. What did concern me, was how much I was consuming. If you consume everyday, you will have a higher concentration of cannabinoids in your system then someone who does so, once per month.

I consumed everyday. I had to flush my system with water so the detectable levels of cannabinoids would not show up on the Mass Spectrometer. Yet, if I diluted my samples, then I would be flagged for having either too much water or insufficient levels of creatine. My sample would come back invalid, requiring me to do it again. Roughly 3-5 days before the service weekend, I would stop consuming, and start flushing my body with plenty of water. I would also consume red meat with almost every meal which contained large quantities of creatine. I also bought creatine supplements and took those as well. When I woke up early in the morning to drive to the Command Center, I would drink mainly powerade and sports drinks to ensure my urine samples had at least some vitamins and were not strictly water. But to make my urine look urine colored I took large amounts of vitamins that would saturate my urine and make it appear urine colored instead of clear, like water. I also took large amounts of creatine supplements and continually flushed my system with water.

I passed every test I ever took.

The Marines in my opinion are also the rebels and the troublemakers compared to other branches of the armed forces.

"Take me to the brig, I want to see the real Marines." ~ Chesty Puller

Most marines that I talked to, consumed all different types of drugs at music festivals, but they chose the drugs that would exit your system in just a few days. Cannabinoids can stay in your system at detectable levels for months, but I did not enjoy other drugs near as much. I stuck with cannabis and consistent exercise. My plan worked and I was never caught by the United States Armed Forces.

One of the times I came home from a long weekend, I really looked forward to a nice rolled blunt with some quality green. I had already contacted Luthor because he was still in town and he brought over some of the best that he could find. Remember, Luthor is a gangster, he had friends that had grow houses. He knew the best weed around, where it was, how much it should cost and nobody was going to "hustle" him.

Luthor, met me at my place and we burned on my balcony with my roommate Austin. Dante and Austin were friends and since Dante lived a few apartments over, he came over and smoked with us. After he hit the blunt he was like "DAMN NIGGA, where did you get this?" Luthor held up a big bag of beautiful weed from one of his boys while ripping the blunt. He let out the smoke and said "$350 an ounce and $1100 a QP (quarter pound)" Luthor always be hustling. Now, it was at this point that Dante and I really began our connection. We finally exchanged numbers after smoking another blunt and he hit me up in just a couple of days.

Smoking weed makes you connect with people in ways that you cannot imagine. Dante is from Cuba and through one of our conversations I found out a bit more about him and his family. His dad was here without papers, is a gangster, been shot multiple times and even snuck in and out of the United States MULTIPLE TIMES. On top of all that, his dad worked like a slave and built his empire in California and they now own all types of industrial land and commercial properties.

Definitely no "goody goody white boy" christian upbringing for Dante. I understood why he was always after money, sleeping with lots of girls, and quite frankly, I was jealous. I put all my sour feelings behind me and realized that very few people in the world emit what I like to call, the honesty vibe. What I mean by this is that people treat each other the way they want to be treated. If you are honest about what you want and are direct with people, giving them all you have then that karma should come back to you. Dante had a different way of looking at things and I was finally starting to realize that there was no right/wrong way of doing things. Right and wrong is in the eyes of the beholder. You can do something that is illegal, in an ethical manner and people will love you for it. From Governments to Religions, Corporations to individuals, we all have the capacity to be ethical, yet rarely, we act ethically. Dante was ethical and very good person.

Being young, I had already gotten into trouble. When I was 19 I was arrested for Underage drinking and had to go do a bunch of community service (which I faked) and then I always smoked weed, so I was constantly in possession of an illegal substance. My definition of what was legal would be considered crazy. I relied more on the basis of ethical practice and doing unto others what should be done unto you. I had also just gotten back from bootcamp and was not scared of anything, except talking to beautiful women. Nothing could slow me down.

Chapter 8

"Fortune sides with him who dares."
— Virgil

A few weeks into the semester I received my loans from the government. I had a few thousand from the military, a credit card with a limit of $7500 and was expecting another few thousand in student loans. All of my loans were sent to one account while I kept my money at another bank. I usually went to one bank, withdrew the loans and then deposited them at my other bank. Except this time, I was a jackass and asked for all the money in not hundreds, but singles. The lady behind the counter at the credit union spilled her drink. The bank teller called the bank manager and said "Well Mr. Loathing, I'm afraid we only have $2,000 in singles, you will have to take the other half in large bills". I left the bank with $2,000 singles and almost $1500 in large bills.

It was amazing.

Having really large stacks of cash just shows how asinine our monetary system is and how a couple of zero's really determine wealth. I had about $2,000 wrapped up in rubber bands and it was placed inside a big box. My roommate Jamal always listened to rap music, came from a poor background and I wanted to surprise him and his good christian ass with a RICK ROSS pile of cash. He was in the living room and I came home with Austin and we had a big box of money. We sat Jamal down on the couch and told him we stole something from Rick Ross. Jamal was in for a surprise. Austin and I told him to close his eyes and we took the top off the box and started putting rubber bands of singles in his arms.

We took the 100's that the bank gave us and put them on the outside of the stacks of money, so it looked like he was holding $200,000 or a decent amount of money. We told him to open his eyes, he "oh my god! Is… is this…" and he started to contort and eventually fainted. It looked very similar to Dave Chappelle from Half Baked when he receives the pound of marijuana.

He woke up after we slapped him in the face. Jamal looked at us and said "I have never seen that much money before, its.. its…beautiful." Later that afternoon, we called Dante over to do the same thing. Dante was super excited took pictures to show everybody in Cuba. Later to put the icing on the cake we went into my bedroom which was the cleanest/most organized and we took all the rubber bands off the singles and put them all over my bed. I was in the living room when Jamal came home from class. I told him to go into my room. All I remember hearing was "OH MY GOD!" he runs back to the living room and asks "Can I lay in it?" I said "Jamal, you are going to do more than just lay it in, you are going to pick up handfuls and throw it in the air".

We played with the money for about an hour, literally like kids on Christmas morning opening presents. It was also really hard not to smile with thousands of dollars all over the place. After we were done playing, we picked up dollars for about 20 minutes and put them in a duffle bag. I kept that money for about a week to show everybody and eventually I had friends coming to my house to ask "Can I play with the money?" Quality entertainment. I kept finding singles in my room for a couple of months and even a few more when I finally moved out of the apartment. (I took one thousand of those singles and I put them in a box banded all up. I gave them to Jamal when he graduated. He was the first person in his family to go to college and he was graduating a semester early. I couldn't have be more proud.)

At this point, Dante knew I was also, all about the money. Dante played poker and was pretty damn good at it. He had a larger nest egg to work with so he could afford to go and hustle at the tables, where as I was a bit more conservative. We continued to bond our friendship, always in search of good trees (cannabis) and even tried to get girls from time to time. Dante almost always took a girl home, regardless of how much she weighed. A winner never quits and a quitter, never wins.

In September, I went to a job fair hosted at the Air Force base. Although I had enough money saved up that I would not have to work the semester, I was accustomed to having a job and could always use some extra cash. Let alone, I was hoping to attend law school and even if the Military was going to assist me, it was going to be expensive. I walked around and talked to people and then I noticed a booth from a brand that we all know and hate, Banco Americo. I was graduating with a degree in Economics, I figured having an in at one of the largest banks on earth was not a bad idea. I would at least learn how lending works, have the potential to move up in the ranks if I was not accepted to law school. I always had options because the labor force is geared towards veterans.

After the first interview, the Bank Manager named Ricardo, closed the door to his office and said something that is hard for me to forget. "I don't know who trained you, but you nailed it, I have 6 more interviews today and I'm going to call and cancel them. You got the job."

Bingo, I was in.

I started at Banco Americo as a teller, this is the baseline that everyone needs to start at. After a few weeks of training, I was given my combinations and certain keys because every bank has high standards of accountability. It takes at least two people to open every vault, set every vault timer, lock most securities and ensure that the bank was ready to be closed down everyday and every weekend. As the newest employee, I was let on a little bit at a time and every week I was given more responsibility or access to different parts of the bank. We had opening procedures and lots of rules and regulations to follow in case something went missing, someone was robbing us, there was a problem with the security system, and the list went on and on.

My branch had two banks within the property. One was a large 5 story corporate office building that remained empty since the mid 2000's and a detached drive through area that dealt only with car side deposits and withdrawals. I started out in the drive through with the senior teller and it was nice for the fact that only the two or sometimes three of us, would be in the small detached drive through. The rest of the employee's had to work inside the bank with the bank manager and deal with all the complicated transactions. The drive through was easy, we listened to music and only had to speak in a microphone, we never had to deal with customers face to face. Whenever there was something we were not sure of, or didn't know how to handle, we sent them inside the main bank and our associates do the work.

The strange thing that I discovered, mainly from asking suggestive questions to older employees, was that the drive through contained most of the money that came through the bank. The Armored Truck would make two stops, one inside the big bank and one out to us across the parking lot in the drive through. Businesses, whether it be a dealership, McDonald's, Strip club, Auto Body, etc would drive through usually on Monday morning after their long weekend with security envelopes filled with thousands upon thousands of dollars. Since I lived in Los Angeles, large corporations and other businesses made their deposits at the nearby Banco Americo and never even had to get out of their car. During one of my shifts I collected roughly $180,000 in a 4 hour period and I was amazed at how much money really went through the bank.

The hardest part about my job was not having the temptation to rob the bank, but seeing how evil the banking system really was. Half the time I would work inside the big bank and I would see mothers holding their children while they made deposits. I could see that they had 4 credits cards maxed out and $64 in their checking account. I would also see people come in to cash their checks for the work week, but because they did not have a Banco Americo account, the bank charged them a flat fee for cashing the check. A man that worked all week and earned a few hundred dollars had to pay some of it to Banco Americo, because he did not have enough money to open an account to negate the fees. Every Friday I would see the same people come in and lose their hard earned money from the greedy banking system. Banco Americo was already making trillions, but they just had to keep squeezing it from those struggling to cross the poverty line. It was depressing, no matter how old or how young, people had the same problems and I can only imagine what their daily lives were like. This job was really starting to get me depressed and It made me realize how lucky I really was and how horrible, capitalism, really is.

At the beginning of December, I took the LSAT for the second time. The first time I got a 147 which is not that good. I needed at least a 150 to be considered qualified for the JAG Program. After more preparation I took the test again and got my scores back just two weeks later. I got a 151! I finally had all the requirements for the JAG program and I even printed up extra copies of my papers to show my commanding officers and those in charge of me at the Marine Corps Base.

Sometime in late December, I remember passing a drug test for the Marine Corps and then talking with a SGT about my future prospects in the Marines and what I was planning to do. I told him how I'm trying to go to OCS (Officer Candidate School) and join the JAG (Judge Advocate General) program. We talked for a few minutes and he said "You know how difficult it is to get selected for that right? They don't just take anybody". I pondered what he said for a second and replied "My recruiter said that after I finished school and I had all my requirements for the JAG program I would be sent to OCS since I already had my College degree". I pulled out my papers to show him how I scored above the requirements and I was super excited. The SGT replied "Oh my god....5 second

126

pause... your recruiter lied to you....Hang on, let me go get another SGT."

At this point my whole world fell in on itself. I was confused, shocked and horrified. I had no idea what was about to happen. I stood there for a few minutes and waited for him to come back with the other SGT and I explained my situation again to both of them. This SGT said "That's not how it works, what happens is that once you make all the qualifications, you go to a review board and they pick the guys that went to OCS first and then see if they want to issue you a new contract and cancel your current obligations with the Reserves" he continued "They usually only take the people that went to Harvard, or West Point for those type of positions, even if you have all the same scores and everything, they leave it up to the Panel to decide, it's not a guaranteed thing" they then asked for my recruiters information. I gave them the information and they saw his rank which was higher than theirs and they could not chew him out.

There I was, trapped in a 6 years reservist contract, stuck in Los Angeles, California about to graduate university, working a job that made me depressed and I had very little chance of ever going to law school because I would not have the money to pay for it. 21 years of my life, aiming for a target in the wrong direction. I learned from other members in the military that I was not the only one with this type of problem. Apparently military recruiters are paid based upon the number of recruits they send into the armed services. They are salesmen, who lie, cheat and do whatever it takes to meet their quota. My recruiter lied to me and had me sign paperwork that he later changed in the computer, without my permission. It would be my word against his, a battle surely I would lose.

I spoke later with my commander who was an officer and he told me even more disturbing news. Apparently the JAG program was not even available for new service members since early 2011. When I signed up, my recruiter lied to me and told me outdated information. After nearly a decade of war in multiple countries, the United States government was not interested in paying for law school for graduates, they had enough lawyers.

My life was falling apart. I scored a 96 on my ASVAB and could pick any job that I wanted in the military. I was not some grunt that joined the military to die. I wanted to become a productive member of society. The first day I arrived to recruit training I should have realized that something was awry. When I presented my paperwork to the commanding officer he told me that he had no idea I was on the way. I went into the admin office and when they typed my name in the database, all of my information was blank. The only thing present was my social security number. My job description, physical fitness scores, address and all other personal information was non existent. They did not even have a contact information about me or who was my next of kin, if I would have died.

That night, I called up Luthor and he brought me some of the best weed I have ever smoked in my life. We started talking. The conversation lasted a few days and we hung out later that week to shoot some pool, and chill. I will be honest, hanging out with gangsters gives you a gangster mentality and I always confided in Luthor and asked him questions that I knew other people would not have the answer to. I could ask him anything, whether it be about drugs, girls, philosophy, politics, traveling, science, whatever. Luthor and I always had good conversation and good connection. I could ask Luthor anything.

One night, he came over to my house, and poured a few Soco and limes, we were getting ready to out and meet some girls. We continued our conversation from the night before. Luthor flopped down on the couch and I was in the kitchen. I looked over and asked him.

"Would you be interested in robbing the bank?"
Luthor finished sipping his drink and replied "I'm down."

"Flava in Ya Ear" Craig Mack (original mix)

Chapter 9

Going back to my original stoner friends of James and Gibrarian, all three of us took a class in 2011 taught by an eclectic professor within the economic department. The title of the course was Economics of Crime. I enrolled in the course because I wanted to learn from one of the most globally diverse professors in our department. Also, who doesn't like to learn about crime? I have always found crime interesting and was frequently committing crimes myself, so I figured the course deserved my attention. The main purpose of the class was to answer a question that we all know and love. Does crime pay?

Throughout the course we analyzed and broke down different crime sectors and court systems, to determine whether our current justice system was in fact doing good, or just costing its citizens lots of money. As you can probably imagine, after only a few short weeks, we mathematically proved the inefficiency of the "justice" system. The police wasted money imprisoning people for small quantities of drugs in order to fill prisons owned by private investors. My professor was Kwabela Kuka Oheama from Africa and he saw the world a bit differently than the rest of us. Professor Oheama did his undergraduate and graduate degree in Africa and then decided to move to South Detroit to continue his studies. If you know anything about South Detroit in the 1970's it wasn't exactly the best or safest place to live.

Professor Oheama did not believe that anywhere in the United States could be more dangerous than Africa. He decided to move to one of the most dangerous cities in the states to continue his research about court systems, social inequality and crime. The first time he came to the United States was when he flew to attend University. He never visited Detroit, and only kept in contact via phone and mail. He arrived at the University, started attending school, rented a small apartment and bought a car. Two weeks into the semester, his car was stolen. He admitted that he lived in one of the worst areas of the city and when he filed the police report, all of the white people at the police station thought he was committing fraud.

They asked see his papers and when he pulled out his passport, they showed him no respect. After he submitted all the papers to look for his stolen car, he left the station, but knew in his heart that the police were probably not going to do anything. A few weeks later, he was walking through a part of town and he noticed a car that looked just like his, but had a new license plate. The police had not contacted him about any new leads so he crossed the street to see if the car was his. Thankfully he still had the keys in his pocket. Professor Oheama opened up the door and stole his car back from himself. Amazing.

When we arrived at the topic of whether or not crime actually pays it was a simple mathematical equation. Yet, at the end of the day, it was all a matter of preference and whether or not you were risk averse. Let's say you commit a crime and earn $50,000, but if you get caught, it costs you $10,000 in court fees and two years of lost wages (prison time). If you made more than $20,000 a year then technically you would lose money on your decision. But if you don't get caught, and you earned less than $20,000 every year, you just earned two years of savings. For someone living at or below the poverty line, that is an inconceivable and incomprehensible amount of money.

My parents were very good at letting their children have no money, technological advancements, proper nutrition or any confidence that they would ever succeed at anything they ever did. I always lived below the poverty line. Meanwhile, my father drove a Porsche and my mother a BMW. Sometimes, my father would even buy a nice piece of steak from the butcher shop and have it prepared and ready for the grill and he would set a box of Mac'n'cheese by the stove and say. "Your mother and I want some time alone, cook your dinner and we are going to eat on the lanai." I was seven years old, my sister six and my brother four.

After my "reasoning" and since I survived for the last 3 years on less than $10,000 per year, I decided that robbing the bank, presuming the proper amount, was a positive economic decision. When you factor in risk, and liability, it was the most logical decision I could have made, assuming I preferred risk. I was stuck in a 6 year Marine Reservist contract, I had virtually no chance of affording law school and I was lied to by my own country, where did my American dream go?

Luthor and I kept talking and one of the nights before winter break, I had a few guys over at my place to drink beers and smoke some blunts. Dante was over as well and all of us talked and relaxed on my balcony. Dante had a few Cuban friends with him and somebody brought up the topic of me robbing the bank. I told them it was difficult and the situation had to be perfect, but of course, OF COURSE, I had thought about it. Little did they know what was underway.

Luthor and I acted pretty low key and continued on with the night. A few nights later I took Luthor by the neighborhood and we went over the plan. I showed him how easy it was going to be, where to stage the car and what path he needed to take. I wrote him a list of things to buy and told him to put them in a bag so when the day came, he could just drive up, rob me and then get away.

We rehearsed a few times, and decided where to drive and talked about what to do if we were caught. Luthor would be on his 3rd strike of committing a felony and would have to serve prison time. He had a lot of experience with both jail and the court systems so he knew the ins and outs and what to do if we were caught. The only thing he was not sure of, was our bail amount, that decision was up to the judge. Luthor had just finished having his record sealed so technically when the preliminary judge looked up his profile, he would come up clean. This was very important because if I was caught working with a career criminal, I could also be labeled a career criminal.

One problem we had was the alarm. I was obviously on camera so I had to be as inconspicuous as possible while getting robbed. We both knew that I had to pull the alarm, but it would be better if I pulled the alarm at the end of the heist. We eventually came up with a decent plan and decided that the amount of money had to be pretty high if we were going to split it 50/50. I looked up the charges and saw that the highest degree felony Level 1 was anything $100,000+. This was our minimum and to be quite honest, most banks including the one I worked at, would hardly ever have this much money available. Even if you added up all the tellers working a shift, to pull off a job like this the conditions would have to be perfect. We decided to wait for the perfect storm.

Another problem we had, was how Luthor was going to get inside. The small detachable drive through had only one door and I obviously had keys, but then suspicion would arise and the police would think I was involved if I gave Luthor a copy of the key. I thought on my feet and came up with an idea that would allow for him to get inside. Everyday, the man from UPS would come by and deliver packages and he would knock a few times on the door. I would then look through the security window or hear the guy say "UPS" and then open the door, hand him the daily mail and then go right back to work. This was the ONLY person that we opened the door for everyday. UPS usually came between 12 and 1 pm.

Another element was communication, we decided that since I would have to call or text Luthor, he would steal my phone and if we got caught, he had all the evidence and we would come clean about everything.

We also collaborated on our story. If Luthor was caught with over $100,000 the police would assume there was another motive for this money. The main reason both of us wanted to steal the money was to pay off our debts and attend graduate/law school. We were both on our own and did not receive money from our parents like all the other fraternity members. If there was anything left over, we were going to buy motorcycles. Simple.

Now to bring my "economically educated, morally driven, statistically placed, decision" before the eyes of any medical professional, I discussed with Luthor the following strategy that he also agreed to. When people work at a bank, almost always there are two people in the same room so there is constant accountability. There are safety protocols mainly for the people that work there and to protect the bank from loss. I told Luthor that we are not going to do it unless for some reason I would be left alone at the drive through. I did not want ANYONE to witness a bank robbery because I did not want to harm their physical, mental or emotional health. The last thing I wanted on my conscience was one of my coworkers going insane for the rest of their life and be paranoid because they were in a bank while it was being robbed. No amount of money is worth someone's sanity so I put everybody else before myself and the situation would have to meet all of the following criteria.

1. I would need to be absolutely alone for roughly 30-60 minutes as scheduled on the weekly time tables.
2. The hours of the that scheduling would need to be between 12-2pm
3. The amount in question would have to be >$100,000 in my drawer from all the deposits I had received that day.
4. Luthor would have to be available

These were very tough conditions to meet, but patience is a virtue.
The bank was always super organized and everybody had their schedules at least two weeks in advance. Christmas season went by and nothing popped up, but when I got my schedule for the new year, January 15 met all the right criteria, except the amount in the drawer, that was always a roll of the dice.

I went into work at 11:30 and my coworker was getting ready to leave and I had to take his deposit envelopes with ridiculous amounts of money inside. "Yeah, some guy from the car dealership came by and dropped off like 80k and Mcdonalds and another few business are in their as well, it's like 126k, have a good week bruh, I gotta study for a test" he said. My heart started racing. I was just given a bag of roughly 126k in all types of bills, it was sealed, able to put inside of another bag with ease. I also had roughly the same amount of money in my own vault. As I put the bag in my drawer I remember saying to myself as I saw my law school tuition before my eyes.

"PAY DAY"

That January afternoon at roughly 12:37 pm Luthor knocked on the door and I went to answer, thinking it was UPS. What happened next may define me as crazy, bold, badass, and original but I don't regret taking the chance to improve my life because "The System" is not here to help "The People". The door swung open and Luthor pushed me on the ground holding a knife and a bag.

"GIVE ME THE MONEY!!!"

Now please understand, we are good friends, robbing a bank, for the first time. There was bound to be some room for error and crazy emotions going all directions. Luthor was a gangster, but still, practice makes perfect, and we were taking our bank robbing virginity. I acted scared (my heart was racing) and slowly reached for my keys while mumbling under my breath.

"Luthor, there is no audio recording,"

Behind his ski mask and hoodie Luthor says "oh… My bad bro, you good?"

Think about it, we are two friends robbing a bank, I am really glad we did not laugh on camera. I reached into my pocket and pulled out my keys. He walked me over to the counter and I opened one of two drawers. The top drawer had small money and the bottom drawer has all the big money, the large bills, deposit envelopes, etc. Both drawers cannot be open at the same time and since we wanted this to be as quick as possible, I got on my knees and opened the second drawer and then immediately laid on the ground, face down.

As I laid on the ground I started screaming directions and he put all the money in the bag, took out the keys and opened the top drawer that had smaller money but still thousands and thousands in loose bills and he took all that as well. He zipped up the bag as I screamed for my life. He ran out the door, it slammed. I laid on the floor for a few seconds while my heart beat like a drum.

I jumped up and pulled the alarm and honestly I was gasping for breath. It was the most breathtaking experience of my life. It was pretty hard to keep cool, knowing I just committed a pretty serious felony. I then had to call inside to the main bank and let them know I was robbed. I spoke with the bank manager Ricardo on the phone briefly and I was instructed to wait for the Police. I went over and poured myself a glass of water, walked back and sat down on the ground until Police arrived. I was in shock and was not ready for what was about to happen. Within 5 minutes the police came cruising up and they knocked on the door. They then had me stand up, open the door and one officer asked for my name.

"Ace Loathing" I replied

"Cuff him" said one of the officers

There is no worse feeling on earth.

As they put me into the back of squad car, I looked through the windshield and who do I see being searched?

Luthor.

Chapter 10

My world was slowing down. I had no idea what to think. As I sat there in the squad car trying to remain positive, I continually pondered "Well, at least I'm not a bootcamp". It made things a bit easier to bare. I also realized that I was read my Miranda Rights, but I was never read my charges. The police cuffed me without telling me why I was being detained.

The car ride settled me down and brought me to a homeostasis. I relaxed and realized a new chapter of my life was about to begin. I could now put on my military attitude and talk with ease. My plan was to remain silent until I knew exactly what was going on. They took us to the station and put us in different holding cells. The officers pulled me out first and walked me into a room and sat me down. The classic, good detective, bad detective began.

"Do you know why you are in handcuffs?" - Good detective (female) who then removed my handcuffs

"I would like a lawyer, please" - Me

"What are you?!? SCAAARRRRREEDD," - Bad detective (obese male)

"We are going to get you! Your partner already told us the whole story, you are going to prison!"

Calm as a dove I repeated "I would like a lawyer" and even smiled at the obese detective. They both looked at me and their whole power trip mentality and attitude went away.

The fat detective continued on saying things to try and make me talk until I was eventually placed in the holding cell room, same as Luthor. People were constantly being arrested and brought in, we were not alone. When I was finally in the same room as Luthor we had a brief talk.

"What did you tell them?!" I said

"Everything, that's why they arrested you," said Luthor

"The whole story?! The plan? Motive? Everything?" I asked

"Yeah man, as long as our stories match up we should stand a good chance in court and they got all the money back which is the most important thing."

I wasn't in that room for more than 2 minutes until they came and got me and took me to another room. This time I had 4 more detectives, all equally fat pigs, but this time they were all bad. They started yelling at me and said "Your partner told us everything! If you deny what he said we have to take this to a FEDERAL level. You robbed Banco Americo which is protected FEDERALLY. We can make this a lot easier on you and all of your charges will not go to the federal level. If you admit everything right now, the case is over and you are only hit with 2 charges. If we take it federally, we have no idea where it is going to go,"

"Now, we also looked up your profile and it says you are in the Military."

Insert another moment of "OH FUCK" shake my head.

This is something I also did not take into consideration, even if I got away unpunished by the court systems, I would still have a lot to pay for at my military duty. I had learned about honorable, general, and dishonorable discharges while at Bootcamp. Having a dishonorable discharge was something I could not afford on my record. I decided right then and there to alter what I was going to say to the police. If I included in the police report what happened with my recruiter, it would only turn out even worse for me. The recruiter was the main reason for my motive, but I decided not to say anything.

As I sat there pondering on whether to open my mouth, my life was flashing before my eyes, while the room was in slow motion. All of them were yelling at me and it almost seemed like they were pleading me to come clean. The whole "federal" angle was something that I had not considered, researched or was even aware about. It seemed that the police wanted to keep this as small as possible and right now they had the case closed. All the money was returned to the bank and the two culprits were in custody. It was at this point I came forward and told the same story as Luthor and almost everyone at the police station started to give us respect.

Think about it, two college kids in their final year of study decide to rob a bank because they didn't have enough money to attend their graduate schools and came from lower middle class families. It wasn't like we were going to use that money to buy a couple kilos of cocaine and fuel a crack war. We were moderately educated human beings that were frustrated with the system. I had several officers and even people that worked at the station, swing by my cell and ask me to tell my story. It was strange, I think the police were so amazed at well behaved, educated, polite people in their station giving their officers respect and telling such a genuine story, they actually felt sorry for us.

"Have you tried more than one girl before?" - Elena

Elena, Rossi, Diamond & Eric

USA & Cuba

"Beaches, Bedrooms & Barcelona" by Ace Loathing

I was finally in the cell next to Luthor and he told me what had happened. He said that as soon as he the ran out the door, he jumped the fence and disappeared into the residential neighborhood. As he crossed the street to get to his car. Two police officers in their squad car saw him. Apparently as Luthor had set up his car, an old white lady in the neighborhood was smoking her two packs-a-day of cigarettes and saw Luthor. He got out of his car and pulled out a bag, then put on a ski mask and disappeared into another street closer to the bank.

This woman decided that it was worth a call to the police. I am not mad that she called the police. I am mad because the police report says she called him a 'black' man. Apparently no black people lived in the neighborhood.

FUCKING PERFECT

Before Luthor had even knocked on the door to the bank, police were on their way to his car, to investigate a 911 call for a 'suspicious person' in the neighborhood. We were doomed from the beginning.

Luthor said he was about 20 meters away from his own car when he saw the police. Thinking they were there for him, Luthor ran with all the cash and tried to escape the neighborhood. The police apparently hit the gas and ran over Luthor with a squad car. He showed me all the bruises and they started beating his ass and this is immediately where he confessed everything and dropped my name. I am not mad at Luthor for what happened, but I guess life had a bigger plan for both of us.

Back to the holding cell, Luthor and I both stayed in there for another hour. I guess the pigs were working on paperwork or something, but we had no idea why we were still there. Remember, Luthor had his car at the crime scene so that was also part of the crime. The police were searching his car and guess what they found. 25 Grams of Cannabis, a lighter and pack of rolling papers. Luthor was now hit with felony possession drug charges.

I specifically remember, and I'm not kidding when I say this, that two black police officers came in with a bag of weed and said to another officer "Yo JONES! Come check out this weed! I ain't EVER seen weed like this before, this is a WHOLE other level."

Luthor looked at me and said

"Fuck....I just bought that ounce too."

Another hour went by and we had our names called and from here we were going to county jail. They put both of us in the back of a squad car and at this point I wasn't happy, I wasn't sad, but I was amazed at how far I'd come and how hard I'd fallen. We talked in the car for the 20 minute ride, but it was really tough, really, really tough.

> "When you're in jail, a good friend will be trying to bail you out. A best friend will be in the cell next to you saying, 'Damn, that was fun'." - Groucho Marx

We went to county and if you have never been to jail before it's not fun, but it's not horrible. The worst part was central booking. Luthor had been to this exact jail multiple times so he knew what to do and I literally had a guide. Both of us went through a medical exam, central booking and then came the time where we had to stand side by side and get our mugshots taken.

I turned to Luthor and said "Should we smile?"

"Ha, might as well!" - Said Luthor

We both smiled and mine was so hard to make. I knew my life was heading down a path of uncertainty and It was difficult to smile, but at least I wasn't going in alone. This photo was then put on the local news and all over the internet. We sat in central booking for over 6 hours. We went over to the window and found out what charges were placed against us and our bail amounts.

Ace

1. Grand theft over $100,000 – Level 1 Felony
2. Scheme to defraud a financial institution – Level 2 Felony

Bond set at $22,500

Luthor

1. Grand theft over $100,000 – Level 1 Felony
2. Scheme to defraud a financial institution – Level 2 Felony
3. Possession of Cannabis over 20 grams – Level 3 Felony
4. Possession of drug paraphernalia - Misdemeanor

Bond set at $25,000

Luthor at this point inserts the classic whistle noise of (DAMMMMNNNN) and says

"That's gangster, we can tell everybody we robbed as much as we want. You gonna have respect inside, don't worry."

I'm waiting at the processing station and after 10 hours of custody they finally gave us a bologna sandwich and an apple. I was starving. Another man got his sandwich but was so devastated by his situation that he could not eat. Luthor asked for his sandwich and he gave it to him. After a few seconds Luthor tore the sandwich and offered me half. The guy sitting next to me asked what I did, and Luthor told me not to answer. I was curious as to his reaction and police were all around so I kept the conversation going.

"We robbed Banco Americo for a half million," I said

The man coughed up his sandwich and his eyes got real wide and says "Bullshit man, you are fucking lying to me!"

Luthor started laughing.

I then said "nah man, come with me over to the window and I will prove it to you."

We both finished our bologna sandwiches and then went up to the window and I read off my case number on my wristband. My charges appeared on the screen. The guy looked at me with the widest whitest eyes and says "DAMN SON THAT'S OG!!!!!!" To educate all of you that do not know, the term OG refers to 'Original Gangster' which is arguably the highest honor you can receive or be called in the criminal world. You can call someone a thief, a hustler, a murderer, drug dealer, but when you call someone OG they don't need an explanation. The shorter term from there is then called G.

As a white dude, you don't just walk around and call people G in jail and I was in California with an overpopulated jail system. When they finally got us to our pods of inmates, Luthor and I were separated. He said that we would see each other tomorrow and face the judge to get our bail amounts. It was then, that I spent my first night, in jail. I woke up the next morning at 4:30 am and ate breakfast (jail food). I gathered my things and went through a long process of standing and waiting to see the judge. They put all the males on one side of the room and all the females on the other. Luthor and I were able to sit next to each other in the courtroom but only had a few minutes to talk because once the judge was in the room we had to be silent.

Luthor told me that this is the part where the judge reads what you did in front of everybody. He would read your prior offenses and then set your bail amount based on what he feels. He also said it was always pretty funny so just sit back and watch. While in the room I saw the slums of society, most of them were people with a severe lack of education, social problems, deformities and to be honest, all of them were really physically ugly human beings. Luthor and I appeared to be the only decent looking/normal people in the room. I watched as a man in his late teens or early 20's fall out of his chair onto the ground looking ghost white. Luthor said he was going through a heroin or meth withdrawal.

The females got to go first and most of them were there for petty theft, domestic violence, small drug possession, or prostitution. The way the judge made them feel though, was awful.

"Mrs. Jones, you are charged with prostitution, SEX, for $20. How do you plead?" It was 5am. I can only imagine the life of a judge. It was hard not to laugh at what he was saying. This judge was better than any television show. When I was called to wait in line to see the judge, Luthor was called a few people behind me. I guess things were in alphabetical order or something.

I went up and faced the judge, thankfully my face was shaved from the day before and my military haircut was still looking crisp. The judge was an old white man and I had a good feeling about my chances. I crossed the little door and went before the judge. I greeted him with a 'good morning your honor' hoping he would react kindly. He looked above his glasses, at me and squinted then he smiled and said 'good morning' in return.

No one else had said good morning to the judge that day and I figured it couldn't hurt my chances. I was already dressed in an orange jumpsuit and we were all criminals to the judge anyways. I stood in a military stance with my hands behind my back like I practiced all summer long and looked at the judge neither smiling, frowning, scared, or happy, but a blank face. I wanted to appear as neutral as possible.

The only information judge had in front of him was the police report, which was nothing more than a few handwritten sentences about the incident. Mine said something along the lines of "Suspect was apparently working with another man to rob Banco Americo." If this does not say something about the harsh nature of the justice system I don't know what will.

Listen to 'Mathematics' by Mos Def.
"A 5 minute sentence hearing and you're no longer free"

This was all the information the bail judge had. He read my charges aloud, but compared to everyone else, he read them quite slowly. I guess he was use to people committing small misdemeanors and drug related felonies. When he saw my charges he gave me much more attention.

"Mr. Loathing... you are charged with grand theft (pause... pause... pause...) of over $100,000

AND

...scheme to defraud a financial institution."

he then asked his clerks if I had any priors. "Prior convictions?"

"no priors your honor" replied his workers

"any prior arrests?" said Judge Heinrich

"none your honor" (my alcohol charges were dropped after I completed community service)

At this point the judge was not looking at the papers anymore, but at me. He stared at me for a good 10 seconds and at this point I was trying to relay nothing except "I don't need to go to be in jail" through my face. The judge took a deep breath and then said "Well Mr. Loathing, based upon your good standing as a citizen until this point and the grave severity of the charges placed against you, I set your bail at $2,500 per charge. Stay out of Banco Americo and do not remain in contact with the co-defendant"

BANG GAVEL

I kept my military face and went out and waited for my fellow inmates. Once in the waiting room I let out the biggest sigh of relief and just realized that all I needed was $500 to a bondsman and I would be out of jail! This did mean however, I was not allowed to talk to Luthor anymore or I could face serious punishment. As I waited in the room with a few other guys, Luthor came through the door looking like he just won the lottery.

"WOOOOOOO!!!!!!! Judge set my charges the SAME and dropped the drug charges to $500."

This was the last time I ever spoke to Luthor in person. He had people coming to bail him out and I knew with a few phone calls I could get myself out as well. I hoped.

I was finally assigned to my pod which was full of about 80 other inmates. There were only a few bunk beds in the entire place and when I was assigned my bed it was next to the entrance and I had a top bunk. This for me, was a luxury. I didn't have to worry about being on the same level as everyone else and I was also by the main entrance so there were police officers constantly walking in and out along with those on duty.

For those that have never been to jail, know that jail is not a violent place. It is an air conditioned "hotel" compared to prison. Everybody has a bed, you can use the communal showers whenever you like, there were books to read and they even had a basketball court with a ball. Jail is a higher quality lifestyle than a lot of people live in the United States and I was amazed and finally understood what professor Oheama was talking about. The private prison system in the United States is horrible and it's tough for me to comprehend. The mentality of politicians imprisoning people for small drug charges and petty crimes just so they can make more money, puzzles me. Those politicians are the real criminals.

To give you a breakdown of what my 80 guys looked like. Over 50% were Hispanic 25% were Black and the remaining were a mixture of other ethnic groups. Also, these were some of the biggest humans I had ever seen. You could tell what type of people were experiencing their first time, they were usually fat, scared looking, and acted like a punk. Jail serves as what I learned inside as the "hotel" between prison and the real world. Those getting ready to go to prison were inside jail and just killing time in the system. The dudes that had been to prison before, were (I do not need to exaggerate) the largest and most animal like human beings I had ever seen. One of which was sleeping right underneath me. His name was Willy.

Willy was African American 6'6", 250lbs and chiseled muscle. I bet if he ever went back to playing sports he would put professional footballers to shame. He was the calmest nicest guy and very sophisticated. You would never guess what he was in jail for. Well, maybe you can, he was a bank robber.

Willy had been robbing banks for about a decade and was really good at it. He went to college, got a degree in finance, sold a bit of weed on the side and started a job that he hated at some financial firm. After working there for a little bit, he was so frustrated with making bullshit money with his "education" that he talked to a few friends and they robbed a bank for the first time.

Andrea

Dublin, Ireland

"Beaches, Bedrooms & Barcelona" by Ace Loathing

Willy had the following strategy. He would get dressed up in a jogging suit and running shoes and go into the bank wearing sun glasses and a drawstring backpack. Except the trick was, that he would have on not one running suit, but two. He would always make sure there was a female teller and he would small talk for a minute and then ask to see her nails because he "liked that color". Once both hands were in his view he would hand the teller a note saying he had a bomb in his backpack and that he needed all the money from her second drawer (I guess he knew that all the money was also in the second drawer) and that she could only use one hand. (this made it very difficult to slip the alarm immediately) The note also said that she could not say anything until he was out of the bank otherwise he would detonate the bomb.

Once he had the money, he would run out of the bank and since he was already in running clothes it looked like he was just going for a jog. He would sprint as fast as he could to a safe predetermined location. Then he ripped off the first colored suit and then continued running down the street in a completely different color and his friend in the getaway car was stationed about 300 meters away and then they drove off.

"I did this for about a decade, we would go all over the country and hit the small banks, credit unions, and ones that didn't have a lot of security. I had over $180,000 saved in my house and the FBI finally caught on to me. They broke into my house when I wasn't home and took my money and raided the place. They even took my microwave, what the FUCK are they gonna do with my microwave? I dunno man, fuck the police".

Now Willy had been to prison, but he had only been to Federal Prison. I asked the difference and he said that since he was robbing FDIC banks, like I did, all of his crimes were Federal and that's who the jurisdiction was left up to. He also said that federal prisons are really nice, compared to state prisons and if you ever commit a crime worth going to prison, it should be at a federal level. "Man, I was at a prison for almost 2 years and we had a golf course, air conditioned cells, higher quality food than this garbage, it is DEFINITELY where all our tax money goes."

Now I understood a bit more about the system, the way things worked and what I was going to do. It was amazing to understand that most criminals are just normal people (excluding rapists, murderers and child molesters) that came on hard times, frustration, or bad luck and made a mistake. Granted, Willy was a career criminal, but it was amazing to hear his perspective and the story of his life up until this point.

When I first took the bunk above his, people were walking around, bartering and trading stamps and letters, for food etc. I have to be honest, I was one of smaller people, not shorter, but definitely on the small side compared to these beasts. One guy came around and was selling something and picked a little fight with me since I was sitting up on the top bunk. I forget what he said, but it made me a little mad so I decided to immediately call him out. He was bigger than me, but chances were he wasn't more gangster than me.

"So what got you in this joint playboy? Didn't pay child support" - I said

"Go fuck yourself, Slinging caine and moving work like half of us in here," - he said

"I bet you got a DUI, fuckboy." he continued

Luthor had told me what a fuckboy was. A fuckboy is literally what it sounds like. Since we were surrounded by dudes, usually the small and the weak ones would be subject to rape and since they couldn't fight back, everyone usually passed them around "bustin cheeks" and called them fuckboys. Being called a fuckboy is also a huge insult and I was not going to be called out like that.

I stayed on the top of my bunk since that still made me higher than him and he was about 5-6 meters away and I said louder so more people could hear me. "OH you want to know what I did, FUCK BOY, I robbed Banco Americo for over $100,000" At this point about 10 people had noticed our conversation and we're listening."Yeah, we'll see about that, Yo! Phone in and find out if FUCKBOY is straight"

Some other guys in the pod called home because we were allowed to use the phone at this time and looked up my name. The article appeared in the paper and it said I stole more than $100,000 from Banco Americo. As soon as the guy on the phone heard the news he told everyone in the pod "DAMN! THIS MAN IS A GANGSTER" The guy hung up the phone and told everyone I was not lying. The other guy who called me out, never even walked by my bunk again the rest of the time I was there.

Fuckboy.

It was at this point that I met almost everybody else in my pod. Everybody gathered around me in a circle and I told the story to about 80 people. I even animated it a little bit to appease the crowd. Everybody was excited and some huge African American guy with face tattoos and gold teeth walked up to me, slapped and pounded my hand and was like "That's gangsta, and you's a gangsta". He was definitely one of the leaders in my pod and I now had the respect of everybody. I had the coolest story of everybody there. Luthor was right, they treated me like a king.

Willy and I quickly became friends and I was thankful for his help to use the phone. I was never given the chance to call home while in central booking. Willy was also quite good at chess, I guess you would be after years of practice. I learned how to use the phones and I only had a few numbers memorized and one of them was Austin. I called him and he couldn't believe that I was calling him from jail. He said he would come and try to bail me out. Him and Dante both got the money needed and went to a bondsman. The bondsman would not accept either of them because they did not own a piece of property or have a current employer. Dante did not have 5k saved up to to come and bail me outright, I had that in the bank, but did not have access to it. I had to make the hardest decision of my life. I would have to call my mother and father and tell them what happened and hopefully they would get me out of there.

When my father picked up the phone, he was in awe, I could hear it in his voice and he was so confused and having a surreal moment I had to say something drastic so I could get out of there. "Dad, I might get killed if I stay in here, get me out and I can pay you back, you get the money back anyways when the case is over." I knew very well that $5,000 was not a lot of money to my parents, they owned two houses (no mortgage payments) and several automobiles, and had lots of savings in the bank because they were misers. It was simply a matter of whether or not they wanted to do it. My father said no but my mother convinced him. I'm pretty sure my mother had more of a say in it than he did. They said they would come up the next day and handle the situation. The car was also at the impound. My father kept refusing to sell me the car for years and it was still under his name. I assumed he wanted his property back. I waited in jail another night and my parents finally came and got me. Before I left jail, I had an epiphany that would forever change my life and I cannot be more thankful that I robbed a bank.

While sitting in jail and watching all the other inmates interact, a woman with a cart came through the entrance in the middle of the facility and then spoke into the microphone. "Medical, I repeat, medical is here. All of you requiring medications, yearly flu shots or those that have any new medical needs, please come see me." It was at this point that I saw people go up and receive their medications, vaccinations and all types of medical treatments. I thought to myself "People in the United States jail/prison system live better than people in the developing world, they even receive health care."

It was at this point that I decided that if I was smart enough to make all the qualifications for the JAG program why not try and become a doctor instead. If lawyers were put in place to "help" people like me, get out of their problems I did not want any part of it. It was in this moment that I realized law was no longer my calling, nor could it be. Medicine is still a lifelong goal, I am not sure exactly how I will make it happen. Life finds a way.

While my brief time spent in Jail was not stress free, I can still recall certain events and how ridiculous my entire situation was. I would always consider myself a creative person, but experiencing all that I have done, is not a healthy mixture for the human mind. For the first time in my life I had respect from my peers. Prisoners. The first time in my life I was popular, was among prisoners.

Great. The first place I finally felt welcomed and even treated with respect, was in custody. I needed to get out of there. While inside, the last afternoon, all of us were instructed to clean the pod. I went to pick up a mop and before I even touched the handle, Willy had slapped somebody on the back and said "get the fuck up, half-pint!" The man was sitting down playing cards. The man was also of Hispanic origin with tattoos all over his body. The small man picked up the mop and I saw another man, the age of 65 say peacefully "Don't worry about cleaning, we got it." while looking at me.

Most of the people inside that I talked to, said that I did not deserve to be in there. This served as another level of motivation. Almost as if life was telling me "You are welcome down here at the bottom, but c'mon man, we think you can do better." My name was finally called and I left to change into my civilian clothes and leave jail. I met my parents outside the station and went to pick up my car, but when we filled out all the paperwork and paid the fees, the people at the impound said "Do you have the keys?" Of course we did not have the keys! They were at the police station and we did not have time to go there and retrieve them. The people at the impound were complete assholes. They only accepted money orders in the exact amounts required. They would not even accept cash. The place also closed early and they would only accept a money order written on the same day. They were trying to fuck over poor people that had limited resources.

Brief example. If my car was impounded by the police during a crime and I had the right to have it back and I was on foot alone, this would be my scenario.

1. Exit the jail and walk 10 miles to the impound station
2. Walk to the counter and learn the amount needed to pay for release
3. Walk roughly 10 miles in the opposite direction to the police station and pick up my keys that were confiscated
4. Walk another 5 miles to the nearest location writing money orders, presuming I had the hundreds of dollars necessary to buy a money order
5. Walk however many miles to the impound station from the money order location, on the same day in the allotted business hours and retrieve my car.

Thank you mom and dad for coming to get me and even paying to release the car. My father said he was keeping a tab, but I now know that he never expected me to pay back that money anyways.

My relationship with my father and his money is another reason I decided to rob the bank. I am very angry at my father because he stole not money, but opportunity from his children, especially from me. In the United States, poorer individuals are eligible for Pell Grants which are free grants from the government to attend University. Those who received Pell Grants were eligible for nearly $32,000 divided equally over the course of 4 years. With these Pell Grants, I would not have to work a job during my time at University and I could concentrate on school. I would not have a luxurious life, but it would provide me with enough to live a minimum wage lifestyle. It would also give me time, which is much more valuable than money. I would not have to waste my time working a low paying job, instead I could focus on school. I applied for my Pell Grants at age 18, but was denied because my parents were claiming me as a "dependent" on their taxes.

At age 18 I was legally an adult, but my father did not see it this way. He viewed me as his property until I was age 24 and he could claim me as a "dependent" on his taxes. If your parents claim you as a "dependent" it means that they are responsible for you financially, during that specific tax filing period. The government looked at my father's tax returns and because he claimed to provide for me financially, I was not eligible to receive Pell Grants during University. He never paid me a dime during those 4 years.

The truth of the matter was, the moment I was kicked out of his house at age 18, I received nothing from him or my mother. The Prepaid college program covered less than 35% of the actual costs of attending University. I was responsible for paying the other 65% along with my cost of living. By claiming me as a "dependent" however, my father received a tax credit, which in turn, placed thousands more into his pocket, annually. To be clear, due to greed and hatred, my father denied me access to over $32,000 in free government money. He instead put somewhere between $9,000-12,000 into his own bank account while claiming to help me with my expenses during University. What hurts me the most is that I fought with him every year about my legal rights to this money. Every year, my father lied to the government claiming to support his "dependents" while they attended University.

To this day, he denies any wrongdoing as does my mother. I assume that he did this to me because the cost of the Prepaid College Program was roughly the same amount that he received back in tax credits. I think he saw it as a "money back guarantee" that I could not fight, unless I had the money to take him to court. Every year of University I went to the financial aid office and explained that my parents were lying about me on their taxes. I even showed copies of my tax returns to prove I was earning more than $10,000 annually. The financial aid office said I would have to take it court and it would cost me thousands of dollars to do so. I never thought that my parents were greedy enough that they would lie about me on their tax returns. I do not know how my parents live with themselves year after year, knowing they robbed their firstborn child of his future, in exchange for a few thousand dollars.

What occurred after I robbed the bank was the most heartfelt. My little sister was in her second year of University and was facing the same problem. My parents were stealing from her. She did not have enough money for a computer when she started school. I had extra money from working and I decided to buy her a macbook. I also paid her rent for several months, directly in front of my mother because my sister was in between jobs and could barely scrape by. My sister worked as a waitress and attended school full time.

After 4 years of fighting with my parents, robbing the bank, going to jail and creating a huge mess for my family, my father finally realized he was wrong. The following year, my sister filed her tax returns as an "independent" and she received Pell Grants for the first time. My sister continued working during University and graduated with virtually no debt. It took a lifetime of work from me to get my sister half of what she was eligible for. I hope the pain and torment of my father is beginning to sink in.

I will never forgive you for what you did Dad. You should be ashamed of who you are as a person, an educator, a husband and a father. As a protest to my father and his actions, I stopped drinking a few years later and have remained sober until this day.

I went and had dinner with my parents because they had to go and work the next day. We talked about what was going to happen and to be honest, we had no idea. I had a court date next month and I already filed the paperwork for a public defender. I owe my parents more than a few thousand dollars for bailing me out. It's just a shame I had to rob a bank to bring my family a little closer together. It was the first time I saw my parents since Bootcamp, the year prior.

I drove home that evening in another state of mind. For the first time in a long time, I had broken my normal cycle. It was almost as if my eyes were recording instead of watching a re-run. I felt alive. I arrived home and climbed the stairs to face my front door. I saw two people, one of my friends from childhood named Silva and a beautiful woman named Veronica.

Chapter 11

"Hypnotized" by Plies, Akon

The first time I met Veronica was before a tailgate at an apartment party in August of 2012. A bunch of people were meeting up to go and tailgate for the first football game of the season. I was there, talking to girls and I had just gotten back from Bootcamp. Let's say I was feeling quite confident. I went to the kitchen passing dozens of people and I saw this beautiful blonde girl. She stood about 5'8" with a voluptuous body holding all the red solo cups and I needed one. American Counterculture injection (red solo cups are usually not handed out at parties unless you have paid for alcohol, they were always guarded by somebody, in this moment, it happened to be Veronica) I had never met Veronica before and I tapped her on the shoulder and asked "Can I have a cup please?" She boasts out "WELL WHO THE FUCK ARE YOU?"

Almost everyone at the party became silent. We both just stood there looking at each other with locked eyes. Veronica was a pitbull, but underneath her Alpha female persona, she was brittle as a house of cards. She cried in front of me in public before. Everyone woman, deep down, is a little girl and I think the little boy in me was talking to the little girl in her. I felt some type of connection.

It was at this moment that my friend Skyler, also from childhood who was one of Veronica's friends said "No Veronica this is Ace, remember? Ace?" as if he was talking to a pet dog. Veronica instantly changed from being the tough girl holding the Solo cups to a googly eyed princess who said "Oh, hi Ace! Nice to meet you, FINALLY." Apparently Skyler had mentioned me before, who knows what it was about, possibly the Military, or the fact that I consume earthly amounts of cannabis.

Whatever the reason, she was smiling and I was smiling. I was also really intimidated by how pretty she was. I took a cup and said "let's talk later" she smiled and I went to have a beer.

I hung out with Skyler more often that year than I had in years prior and we consume lots of cannabis. After I had that first interaction with Veronica I asked Skyler who she was and I got the scoop. She had a similar background to me, but even more christian. Her father was a preacher of the christian church and at times in her life she was even more brainwashed christian than I was. When she came to college she finally broke free, drinking, drugs, lots of sex and even got a job that most people would look the other way at. Veronica was an exotic dancer at a high end Gentleman's club.

As I arrived to my doorstep and found Silva and Veronica there, I was really thankful that one of my oldest friends was there to support me after I got out jail. I was however, curious as to why Veronica was there. Veronica displayed signs of hybristophilia. Apparently robbing a bank is rather attractive. Not many women can say they know a bank robber, or let alone, slept with one. I however was not focused on anything except the fact that I was going to prison for robbing a bank. It was only a matter of time.

When I opened the door and took them inside I went to the kitchen and poured myself a glass of water. I was thirsty and stressed beyond belief. Silva and I began talking, just bullshit conversation, but it calmed me down. I remember being at the far end of the kitchen and Silva was on my left and Veronica was on my right. It was silent at this point and I was still wearing the clothes I was arrested in, a formal blue dress shirt, black pants and tie. Silva asked me some question "So how do you feel man?" and it was at this point that I walked up to Veronica and put my right hand lightly around her throat, I still had a very serious look on my face because all I was thinking about was prison. I looked Veronica right in the eyes and said "Have you ever wanted to kill somebody (I squeezed her throat a little harder, then turned my gaze towards Silva) "for their mistake?" (slowly letting go of her throat) I exited the kitchen, I was in another world. I am sure I gave Veronica butterflies, at least I hope I did.

Veronica and Silva hung out for another hour as all of us shared a blunt on my balcony. I really needed a good burn to calm me down. We talked about what was going to happen and Silva was there for me in case I needed anything. Veronica was quiet the entire time and I had no idea what she was doing there. Looking back on it. I had just come out of Jail and instead of wanting a girl more than anything, I wanted certainty of my future.

If Veronica ever has a chance to read this story, I want her to know that I am truly sorry for the way I treated her the entire time I knew her. You are beautiful Veronica, you have a wonderful personality and I think it takes a crazy christian upbringing to make a woman become a stripper and face torment from men. I wish I was more direct with you, but my lack of experience with women was a detriment to our interactions and for this I am truly sorry. But let it be known that I have also, broken free! I have slept with dozens of women in the last few years, developed some relationships, and I do my best to keep all of my girls happy. I learned since 2013 and I hope that one day we can meet again and show each other how much we now know.

After Silva and Veronica left, Dante came over. He was angry. The first thing he said was "Nigga why the FUCK didn't you tell me?!? If you told me, we would have gotten away with it... $100,000!!! do you know what we could do with $100,000 ???"

Leave it up to Dante to be impressed and disappointed that he wasn't in on the plan. It was at this point that I knew Dante was on my side. Dante didn't mind getting into trouble, well, he had never actually been caught doing anything illegal so he didn't know what trouble felt like. I didn't have a job and had little chance of getting a new one with felony charges on my record. It was about time that I joined Dante in the business that he was already good at. Moving work. Dante moved many 'substances' through the University system.

That Friday, we all received our financial aid for the spring semester and I knew exactly what I was going to invest in. I was already buying weed by the ounce to save money and I knew plenty of people that were already buying weed. All I

159

had to do was get my product out there and start selling. The only thing that was holding me back were my roommates. Topher was drug free and this new guy that lived with us was always in his room playing video games. If I was going to set up a trap house and sell weed, I would need to make sure my roommates would never find out.

I took the following precautions and always sold my product in the following manner.

1. I bought a vacuum sealer so I could keep my product air tight and smell proof.
2. I disguised the product and put it inside small Doritos bags. I would then vacuum seal and heat seal the Doritos bags back to their 'unopened' status making the weed disappear.
3. I only sold to college kids
4. I tried to only sell to females
5. I bought a separate phone from Metro PCS that only had calling and texting so I had a burner phone and nothing would be tied to my number.
6. Every time I prepared, opened, closed, sealed or touched anything, I would be wearing surgeons gloves. This would keep my fingerprints off everything.
7. I only worked during the daylight hours
8. I charged a delivery fee if people did not want to come to my place
9. I was always very welcoming and a good host, I would make people drinks, smoke them out and make sure every time they came to my house they understood I was one of their friends and they should feel comfortable.
10. I cleaned my house and room everyday, military standard
11. I bought a triple beam scale that everyone used in chemistry class and my customers always weighed their own product right before their eyes. I was never going to hustle my customers, I needed them to trust

me and have a positive experience, so they would tell their friends and come back.

I also knew that deep down, weed did not make that much money, you could get it from anywhere so I asked around and kept searching for something else that I knew everyone in college wanted to try. Magic Mushrooms.

It was tough, I asked around a lot and then one day a friend of Austin's came over to visit, his name was Benny. I knew Benny from before, he lived in the same building as Austin, Jamal and I during freshman year. Benny didn't do any drugs because he wanted to go and work for the FBI when he graduated. Every time I asked him to try cannabis he would say in a funny way "NO NO NO, thanks but no thanks, somehow, some way, there is a little old lady who is going to see me stoned and then that lady is going write it down in her journal that she saw me stoned and then when the FBI does a background check she is going to come forward and tell everyone that I was stoned, just once, on your balcony" Benny was a funny guy.

As Austin, Benny and I were talking on my balcony, I told Austin that I was still searching for mushrooms. Austin wanted to try them as well. I had done mushrooms with James and Gibrarian for the first time on spring break in 2011. It was the most positive spiritual experience of my life and completely changed the way I viewed every living thing from that moment on. Psilocybin has the power to save the world and I hope everyone can try it someday. Benny said that his girlfriend over in San Diego had some old roommates that use to grow mushrooms in large quantities. I asked for her contact info, shot her a few texts and gave her a call. Benny said he was going there next weekend to visit her anyway. It was now getting close to spring break and I knew that everybody dying to take a "trip". I saw a demand, and hopefully I had just found the supply.

I drove down to meet Benny and his girlfriend in San Diego and to meet these roommates that supposedly had large quantities of Psilocybin mushrooms. We ate dinner, talked about what was going on and I had already secured a price. $1500 for a half pound. A half pound is over 200 grams of mushrooms. Any amount of mushrooms is considered a felony and since I had a really large bag it didn't make a difference. Besides, I thought I was going to prison anyways. I had seen pounds of weed and large quantities of other drugs, but never a bag of mushrooms that had to fit inside of a suitcase. These bags were HUGE! One of the mushrooms was 15 grams by itself and we called it the umbrella.

I knew that I had a great looking product and I even took a small dose to make sure they would do the trick. The guys who sold them to me said that 1.75g was enough to make anyone have an experience if they had never had one before. Seasoned veterans could take more if they wanted, but these were pretty strong specimens. I figured at 20-30 euros a "trip" I would triple my money and have a solid amount to live off of the rest of the semester.

I tried constantly to find work, but I always came up with no for an answer. It is almost impossible to find employment legally with a couple of felonies on your record, even though I had employment history since 2004. The situation was quite frustrating for someone who was in their final semester of undergraduate education. I used almost half of my money from my financial aid on those mushrooms in hopes that they would sell at University. I drove them back to Los Angeles and got to marketing. My goal was to become the mushroom man on campus.

I already had my core group of friends from childhood that wanted to try them. This group included, Silva, Skyler, Sam and some new friends Bruce, and Tu. Veronica had a few friends as well that wanted to try them and from there I began to make an entirely new group of friends. All the people mentioned before listened to electronic dance music (EDM). I was super depressed and constantly thinking that I was going to prison, these people really emerged as my new friends in a time of need while I was losing my mind.

As spring break approached I knew that the days leading up to it would be my busiest days. I needed a few weeks to let people know and then people could come pick up from me and then head off to their spring break destination. I went to a few guys in the fraternity system that I knew, but I had to be careful, because half of the greek life system was against drugs and I didn't want anyone knowing I was the man behind the mask. The guys in greek laid the foundation and I moved almost 100 trips right before spring break. I cleared about $3000 and already covered my costs. I still had about $1000 left to sell, but I would need more money to pay my rent and feed myself. I continued to sell weed and other small amounts of mushrooms over the spring break. At the end of the break, I earned enough money to pay off my rent for a few months until my final court date, so I did. I would still need money to eat and survive the rest of the semester. I continued to sell weed since I was unable to find other work.

When my parents left to go back home after they bailed me out, one thing they told me was that I was still on my own and if I wanted to get a lawyer it was going to come out of my own pocket. Hiring a private attorney is expensive, let alone finding one that would take the case. My case was complex, and most lawyers don't like hurting their winning percentage. In the middle of this mind bending depression, I had my first meeting with my public defender. I woke up and drove to her office and after I waited in the lobby for almost an hour I went inside to speak to her. She was short, fat, and had very poor people skills. This woman had graduated almost a decade earlier from law school. She had very little confidence when she spoke, except when she told me one line. "You are GOING to prison, it's not a matter of if, it's only a matter of how long." Great, just what I wanted to hear. In the back of my mind however, I had higher hopes.

I asked what steps were necessary to prolong the court case so I could at least try and finish the semester and have my degree before I went in. She looked at me and said she could file for an extension and maybe give me 6-8 weeks into the summer and hopefully everything would be okay. We filed the paperwork and I would see her in court in a few weeks. After another week or so, I got a call from a number, on my personal phone that I did not have saved in my contacts. It was the area code of my hometown and after I let it go to voicemail only one name came to mind when I read it aloud. Scott.

It had been a long time since I talked to Scott since he had gone off to college a few years ahead of me. But now that I remembered, he also attended USC, or at least graduated by now since I was in my senior year. I quickly give it a call back, he answers and I said "Scott?!?" He said "Ace how you doing buddy?" I responded in all honesty "Well, Scott I've been better" Scott responds "I can imagine, listen man, I heard about what happened and I want to let you know that my father is working on it, you are not going down without a fight" My heart stopped and I think I even teared. If god wasn't real then I think the divine forces of mother nature were on my side. "Come down to my house for Easter man, my father wants to talk to you and I think he might have a solution to your problems,"

"I will be there Scott, thank you man." I said.

"Good to hear from you man, stay outta trouble, see you soon." Scott hung up the phone.

As I hung up the phone I wanted to vomit at what just happened to me. A true friend had to come my rescue in my time of need. Scott's father was one of the biggest lawyers in my hometown. Although he was not a criminal defense lawyer himself, he had the best connections of anyone I had met in my life. Easter weekend was spent with Scott's family. I drove to their estate experiencing mixed feelings of hope, humility and fear. After we ate dinner, I spoke with Scott's father alone, watching the sunset. He spoke to me in a way that I had never heard anyone talk before.

"Now Ace, I looked at your case and I'm sure you researched everything as best as you could and realized that because of the charges, you scored prison time. A maximum of 41 months."

(Note: In the state of California, they have a score sheet that summarizes your criminal charges and depending on the

164

severity of the charges, you earn points. If you score a minimum number of points, you have to serve MANDATORY prison time, regardless if it was your first offense or not)

"I realize this"

Scott's father then said something that gave me hope and proved the point to me that in this life, it is not what you know, but who, you know.

"This does not mean you are going to prison, with a good private attorney working on the case and the off chance that he knows the State attorney, we can work out some compromise, I made a few phone calls and found out who your State attorney was, and I also found a private attorney who has a relationship with him. Since this is your first time with no priors you stand a good chance in court."

Scott's father then explained the court system and the process. When someone is arrested, they have a file made with all the specifics of the case included. To speed up everything, the only information presented to the judge was my name and the current charges against me.

When I went and saw the judge the first time at my arraignment and made a plea of not guilty, the only thing she knew about the case was my name, and the charges against me. A judge works on many cases at once and does not have the time to open up and read through the specifics. She was working on a million things at that time and I was just another page on her docket. I would have several court dates prior to the "trial by jury date" to see if the State prosecutor and the defense worked out an agreement. This is all put in place to not waste the judges time.

As a brief example. I rob a bank and I have arraignment, hearing, pre-trial, possible pre-trial extension, and then trial. 5 Court dates. If the punishment assigned to me for my crime is 41 months prison, any time during the different periods (hearing, pre trial, trial), I can plead guilty and accept the punishment and the case never goes to a judge. The job of the State Attorney is to work with the defense attorney and come up with a punishment that is still acceptable for the crime, but less severe than the maximum.

If you have a public defender that is over-worked with a bunch of cases he/she almost never gets a chance to talk with the State Attorney because he/she is a busy person seeing hundreds if not more cases at a time. If you miss the chance to speak with the State attorney, you missed your shot. This is the problem with public defenders, they have too many cases and not enough time to focus on them. Let alone they are paid like shit and could care less about what happens to you. You are just another number in the system.

A private attorney on the other hand is very well paid, so well paid that they can take a load that is suitable for themselves and actually get something done. They are not commanded by a local office to tell them what to do. My Private attorney Bobby Jackson had the ability to take his own cases and choose his own battles, almost securing his own success rate. What Bobby was planning to do was negotiate with the state attorney (someone he had worked with prior) for a punishment acceptable for the crime, but would also set a precedent for my charges, hopefully avoiding prison.

Elvira

Stockholm, Sweden

"Beaches, Bedrooms & Barcelona" by Ace Loathing

Now, just because the State attorney and the Defense agree on a punishment, it is still up for the Judge to approve of the sentence. If the judge does not approve of the sentence then I was right back into the court system and the private attorney and the state attorney had both failed their objective.

Scott's father, knew Bobby from back in the day and Bobby worked with the State attorney years prior. The triangle was complete and the only thing left in question was the money. Bobby was asking $7500 and from what I could infer from Scott's father, this was a ridiculously low amount to try a case of first degree felony bank robbery. I think he was going to pay Bobby some real money on the side to cover his losses. Brian knew that I came from a comparatively poor family. I told him that I did not have that kind of money and my parents were not going to help me. He asked for the email and phone numbers of my parents and he said he would do his best.

I left with some Easter leftovers and headed back to University with an emotionally filled heart and stuffed stomach. I could not believe the luck that life was giving me. I had my rent paid for the semester, the potential of having a private attorney work on my case and the possibility of even being able to graduate with a degree in Economics. All I had to do now, was lay low, pass all my classes and I might have a chance of NOT going to prison. The only underlying part that troubled, stressed and tormented me to no end, was the fact that I scored MANDATORY prison time and it was hard to not think about what was going to happen to me, all day, every day for the next few months.

Chapter 12

The rest of my semester was spent in the following manner.

1. Sell enough weed to pay my expenses, eat well, go to clubs, concerts, consume alcohol, and be able to smoke as much weed as necessary to keep the stress levels of ever looming prison off my back
2. Go to class and pass all my classes. This was already a problem because I failed the first round of tests and would have to get between A's and B's to finish out the semester with high enough marks required to graduate
3. Surround myself with friends so I would not lose my mind.

I did not even think about getting a girlfriend. The last thing on my mind was sex, a relationship or having to put woman in the position of having her boyfriend go off to prison. I had never looked to a woman for strength this far in my life and I was not about to start now. One of the biggest regrets that I had was not making a move on Veronica. I was socially awkward and only hooked up with a few girls during my time in the fraternity. I was 21 years old and I still had virtually no existence of a sex life. Years later I finally learned a bit more about myself. I have slept with dozens women and even had a few relationships. Practice makes perfect.

Something I did not know about Veronica until much later was that she slept with almost all of my friends. I had no idea and as I met more and more people, they too, had also slept with Veronica. Everybody was always making jokes about Veronica's last name which was Bach. Whenever a bunch of us were hanging out, people would say "Veronica COCK, AAHH, MORE COCKS in my MOUTH, give me that good head Veronica! LEGENDARY BLOW JOBS"

things of this nature...

Everybody always laughed and it always ended with a "Go kill yourself _____" from Veronica

I guess they weren't lying.

Years later, I now realize that the best thing for me, besides, drugs, alcohol and partying to relieve my stress, would have been to pursue a relationship with Veronica and actually have had a sex life with a beautiful woman that was attracted to my character. I really fucked this up, but the crazy christian brainwashing that I endured as a child was always making me feel guilty about sex, even though I experienced it multiple times. It was hard to not fear the act. I could not convince myself that the experience of pleasure was greater than the risk of conceiving a child or committing a sin against god. Veronica would have made a great match, after all, her father was a pastor. A bank robber shagging a stripper. Nice.

Scott's father made a call to my parents and convinced them of the severity of not having a personal attorney in a time like this. It took several phone calls and finally my parents decided to fork over the money and take the chance. In all seriousness, it truly was a risk. The judge would have to agree with whatever the state attorney proposed and if she said no, I was going to prison. My parents really wanted me to graduate and told me that it was my number one priority. I had already lost over 20 pounds by this point and it was hard to focus on anything. I ended the semester by passing all of my classes. I was set to graduate, all I had to wait on now was my court date.

A few weeks before graduating I logged onto my online account with the school and looked up my graduation profile, but it said 99% completion.

Huh? What? I passed all of my classes, why does it say I do not have the credits to graduate? I peered through my graduation requirements and one of them was that I needed to have a 2.0 in all my core classes which were upper level economics courses. I always took hard classes and received mainly C's. After looking through my course grades I had earned two C- which pulled my grade point average overall for that section down to a 1.98.

Are you serious? So because I did not have a 2.0 in my core classes I was not allowed to graduate. I set up a meeting with my counselor and asked what I could do. Large Universities are a complete joke when it comes to a counselor. I went to the office and it was like waiting in line at the Department of Motor Vehicles. I waited for almost an hour and I was finally called to visit a counselor. Guess what he told me? The exact same thing I read on the website "Well, the University will not allow you to graduate if you do not have above a 2.0 in your core classes."

I then explained that I am about to go to prison and it is a miracle that the stress of this semester has not already killed me. "Is there anything that the University can do?" I asked. "Yes, you can enroll in summer courses and re-take one of your classes hoping that you get a better grade so you can graduate." I also remember asking if there was some way I could appeal my situation. They told me that the appeal dates had passed a few weeks ago and I was not eligible.

Fucking perfect, so now I have to come up with more money, stay in school over the summer just so I can take one class so I can graduate. When will I ever get a break?!?!

I went back to my room and smoked ridiculous amounts of weed and realized that I needed to come up with several more thousand dollars to take one fucking class to graduate. I then performed some research on my financial aid. I did not use my student loans my freshmen year so I should still have a few semesters left. I looked through the horribly designed websites for student aid and found that I had two semesters of credit left so I should be more than okay, all I would have to do is come up with money for rent and food.

I enrolled for the summer semester with two court dates looming in coming weeks. I browsed through classes and found the ONLY class available for my major that could increase my GPA. My major was Business Economics, which had less than 50 people in my graduating class, regular Economics, had almost 800. Most people chose something in the business college like marketing or finance, or they chose the "soft" side of Economics which was all theory and no calculus or applied mathematics. The University only offered one class during the entire summer semester that would satisfy my requirement, International Economics with Calculus. It was offered only once per week on Wednesdays for a 3 hour segment. I looked at my court schedule and guess when I had BOTH of my court dates.

Wednesday.

The teacher was even nice enough to post the syllabus. The class consisted of two tests and a final. Guess when both of the tests were?

On my court dates.

I was losing my mind.

I would have court in the afternoon and the class in the evening on both of those days. When I went to the first class, the teacher said that all information for tests would be given in class, the book was merely a reference. The final grades would also be given in a form of A-F with no plus or minus. If students think studying for an exam to graduate college is stressful, imagine how I felt. I would have to set a precedent in the state of California for First Degree Felony Grand Theft to avoid going to prison, AND STUDY for my final class to graduate with a degree.

I went home and smoked copious amounts of cannabis. Thank god I was selling it, I would have never been able to afford my habits at the prices I was charging people.

The first court date rolled around and Bobby asked for an extension. Let me say, Bobby knew what the fuck he was doing. During court I watched other lawyers talk to the judge and a lot of them were absolute clowns. They demonstrated poor levels of professionalism, while others were blatantly unprepared. Developing a relationship with the judge was crucial. I felt sorry for some of the other defendants, their lawyer was garbage. Bobby came to court wearing a suit and holding nothing but a small folder with my information. He greeted the judge and said "Your honor, council requests to approach the bench"

"Granted" said the Judge.

I had never seen this before, even on television. Bobby walked right up to the Judge and she leaned in and they had a private conversation. The court reporter even stopped typing because she could not hear what they were saying. He talked to her for about 20 seconds and then she banged the gavel and approved my extension. It was over. I had another meeting the next month.

We had already asked for a lesser punishment involving jail time, and some probation, but it was denied and we had nothing to bring before the judge. I went to class that day and took my first exam, the third week of a 10 week semester. Guess what score I scored? 78%. A Grade of 'C'.

"Why I fucked 'em both when they said they sisters?"
- French Montana

Mahin & Estera

Tehran, Iran

"Beaches, Bedrooms & Barcelona" by Ace Loathing

Fuck! I would have to get at least a B on the next exam and the final in order to have a B for the course. A few more weeks went by and these were the most stressful. Robert was only paid for until the final pre-trial court date. If I chose to go to trial, it was not part of the agreement and I would have to go back to the public defender, or represent myself. She was already flustered with work and if we went to trial, we would likely lose and my punishment would be 41 months prison time. Talk about stress. The plan with the state attorney would have to work now or never. Robert along with the state attorney had done some research and the best plan they could come up with was 4 years of probation and 50 hours community service.

Probation? Really? You're telling me that If I set this precedent, someone can rob a bank for a 1st degree felony amount and only get probation? Robert and the State attorney said because I was a first time offender, it was highly possible. My judge was also the youngest female to ever have her position and loved to set precedents. I was a white male with no priors and about to graduate college. It would not be favorable for the "rehabilitation" of my character to send me to prison. We had a chance.

I sat there thinking, "Wow, having a private attorney, you can do anything, this is amazing." There was however, one catch. I could earn probation but I would have to be convicted and would be labeled as a felon for the rest of my life. Ouch. I weighed out my options, I would be a felon, but I would not be going to prison and face harsh conditions and the possibility of being murdered or severely injured due to my size. There was also one underlying factor that weighed heavily on my decision. Luthor.

Remember that Luthor was going through the same court process as I, however, I was not allowed to speak to him, even though I wanted to. He was on his 3rd conviction of a felony so prison time was mandatory, just a matter of how long. When we were in jail, a guy came over to Luthor and was like "Yo Luthor! Long time Dog, u good?" A little bit later when we stood in line to change clothes into our orange jump suits, another guy in line was like "Yo Nigga, Luthor is back!" Luthor already knew people inside. This truly scared me. If he was 100% going to prison he had a much different life to think about then I did. I still had hopes of not going to prison. Everyday that Luthor would be sitting in prison I would be out free. Every time he woke up, for years, the first thing he would think, is "I'm in here, and Ace is out there. Free."

Since Luthor already knew people and how the system worked, I was afraid. If I was sent to prison, I thought my chances of being killed would increase. It was difficult to study for any test. When Luthor was done with his sentence, who knows what prison might have done to him. He was a gangster and prison is the last step on that journey. Hopefully he would never have to go back, but a lot of people that I talked to said Luthor was going to come out of prison truly evil and maybe he was called to be a career criminal. I would not put it past him to seek vengeance or retribution. He had electrical engineering degree, but he liked to take risks and going to prison with 1st degree felony bank robbery charges made him a badass. He already knew the drug game, carried a gun illegally, nothing was scary to Luthor. I had a fear that Luthor would turn into a criminal mastermind and would have me killed if I was imprisoned. I confirmed the plan with Bobby and said, let's try it. If the judge declines it I'm going to prison anyways, it can't hurt.

I arrived at court (the day of my 2nd exam) and met Bobby and we talked for a few minutes. He asked me if I was ready to face the judge. It was now or never, all the money that my parents and I invested was either going to pay off, or I would be back to the public defender and serve prison time. I was called to the front of the courtroom and Bobby stood behind me, along with the State attorney. The judge asked if the State attorney had come to an agreement and it went something like this.

"Good afternoon your honor, the State attorney's office would like to brief you on the case and then offer the said plea bargain. The defendant Ace Thielmann Loathing worked as a teller for Banco Americo. In early January he conspired with a fellow University classmate and participated in defrauding Banco Americo. The amount in question was roughly $250,000 and the co-defendant was immediately apprehended by local authorities. Both Defendants immediately confessed, all money was returned and the bank suffered no insurable losses. No civilian or employee was present during the act and Mr. Loathing and the Co defendant were the only persons involved in the matter. Mr. Loathing currently attends the University of Southern California and graduates this semester with a degree in Economics. The co defendant also attends the University of Southern California and is in his final year of study. The defendant currently has no priors and it is his first offense, ever, in the justice system. The State attorney's office offers a conviction with a sentence of 4 years probation with a minimum of 50 hours of community service as the best sentence for his rehabilitation."

It was at this point the judge looked at me, for a good 10 seconds (the longest 10 seconds of my life) and the entire courtroom was silent. The court reporter stopped typing and it was just me and the judge. I had on a business suit that I wore for Model UN conferences. She kept staring at me, looking deeper and deeper into my soul. After a few more seconds, she agreed by nodding her head. She ordered me to probation, banged the gavel and moved on to the next case. My heart was racing! Oh my god! I just beat the system, I am not going to prison! Sweet, sweet victory!

Bobby told me earlier that because the courtroom was always a fast paced environment, the judge might not have fully realized her decision and it was better for me to immediately disappear from the courtroom and leave no chance for her to change her mind. As I quickly walked to exit the courtroom, I could not help but think, "I got away with it... I actually got away with it..."

Bobby and I walked down the hall to where I would fill out my paperwork and set up an appointment for my first probation meeting. As soon as we got in the elevator and it was just the two of us, Bobby turned to me and said

"I didn't think she was gonna buy it,"

"ARE YOU FUCKING KIDDING ME? Really Bobby?" I replied.

"You robbed a BANK... This is going in my top 3, good work Ace" said Bobby as he took out his handkerchief and polished his glasses.

Even my attorney thought I was going to prison. Wow. At least he lied to me when I needed it the most and it paid off, but, wow. The worst was behind me now. All I had to do was pass my class with a B and I would have a college diploma.

One of the real problems with the University system is that the teachers really know how to play the system and sometimes I even feel that some teachers work with the University to keep students for longer periods of time just in order to make money. At my university, students were able to withdraw from a course and have it not count against their GPA up until a few weeks before the end of the semester. Let's say a student was not doing well in the class, or had a "situation" that yielded poor semester performance, they had 3 chances to withdraw from courses and have it not hurt against their GPA.

My teacher structured the second test during the Drop week period and would not release the test scores until the following week after the period closed. Since I did not have the money saved to try take ANOTHER full semester at the University for one class, I would have to take the test and get my grade after the drop week ended.

There was another rule that really made graduating quite difficult. You are only allowed to take the same class 3 times. If you do not earn the passing grade the 3rd and final time you were required to switch majors. I was already on my second attempt, so I could not drop the class and save one of the those spaces. I would have to get a B in the class. I took the next test and earned a 78% 'C'.

FUCK! This means that I would have to get almost a perfect on the final to bring my grade up to a B. I studied and studied for the final, worked with the teacher, but she she was only available once during the 3 week period leading up to the exam. After weeks of studying guess what I earned?

79% C

Insert face of defeat. I had beaten the court case, but I did not earn the grade I needed to graduate. I had one class to take, and I couldn't do it. I at least improved one of my grades from a C- to a C. Guess what my new GPA was?

1.99

Fuck the system... Now, somewhere towards the end of the summer semester before the final court date I tried a new substance to help deal with my problems. It was supposed to make you feel really good and actually be the chemical reaction of happiness in your brain. Some call it the mother of all rave drugs, MDMA, while those in my circle gave her a name, Molly.

I will be honest, taking MDMA the first time was mind blowing. It was an orgasm that lasted for 5 hours and got better as you danced. I could not believe what I was experiencing. It was a constant pleasure that rivaled sexual experiences and when people touched you it amplified. Looking at lights, listening to music and actually FEELING the music was unreal. It also makes you super nice and you go around conversing with everybody. You would have no fear and everyone was super happy, ready to fall in love with each other.

MDMA was also the base to whatever else you wanted to put in your body. You could mix Molly with anything and it would make that substance more intense. Let's say for example, the feeling of MDMA was dying down after two hours into your first dose. You could then smoke a cigarette or take a hit of weed and the felling (known as "rolling") would come back, and if you took a shot, the feeling of the alcohol, would enhance the roll. Taking the drug by itself, was nice, but it was meant to be mixed with other things and enhance your favorite intoxicants to a level unparalleled. There was however one problem, it was really hard to find.

Since Veronica was a stripper and had all types of access to people and narcotics, she showed me the differences and actually educated me on the qualities and was a seasoned veteran at taking MDMA. The drug was hot and a new Rapper named TYGA and even WIZ KHALIFA made a song about it just a few months prior. Molly was different, it was a small crystal that you put inside of a gel capsule and swallowed. It would last for a few hours and you could take a little more and keep the feeling going. After the second dose, you couldn't really get the feeling back, because all the chemicals were exhausted in your brain.

It was also considered a hard drug. Veronica had a very good definition of what was a hard drug. The amount that you take to have fun, if can't do it every day and wake up feeling fine, it's a hard drug. This was a good definition. Cannabis, you could smoke, or vaporize as much as you wanted and you couldn't overdose, nor feel horrible the next day. But, if you tried to take these microscopic amounts of Molly two nights in a row, you would feel like shit and want to kill yourself. MDMA is not addictive, but the feeling is nearly impossible to create with other substances. The first time that someone does Molly will be their best venture. The experiences after that will feel great, but not as intense as the original. It was also not advised, medically, that you consume this drug more than twice annually. It wasn't something that you could do on the weekends, or even once a month. It was a HARD drug.

The first time I tried Molly was with some of the new friends I had made through Skyler and Silva including Veronica. I went to the best electronic nightclub in town and danced my ass off, made out with a girl and felt literally ecstasy for 5 hours. It was amazing. One thing that really made me wonder about Molly was the price. Molly was expensive. A solid night of Molly would cost you anywhere from $20-30 per capsule and each capsule would contain anywhere from. .1-.2 of a gram. The human body did not need much more than this to have a reaction. This is not a drug where taking more causes a greater effect. The body can only handle so much. If you wanted a gram, you would have usually have to pay between $100 and $150. A gram would work for 3-4 people over the course of an evening. Everyone searched for Molly.

Veronica got a few grams for a deal from one guy she knew at the strip club and it was nearly $80 a gram. I was already selling weed and understood that once you step into the underworld, all you had to do was ask and you could get larger amounts. The more you bought the cheaper it was, this was true with any drug so I asked Veronica to ask for an ounce (28 grams) from her guy and see what the price was. A week went by and Veronica told that it would be $1500 or roughly $53 per gram. Better, I thought.

Molly would only be sold in. .1 or .2 gram increments and if you were lucky, somebody could sell you an entire gram. It was in high demand and I had already taken it myself and knew it was harmless if you used it only a few times a year. I called up Dante to see what he could do. $1500 seemed expensive. A price like that was $54,000 a kilo, making it more expensive than cocaine, but less than heroin. The production of Molly was not simple. I knew it took a few days, the right chemicals and a chemist to make MDMA. We were going to find it cheaper and make a killing on the college scene. I needed money to finish my degree and I could not find a job, desperate times called for desperate measures.

Dante and I kept talking to people and one day Dante called me up and said, "Yo, I think I met the Plug, I'm gonna go see him tonight just to talk" The "plug" is the guy that controls the operation, he has whatever quantity you need and in case things are not going well, he "pulls the plug" and would disappear. Dante admitted to me that driving to meet this guy at a gas station in another part of town was scary. He didn't know if he was being followed, if the guy was a cop, or what. Dante liked to make money and I was one of his main guys connected to the rest of the University. Dante would always be in charge of getting supply, holding it and then distributing it out to a few guys like me, who would then make all the small sales. Dante had the power to make less transactions but at higher prices. I was one of the guys talking to lots of people and being a "face" within the system. No one knew where I got my supply from and nobody except for a few of us knew Dante. We ran the University.

"What's Golden" by Jurassic 5

Chapter 13

"D# Fat – Original Mix" by Armin Van Buuren, W&W

Dante arrived at the gas station, a little nervous, waiting for a guy to come up on a motorcycle. He said he would be wearing white. A few minutes later, a guy pulled up on a white SUZUKI wearing a white jacket. Dante just saw the plug. Dante got out of his car, while the guy was parking his motorcycle. Dante looked first at his bike, everything was custom, it was brand new and cost at least $15,000. He then looked at his wrist and saw a full rack of diamonds on a nice Breitling watch. This guy wasn't playing.

The plug took off his helmet, and looked at Dante with locked eyes. Not even a second after they make eye contact the guy breaks out and says "Dude, I think I know you from somewhere! Dante responded "I have the EXACT same feeling!" The guy got off his bike and was like "Awesome! It's so nice to NOT meet somebody sketchy in this business if you can imagine, let's get something to eat." They grabbed a bite to eat, talked and joked a little bit. They have no idea where they met, but they had seen each other before in a casual environment, probably at a party or something at the University. Trust is the biggest problem when working in illegal business and Dante had just earned instant trust with the plug. He was probably a few years older than us, but not by much. They finished eating and the plug said, "Well, did you want a cookie? (ounce)"

Dante answered yes. The plug handed him a bag of candy sealed just like we did with our Doritos bags.

"Six hundo, and don't worry man, no rush, get your business set up and hit me up in two weeks. I am glad that we met again man. Later!" *Bump fists*

The plug hopped on his motorcycle and rode away.

Dante got back in his car and drove home. He could not believe what had just happened. He called me almost immediately and said "DUDE you are never going to believe what just happened..." Dante brought the goods to my place and we talked a little bit, he had never had this much stuff before, so we opened it up to see what it looked like.

A brief note, one of the biggest problems with street Molly was that a lot of time, you would only get a capsule filled with something that looked like sugar, it would be small and grainy and people could cut it with other things and you would never actually know if you were getting the real thing. The largest crystal I ever saw was about the size of a large peppercorn. Veronica claimed that she bought a gram that was almost the size of a tic tac.

I went and got some pyrex tupperware that I had bought just for the occasion. Even the dust from this substance was enough to get you high, we put on surgical gloves and masks and were really careful. We also did not want to lose profits, people would pay $15 for a .1 every small piece mattered. I opened the bag so we could see what was inside and what we saw blew our minds. The crystals were not the size of peppercorns or even tic tacs. The largest one appeared to be the size of a golf ball.

We were in shock. This was unbelievable, most people will never be able to see something like this. Even if someone was lucky enough to even find Molly, it would be in a small amounts for a dosage. We sat and looked at the crystals for a good half hour. Dante said that it was $600 per ounce and if we worked our way up he would do a kilo for $12,000.

Some math.
$600 / 28 grams = $21.43 per gram
28grams * $110 per gram = $3080 income per ounce = $2480 profit per ounce
28/.2 = 140 doses of .2 or 280 doses of .1

This means that I would have to sell 280 capsules of .1 at roughly $10-15 per capsule to make enough money to get me through a final semester of college. Or just sell 28 grams.

I was still pretty depressed from the bank robbery and not passing my class. I weighed out a few doses and decided to go hit some clubs with Dante to "test out" our new product. I was an honest dealer, I would never sell anything without doing it myself. I weighed out about .4 and each capsule had about .1 inside and we hit the club. I popped the first one, and about 45 minutes went by and I started to feel it.

"Good" I thought, if this is only a .1 and I already feel it, we can definitely sell this to people and they will come back. About 45 minutes later I took another .1. Another half hour went by and then the feeling of ecstasy I experienced my first time on "Molly" came back and I was ROLLING like the original time. It was at this point that my subconscious took over and I wanted more. I popped the third capsule. Another 30 minutes went by and the feeling was indescribable. My eyes were super dilated, I was dancing, enjoying the music and feeling nothing but pleasure. This was MDMA in its purest form. No one at our University was ready for this, we were going to have the Ferrari of all products and no one could beat us.

I then realized that I still had another capsule left and the club was going to close in about an hour. I popped the 4th and final one and the feeling was just as intense as I had ever felt. I was quite happy. I might actually be able to finish my degree and hopefully have a chance at gaining employment with a felony on my record. I kept dancing and finished out the night, afterwards Dante and I, went home.

Another factor that people always considered whenever they bought Molly was their metabolism. For normal people, that hardly ever exercised, taking .2-.4 throughout an entire evening would be more than enough. Their heart would accelerate, they would dance, and if they wanted to amplify the feeling, they would smoke a cigarette, rip a bong, drink some alcohol etc. Athletes and those that exercised and lifted weights, would usually consume more. They were accustomed to having an accelerated heart rate and the feeling would not

185

take effect as easily. I was always training and would consider myself a heavy user compared to most people.

Our product was good, people would not need to buy more to feel the same effects. Yet, I was always scared selling people more than I knew they could consume. I waited about two weeks and I decided that I was going to take a large quantity and make SURE that I was not going to sell something to a person and have it kill them. Molly was always coming up in the newspaper as the killer of people at music festivals. All of us in the rave community understood that those individuals died because of dehydration, lack of nutrition and long exposure to heat while taking Molly. It was not the Molly by itself.

I weighed out 8 capsules of .2 and picked about 5 hours worth of good music and decided that I was going to stay at home and see what Molly was capable of. I had the house to myself that weekend, my new roommates were never home so I figured it was the perfect way to safely try it out. I popped .2 and about a half hour later I was starting to feel it. It was not nearly as strong as last time, but since I had done it two weeks prior, I expected this. I then continued to administer doses at roughly 30 min intervals. The feeling did not get any more intense after a full gram, but I kept going and my chest was getting tighter. I didn't care. I finished off the night and I'm pretty sure by this point I caused severe brain damage, I then smoked some weed and slept. I woke up almost 24 hours later, with a very stiff neck, but at least I knew that the MDMA was not going to kill anybody.

The next few days I was super emotional, not suicidal or anything, but it would appear almost as if I had bi-polar disorder. It was also very difficult to remember anything, heavy MDMA consumption had really turned my brain to mush. I called up Dante and I told him that I took another dose and I should have really listened to his advice "DON'T do that SHIT. It's gonna fuck with your brain and turn you into a vegetable" Thank you for the words of advice Dante, but my hubris got to me and I started to head down a very, very dark road.

I got a few guys from greek life to come and try out the product. With the quality I had, I could charge as much as I

186

needed, make lots of money, let alone give away some free samples. I had to keep my identity limited to as few people as possible because I was already on probation and if I was caught with drugs, my life would be even worse. Molly was a harsh prison sentence and I did not have anyone to help me if I was caught this time. I needed the money and had limited options, so I proceeded with caution.

My hope was that once a few of these fraternity guys with money tried my product, they would want to buy it in large quantities. They had a safe way to buy it, let alone, sell it to their fraternity members and make some money. I called a few of them over just to chill, guys that I smoked weed with and ones that I could trust, even though you can never trust anybody. They all came over and I had some good weed. I rolled up a blunt, we each had a beer and I brought up the topic of Molly. One of the guys had never tried it and everybody else was pretty much on the same page that it was the sought after, high of the year.

"Girls love it bro, they mix it in their drink, it dissolves and then they love you the rest of the evening."

Having sex on it is great." said one of the guys. "Have you guys ever actually seen crystals? I can only find the powder stuff."

(I had an ounce in my room)

"One time I got a .2 and it was all one big crystal" said one of the guys

"yeah man, people are paying $100 a gram for that shit" - said another

"I will be right back." I went downstairs and got my pyrex with all golf ball crystals and brought it back upstairs.

"Everybody listening? DON'T TOUCH, but THIS is what MOLLY looks like."

I pulled the cover off the pyrex and everybody was in awe.

"Where the fuck did you get this?"

"JESUS"

"Loathing's a Gangster"

"This looks like something from the Legend of Zelda"

Everybody started laughing.

I talked to the guys and said that I have a good connection, but I cannot be seen in the greek system. They were all minor hustlers anyways and I knew that they could move 280 doses of .1 a lot easier than I could. I sold them the first ounce for $750 and said that each one after that was $1000. I should have charged more. I kept some for myself, and close friends that wanted some, but I had hopes that they would be able to move about an ounce a week, and I would earn roughly $400. I was still selling weed to about a group of 10 people, and I had some income to eat and finish the semester. I was living month to month, but at least I was scraping by and staying off the radar. I did not want to attract attention for selling Molly even though I could make great money. I had to stay low key even if it meant being poor.

My probation officer meetings started in August and I had to check in once per month and complete my 50 hours of community service within the first 3 months. I opted to volunteer at the botanical gardens on my campus, pull weeds and spend some time with nature. I went there with my paperwork and the lady was a complete Nazi. I was the only person to show up that day, I followed all of her rules about

188

paperwork and phoning in ahead of time, and I was 15 minutes early, ready and eager to work. "You are the only volunteer today, and I don't know who you are so I cannot trust you, come back next week." She then proceeded to slam the door in my face.

Thankfully I had already developed a good relationship with my probation officer. The first time we met, I was the only person that she had talked to all day that actually had their paperwork and greeted her with a "Good Afternoon, officer". She explained to me, that she had a son, and was currently finishing her master's degree and was beyond backed up with work. I explained that I was in my final semester of Undergraduate and having a very difficult time finding work, she told me to keep looking and something should pop up. I was not allowed to leave the county which made finding work impossible. My area had a large number of people currently on probation, along with an enormous amount of felons competing for real jobs.

Every month I had to check in, fill out my paperwork, possibly take a drug test and show that I was on track with all of my probation requirements. If I failed probation 3 times, I would be sent to prison and serve the full original sentence of 41 months. I had to complete my community service within the first three months and maintain employment, or be enrolled in school full time. Since I was in school, all I had to do was stay drug free and get my community service done. My probation officer was very understanding of my situation and saw that I was actually trying to do something with my life. She gave me first choice on when I wanted to meet her every month. I always chose first thing in the morning so at least she would start her day with a smile.

I was always a little suspicious of any police officer, I trusted her, but always in the back of my mind questioned her motives. I went back to my apartment and continued to sell narcotics and looked online for my final class so I could plan the rest of my semester. The class I needed was offered only once per week on Mondays and with a new professor. I was only thinking positives at this point, and elected to take the class hoping for a great experience.

189

Coloma

Salvador, Brazil

"Beaches Bedrooms & Barcelona" by Ace Loathing

The first week of school began and I realized that semesters during the summer were different than those in the fall and spring, when it came to financial aid. I would have to take a minimum of 12 credits to satisfy my "requirements" of being a full time student, or else I would not receive financial aid. After I did the calculations, I would not have enough money from financial aid to cover the semester. The main reason for this was because USC created a bunch of fees for individuals who had to "repeat" a class. It was my third and final time taking International Economics. USC decided to charge me over $600 extra to take the class the final time. It was a "new policy" this year and I could only imagine it was designed to put money in the pockets of the evil and greedy that ran the school. There were empty seats in the classroom after the first week. Rat bastards.

After I did the math I was few hundred dollars short and if I did not pay the money by the end of the ADD/DROP week, I would be removed from that semester. I called up my parents and begged and pleaded with them and finally my mother stepped forward and said "Just finish, that's all we ask". She paid the school the last of the money needed and I was able to take my final class in hopes of graduating that semester.

Class began and I took a few online classes to satisfy my requirements so I could get financial aid. The only class I had to pass with a B was International Economics, for the 3rd and final time. I went to class on Monday and met the professor. He was an elderly man and gave us the syllabus. The class was only once per week, we would only have 13 classes that semester and then final exams. Two holidays occurred on Monday that semester knocking the total number of classes down to 11. This professor was "just placed" as the Department Head of the College of Business Economics and said that he had conferences and other things to do on two more of the class periods. The class count went down to 9.

Oh fuck, I thought. How are we going to get 13 classes into a 9 class period. He will probably make the course easier or modify it or something. "We will move ahead as scheduled and you will be responsible for the reading and all chapters not covered in class" AAHHHHH. His style was completely different than the two different professors I had before. I wondered what his tests were like.

"We will have 2 tests and a final" which I was used to "I also do not give + or -" god fucking damnit, I thought. "Your tests will be 25% each and the final. 50%." What a nightmare. "Also, I am requiring that you buy the book that I authored you can find it at the bookstore." (The book cost roughly $380.) What a crook! Just like my finance professor a few semesters prior, he too published a new book EVERY year and made the book a requirement because the book was published by his publishing company. This professor made money off every student in class. Luckily he kept a copy of the book on reserve at the library and I would not have to buy it. Universities really are a business. It takes one to know one, but they are also criminals. This professor also made the second test after the drop week, so if you didn't do well enough on the first test, you would not know your grade on the second test until it was too late to withdraw from the course. CRIMINAL.

I saw that the first test was 6 weeks into the semester. I would have to study up and hopefully earn an A. I only had one little problem. I was really into this girl when the semester started, she took up a lot of my time and would even ignore me for a few days after we hooked up last, but I couldn't get enough of her. It's a shame that girls name... was Molly.

I had virtually an unlimited supply of Molly at my disposal, I would take it almost once a week and not in small doses. anything from .4 to even a full gram. I was rotting my brain and wasting my life away. I could not find work, I could not smoke as much weed because I had to potentially pass drug tests once a month and most of the friends that I had, moved on, graduated and I was starting to feel very alone.

I took a bunch of capsules and went to a house party in my building, I rolled up a blunt in the middle of the party and I was one of the older people there. Most kids were probably drinking underage. I brought a massive bag of really good weed with me, close to 15 grams and started breaking it up in the middle of the party on the coffee table. People slowly started watching what I was doing. I could tell that most of these people were between age 18-20 and in their first two years of university. Cannabis was still illegal and I bet for some people, they had probably never seen it before, let alone the quantity and quality I was handling. There were a few black guys at the party and one of them picked up my bag and asked where I got it. He complimented it and turned to the other guys and then they asked how much it was to hit it. "When I'm done rolling, you can hit it first, all I ask is that you take down my number. I'm your new dealer" we bumped fists.

"Aight G" he said.

This kid just called me G... If only he knew. Rolling a blunt is not difficult, but if you have never rolled one before, you would embarrass yourself the first 10 times. Most people are afraid to roll. I on the other hand rolled a few blunts a day, for almost the entirety of my collegiate career. It was easy. I used this method at parties to impress people I had never met before and to show the "tough guys" at the party how soft they truly were. Gangsters are usually the ones associated with rolling blunts, hippies smoke joints and stoners usually have their bong. To each his own...

I broke open the blunt (White Owl White Grape) with one hand, something that I had practiced multiple times so I could do it as a party trick and shook the tobacco guts into a solo cup. All of the weed was already ground up on the table. and instead of putting the weed back where the tobacco was, I flipped the blunt over and rolled it inside out. The black guys lost their mind.

"This guy is serious." one of them said. I started filling the blunt and there was about 2 grams ground up on the table along with the big bag. One of the guys said "How many blunts are you going to roll?" with a pack of White Owls sitting on the table.

By now, this party of about 30 people had 10 of them focused on me, twisting the green. I looked away from the blunt, still stuffing it and looked the kid right in the eyes and said "One" Again, the black guys lost it. "NOoOooo way, impossible. LOOK at all that weed." Practice makes perfect.

I stuffed all two grams inside the blunt. It was still open and it looked like you put too much inside a burrito. There was literally a mountain of weed and one guy at the party said "You can't do that, there is nooooo way." I started twisting one end while balancing and pushing it down, slowly but surely. I got about halfway and I think everyone at the party was looking at me, I was still going strong. I was also, already high as fuck off cannabis, I was in my zone. I keep rolling and rolling and then finished it up at the top.

If you can get past the rolling part you face another challenge. Sealing. The trickiest part for some people was sealing up the blunt and making it stick together so it would not unravel. In the movies, and I think they do this on purpose, you always see people lick and lick the blunt, so it becomes wet and it sticks together. People that know how to roll, only use a very very very small amount of saliva to seal up the blunt.

I looked around and I saw a girl looking at me with big eyes. I asked "Do you want to lick it shut?" She froze up and said shook her head looking a little scared and said, "I don't know how" I reach out with my other hand and wiped away some hair from her face. I said "Just put my finger in your mouth" She smiled and did so, grabbing my hand and everything. Groupie...Everybody at the party was still in shock and some of the other girls at the party were looking jealous that I didn't choose them instead.

I pulled my finger out of her mouth and it was little wet and I ran my finger along the edge of the blunt, getting it just a little bit moist. I finished sealing it up, flicked it around like I was about to play drums and handed it to the leader of the group. The rest of his crew made an over exaggerated "DAMN" like you would find watching Friday with Chris Tucker and Ice cube. "You... You... You didn't even lick it" said one guy with eyes like he just saw a ghost.

"I'm gonna go get a beer, spark it up" I was now the king of the party. I got a few phone numbers and from there I had a feeling I would have enough clients to get me through the semester. Selling weed was easy, and thankfully I had a two semesters of practice and was able to choose who my clients were.

I only worked with girls. It was was a double edged sword. Having women at my house meant that I had a very small chance of being robbed. When they asked if they could bring friends to come and chill, I would say yes, presuming they were not guys. I always had the fear of being robbed. The less guys I talked to, the better. Dante and the rest of my friends would have plenty to choose from and there were almost daily, different college girls coming through. They would tell their friends and the cycle would continue. The only problem was, I was pretty fucked up mentally from all the Molly. I was consuming on almost a weekly basis and it was starting to take effect. Some girls would come over, and buy only a $10 bag, hang out for a while and expect me to entertain them for hours on end.

I was never able to put 2+2 together and realize that most of these women were actually attracted to the "bad boy" that I was. I didn't feel like a bad boy, hell, I was depressed to the point that I wasn't even thinking about sex. I guess my crazy christian brainwashing and my lack of emotional intelligence really bit me in the ass. Girls were literally throwing themselves at me, young, attractive and ready to fornicate girls and I was not even interested. My philosophy was to pump them full of weed, play music and make them feel comfortable in my house. Because of my childhood and abusive drug behavior, I was 100 percent not interested in the girls for sexual intercourse, only their money, so I could survive. I can remember one time, this sexy girl from Jamaica came over, buying only a $5 bag. I regret not sleeping with her.

I was only thinking that she was wasting my time when I could have more customers come through. She was obviously thinking about hooking up with me, but I was not even motivated. Another girl texted me and said she wanted to come through. She was a blonde girl in a masters program involving biology and anatomy. Cute, blonde and the complete physical opposite of the Jamaican girl. I told the Jamaican girl that another customer was coming through and she needed to leave. We were in the kitchen and I'm trying to walk her out and she is just giving me the "look". (oh my god, am I ugly? FAT? what's wrong with me? Why aren't you trying to kiss me? have sex with me? Anything!?) Then the doorbell rang, it was the master's student, the blonde girl.

I opened the door and kissed her on the cheek and gave her a hug as I did with most girls that entered my place.

She said hello to the Jamaican girl and flopped down on the couch and took off her shoes. The Jamaican girl glared at me, then looked at her and said "Sorry, I was just on my way out" then the Jamaican girl looked back at me with a very sad look. I never heard from her again, unless it was over facebook saying "What's wrong with me? you never talk to me anymore? bla bla bla."

The blonde girl was in my living room and pretty much the same thing happened. Except the blonde had come through a few times before and was here to pick up her weekly amount because she smoked almost everyday. We talked for a bit, rolled one up and then when she got up to get something out of the fridge. When she came back, she sat down right next to me on the couch and started rubbing my neck. At this point I had no emotions, I might as well had been a robot. The last 10 months of my life caused me to lose almost 30 pounds, I was stressed about passing college, passing my drug tests for probation and I was abusing drugs at an alarming rate. My life was a mess.

When I did not respond to her actions, she pushed even further and started running her hand up my thigh. I stopped her and said "I don't fool around with my customers" She thought I was teasing and leaned in to kiss me and said something witty in response. I had a very tough time recognizing attraction. My brain was rotting and it was crippling my life. I had opportunities with women all the time and I just was not able to understand and have real feelings.

I diffused the situation and she became very confused, apparently I really turned her on and she even said things like "I want your cock inside me, don't be shy". It was at this point that I decided she was crazy. I told her sorry, and she started to cry, I lit a candle and got her some tissues. She then cleaned her tears and left. I never heard from her again.

A few days went by and I didn't have any sales, I was running really low on money and I had to pay rent in a few days. More time passed and I had to use all of my money to pay rent. I had less than $20 to my name, but a few hundred in cannabis and Molly so I figured I would be fine. I bought some rice and eggs to get me through the next few days. That entire semester I hardly ever had enough money to drive my car and without a car I was riding my bike everywhere, including miles away to get groceries. My life was in a downward spiral.

"Mind Playing Tricks on Me" by Geto Boys

Chapter 14

I took my first test, and midway through the semester I received my grade. 79/100. I was furious. I needed a B average to graduate and if the first test was any notion on how I would do for all the others, I was already worried. I talked to the professor and he said that the first test was the easiest and most people do worse on the midterm and final, exactly what I wanted to hear. It wasn't impossible, but an uphill battle all the way.

Somewhere during those weeks I had my monthly probation officer meeting. I took a drug test, but thankfully she was only testing my piss for cocaine. I already flushed my system anyways and was not worried about passing. I passed the test and we talked about school, the job hunt and my community service hours. Since the NAZI lady refused to give me hours one of the weeks, I was 3 hours short this month on my community service. My probation officer looked at me and told me it didn't matter, but I did not believe her. I counted a strike against myself. I planned to have all my service done by the end of the month anyways, but just to be safe, I put one strike against myself.

Going back to the 9 classes I had on Mondays. We were already through 5 of them when we received our test scores for the first test. The next test was in just a few weeks and it would be during that week I would have to decide to stay in the class, or drop out of college. I would have to try and find work and come back to take my final class again when I had the money saved up. Remember, I would have to change my major if I did not pass this class with a B for the 3rd and final time.

The week before the test, the last half of the class was used as review. Since everyone struggled with the first test, we all planned to be there for the review and hopefully the professor would give us exactly what we needed. The problem was, I had just landed an interview with Men's Warehouse at the EXACT time I had the class. I really needed a job and wanted to stop moving work and Men's Warehouse was a sales job where I could earn over $30,000 annually. The real selling point with Men's Warehouse was that they did not care if you were a felon. They even advertised that they hired felons. I used the reasoning of my father in this instance and thought something he once said "I don't know why people worship gold, I mean, if you were starving, gold is worthless, you can't eat bars of gold" I took his logic and thought "Well, I can't eat my textbooks, I need money, and I will 100% go to prison this time if I am caught. I am going to skip the lecture and go to the interview".

I did really well during the interview and had almost an hour to get back to campus and maybe catch some of the class. Just as I got in my car and drove down the road 2 minutes the interviewing manager called me on my phone and said, "Hey Ace, can you come back? the District Manager just came in the store and I want you to meet him" I said yes and immediately turned my car around. We talked for a few minutes and he told me that his physical biological brother, was the hiring manager for this area. He said he would put in a good word and that I should get a call early next week.

I left the interview feeling super confident, but I had just missed the end of class. The professor never responded to emails, and neither did any of my 20 classmates. I had no idea what was going to be on the test. I received a call a few days later from the hiring manager asking when I was available. I told him that I had a test on monday and after that, I was free. He told me to come in an hour after the test and he looked forward to meeting me. I went to the library and used the book for the class and studied the best I could from my notes and the lecture. I went in that Monday ready for the test and ready to get my A or B and get the hell out of University. I opened the test and the questions were unlike anything I had seen before. There were new equations that were different from the ones I studied in the book and I looked around the room and saw almost everyone with the same type of face of "WHAT THE FUCK IS THIS?".

Not a single student finished the test before time was called. All of us were struggling to put anything down on the paper, let alone answer the proof questions using econometrics. It was the exam from hell. After I handed in my test, which might as well have been a tissue with tears at this point, I got in my car and headed to what was hopefully going to be golden ticket out of the hell that I was in.

I went through the interview and this guy was not feeling me. I'm not sure if had a bad cup of coffee, or if he thought I was going to be a bad team member, who knows. He said one thing to me that made me snap and it was both a blessing and a curse. "You just aren't selling me on it, why do you deserve the job over somebody else" It was at this point I said something along these lines... "Listen, do you respect honesty? Men's Wearhouse hires those with a felony conviction. I use to work for Banco Americo and I conspired with one of my fraternity brothers and we robbed them for over $100,000 while I worked there. I just went through 8 months of thinking everyday, I am going to prison. I beat the case and I am on probation. I have one class left to earn my degree in economics and then I'm going to get hit with $30,000 in student debt. I have not found work in 8 months and I'm losing my mind. I like to make money and I will lie, steal and do whatever it takes, so I can continue my life. I will lie to the customer and make sure that our store is number one in the company while our pockets get fatter." He sat there silent for a few seconds and said "Okay. To be honest, you were not even in my top 10 when you walked in the room. You are now in my top 2, and probably the most genuine interview I have ever had as a manager. Let me sleep on my decision and I will call you tomorrow." I left the Mens Wearhouse and went home.

The next day I received a phone call and the manager said "Listen Ace, I'm going to look for somewhere else for you to work in the company, but my gut feeling is telling me to hire the other guy, I'm sorry." Looking back on what he said, I had a feeling he wanted me to try and sell him right there over the phone and then say I was hired. I was too busy being frustrated at potentially failing my test and having to chose in the next 3 days on whether to withdraw from the University to

200

think that far ahead. Click, he hung up the phone and it was all over.

For the next two days I had a very tough decision to make. If I stayed past the drop week, and did anything less than a C on the last test I took, I would not have a chance to pass the class with a C. I would also have to change my major and take another two full semesters at the University just to earn a degree. If I dropped the class, it would withdraw me from the University and I would no longer be a "full time student" and I would have to let my probation officer know. Withdrawal from school might count potentially as my second strike towards imprisonment. I had until midnight Friday to make my decision and I would see my probation officer the following Tuesday. I went for a long run to clear my head. I was having trouble thinking and was still abusing Molly. I think if I wasn't smoking so much weed to help me recover, I might have actually turned into a vegetable. Thank you for saving me cannabis.

At 11pm on Friday, I withdrew from my class and kicked myself out of university. I figured that spending money for another semester instead of two, was worth the cost, even if it was setting me back even further. I made a few sales that day because weekends were always good for business. I sold some Molly and made almost 200 dollars in an hour and decided to go clubbing. I even brought a girl with me this time to dance, you might remember her. Her name was Molly.

I think I took MDMA close to 20 times in a 3 month period and as I entered into November, my life was falling apart. I went and saw my probation officer and told her that I had to unenroll from the University in hopes that I would be able to pass again in the spring. She looked at me and typed a few things in on the computer, said all was good and we set up our next appointment. I did not believe her for one second and considered myself at 2 strikes. One more to go and I would be in prison with Luthor, except I would be serving my full sentence of 41 months.

During November, I went with Tu and Bruce to a music festival in hopes of making enough money to pay my rent and eat decently the next few months. The main stages were trance and other forms of electronic music. There was a rather large group of us and I sold nearly a thousand dollars in MDMA that weekend. Selling substances at festivals was not what I wanted to do with my life, but it paid the rent and I was able to enjoy a great festival with friends that I will keep for the rest of my life.

That month all I did was apply for jobs and go to interviews. I went all over the city trying to find something that would cover my expenses so I could at least work and start saving again for another semester of classes. I did not tell my parents that I un-enrolled, or my situation, we never talked to each other about anything in 22 years of my life, why start now. I was so broke for money, that I asked Dante to front me more MDMA so I could hopefully make some sales and get some food in my fridge. It was now about November 20th and I had no job, no money, debt to my plug, I was not enrolled in school and my next meeting with my probation officer was the first week of December. I was freaking out and thinking that I was going to go to prison. AGAIN.

I called up my father and I told him that I wanted the title to my car and I could afford to insure it under my own name. My father and I always had a very large battle about my car since I was 16. He would not put the car under my name so it was never my asset, but he demanded that I pay the insurance since he was letting me use his car. I also paid for all maintenance, tires, and over $12,000 in GASOLINE since the car was "given" to me. By this point I had calculated over $15,000 in car related expenses. 6 years later, "his" car was now worth $1,000.

I was coined a "Model UN asshole" by my father. I made the argument that If I was going to pay the insurance for my car, and I am on the insurance for ALL of his cars, why am I allowed to drive only one car? He had a Porsche, a Tahoe and my mother had a BMW, but I was only allowed to drive my car by his rules, even though legally, I could drive ALL of his cars based on the insurance policy. We fought and fought constantly and then he finally agreed to pay the small fee of insuring my car ($140 every six months) on his policy because if I took out my own policy it would be astronomical in comparison. We then came to the agreement that if I ever wanted the title to the car, I would have to pay my own insurance, and separate from his policy. This was the agreement and we stuck to it for over 6 years.

My father was happy to no longer be related to me and told me he would come up that weekend. I cannot believe that my parents did not care about their son to help him out when he was the ONLY one in school. My sister dropped out of college because of money and my brother dropped out of high school because he wanted to escape my parents. My parents, meanwhile, were remodeling their second home and had just spent another $15,000 on new renovations. My father raced cars as his hobby and had over $20,000 invested on race equipment, cars and track fees during the past few years. My parents were even so brainwashed by the church that they paid over 10% of their money in the form of an offering EVERY year since I was born. Over $10,000 was disappearing into the pockets of pastors EVERY YEAR OF MY CHILDHOOD, but my parents didn't even think twice.

One would think, of all the money they spent on material items, they would have invested a little bit in their children so we would not have to work 25-40 hours a week while attending University and actually finish school on time. I guess owning a second home in another state and racecars, takes priority. I was not even eligible for food stamps because my father claimed me as a dependent on his taxes. Granted I lost the food stamps after I picked up my felony, but during 4 years I was unable to get assistance from the government.

My mother and father drove up in the morning and I could not believe the way they treated me. My father had all of the papers in a folder and he came down to look at the car. He then started removing the license plate. To be honest, I don't think I have ever witnessed him happier. As he undid the license plate, he picked it up and looked at it like a winning lottery ticket. My mother barely said anything because my father controls her, she always looks helpless and scared. She asked about school and I said I would get my test back this week. Another few minutes went by and we headed up to my apartment to sign over the title. My father MADE SURE he

203

received all of his documents as if I was going to commit identity theft against him. Silly white people. He signed the title over to me and I signed the other half. I no longer had a license plate, I would have to ride my bike a few miles to the DMV and pay over $115 to get the title, just so I could sell my car. I had about $150 to my name, but over $2,000 in MDMA. Hopefully I could make it happen.

My father signed the papers, and I don't even think he asked me about work. I was without a job for almost 11 months and he just smiled. My mother looked at me and understood I was hurting. It was at this point they said goodbye. My mother tried to give me a hug, but I could care less. I know every mother loves their children no matter how old they are, but love doesn't pay the bills and the faith of god doesn't put food in my stomach. My mother looked at me scared and I looked back at her with nothing but hate in my heart. She let her husband control her and no matter what I said, she would recite some scripture and show how truly brainwashed and helpless she was.

All throughout my childhood my father never hugged his children. He saw his children as "work" and whenever he came home from teaching elementary school, he would put his briefcase in his room, change his clothes and then start binge drinking. He would yell at us to do chores and make sure our house was ASPEN QUALITY clean, inside and out. He never hugged us or kissed us when he saw us. Never.

Some of my friends pointed this out to me when I was in high school and said that it was weird. I guess since I never knew any different, I never noticed. Ever since I was little, my father treated me like a business deal and gave me a handshake. This is what my friends noticed first about my father. The brief times, my father was ever in public, he was heavily intoxicated, but hid it quite well. I think my friend Sam, who briefly dated my sister and took her to prom said that it was strange of a father to only give their children handshakes. Not hugs. My father never even hugged my sister, only handshakes.

The final stroke of the pen sealed the deal and I was officially out of my father's life, he shook my hand and left my

204

apartment with my mother. I don't even think they were at my apartment for 20 minutes. They drove nearly two hours to take what was theirs, I would not have wasted time either. At least I had the title to my car and the chance to pay my rent, and hopefully get my life together and not head to prison.

As my meeting with my probation officer came closer, all I could think about was prison and how I was turning my brain into a vegetable with my abuse of MDMA. Since I was use to researching and validating my claims because of Model United Nations, I was constantly reading medical studies about long term effects of MDMA use. These studies motivated me to stop, which I did that same day, but I somehow stumbled upon an article from the Netherlands that would forever change my life.

The article was about the Eurozone and travel restrictions for felons. It was almost December of 2013 (the most stressful year of my life) and the article mentioned that felons from the United States, might not have access to the Euro zone starting mid 2014. I read that it was up for vote in the Netherlands and it was right then and there that I began thinking towards the future. The Netherlands is one of the most liberal places on the earth. You can purchase cannabis, prostitution is regulated and legalized and they are also one of the wealthiest countries in the world. Almost all other substances people fear, are tolerated and even sold through registered channels, in Holland. I had a passport, but never used it. As I kept thinking about the direction my life was heading the only thing on my mind, was Amsterdam.

Maybe Amsterdam was the cure? I lived 22 years in a Christian mindfuck prison that was leading me nowhere. I rationalized that if I was going to become a bum on the streets, I would rather be in Europe, than the United States. I even convinced myself that with 5 days left until my next probation meeting and the Thanksgiving holiday just hours away, it was now or never.

I rode my bike to the DMV that Monday and got the title for my car. I then immediately, put the car on craigslist for $1000, just below Kelly Blue Book value. It sold within the first hour. I then took my Macbook pro and dumped everything I had, onto a hard drive. I put it on craigslist for $950 and ended up selling it for $850 within hours. I counted my cash and after I sold everything and converted all my coins, I was left with almost $2100 in cash.

I called up my brother, he was doing the best out of my sister and I. He dropped out of high school and started working full time at Olive Garden as a line chef. He slowly began to hate his job, but he could smoke weed whenever he wanted so he was happy. I kept him updated on my situation and told him my plan to flee to Europe. He was all for it. "Ace, you have ALWAYS wanted to go to Europe, you get one life, live it."

One major problem regarding my plan, was that I was in the probation system in California. I started researching like crazy how Airlines track felons and if parole/probation would set off any alarms at the airport. I read through forums and articles and procedures and laws and all that I could find, was that the three days surrounding Thanksgiving were the busiest in the airline industry. One forum post said that he was a felon, currently on probation and flew to the Caribbean from the United States without a problem. A few more forums said that because so many people fly during the Thanksgiving holiday, they only stop and search people that match names on a terrorist list. There are millions of felons in the United states that want to visit their families during the Thanksgiving holidays. Enough forums and travelers said that they were felons and experienced problems while traveling, but NOT during the Thanksgiving holiday.

Thanksgiving was the next day and my brother took off work to go visit my sister. I told him to come to Los Angeles and drive me to the airport in San Fransico before he headed to see my sister. It was going to be the last time he would ever see me. He agreed. I started packing to flee the country.

My mind was racing. What should I bring? What would I do if they catch me? How much will a flight cost me at the airport? Should I dress down? Dress up? What would the weather be like? How will I find work? How long will my money last? It didn't matter. I was set on going and my brother would be here in a matter of hours. A deranged thought came to mind when I looked at the bookcase in my room. "All of those textbooks and works of literature, all my yearbooks, everything, I'm leaving it behind. I don't even have a diploma, well fuck it, I didn't learn anything anyways. My last class to graduate is International Economics. I guess it is about time I studied abroad".

I came across a backpack that I acquired from my sister that was one of her old soccer bags. I wanted to travel light because I knew that I would be on foot. I put on the warmest layers that I had, and packed a few changes of clothes, my military boots, extra shoes and a brief hygiene kit, my passport and cash. I would figure the rest out when I landed.

I looked online to buy my ticket, but read on a forum that I had a very large chance of getting caught If I entered all my information online and tied it to my passport number. The computers would run checks of information if I bought my ticket ahead of time. I decided also to go to an airport out of my county to help my chances of not being arrested. I planned to buy my ticket in cash, the day of, hoping, to make it out of the airport and eventually, out of the country.

As I finished packing, my brother pulled up in his car and came upstairs. We hugged (The way our parents never did with us) and looked at each other knowing that I was about to begin my journey. We went through my room and I gave my brother all the things that he wanted, tools, electronics, whatever he cared for. I also packed up all my documents such as social security cards and birth certificate so he would have them for safekeeping. Neither one of us had left the country before. I closed the door to my apartment and could only think that I was closing the door on my old christian brainwashed, drug abused, sexless, and reckless life. I had almost $2,100 and I knew that my airline ticket would be a lot of money. I would rather die on the streets of Europe than become a junkie or end up in prison. I locked the door and left my apartment. Things would never be the same.

When we got on the highway, we drove about two exits and it was extremely crowded due to Thanksgiving traffic. We pulled off and decided to take the backroads. It was a truly surreal moment, the scenery was totally different and both of us realized it. A brief moment of clarity. My brother and I drove to the San Fransico Airport on black Friday and almost no one was there. Wednesday and Thursday were obviously very busy, but Friday everyone was already at their destination for the holidays. I only had cash and could not risk buying a ticket online, I went to every kiosk from American to United and tried to find the cheapest ticket to Europe. I was dressed nicely and I explained to the woman working at the kiosk that I missed my flight to Europe. I explained to her that I just gotten out of the Military and I had 3 week vacation planned. I needed to get to Europe as soon as possible so I would not miss the rest of my vacation. I tried for almost two hours to find a ticket that was not going to leave me bankrupt. Amsterdam was too costly. There were cheap tickets to Moscow, but the weather was so cold that I could not risk being outside. One of the ladies finally found a ticket to Barcelona, I would fly first to New York and then Barcelona.

Final Price. $1857 Ouch. It was actually cheaper to buy a round trip than a one way ticket. I picked a date just before my 3 months in the Schengen were up. I would at least have a bailout plan if things didn't go well. Having a return trip ticket would also help me get through customs, and validate my story or so I thought. The Thanksgiving holiday was my only chance to escape and as I paid the money and booked the ticket, all I could think was I hope I don't get flagged, caught, and then sentenced to prison. I bought the ticket and had a few hundred dollars left. My brother and I left to go and have dinner because my flight was leaving the following morning. I planned to sleep at the airport. We went and had dinner and because it was black Friday, almost everything was closed except TGI Friday's. Ironic, but I guess I had just bought a new life for Black Friday, which was quite the deal.

It was tough to stomach my food. I was getting ready to run away and begin a new life. I was so thankful for my brother being there. He was the only one I could trust with my secret. Not many people can say they have a fugitive as a friend, let alone, as a brother. We finished eating and he took me to the airport. We hugged and both of us were in tears. Leaving him was one of the toughest moments of my life. I will admit it, I was scared as fuck. I would have to pass through Los Angeles, New York and Barcelona to make it into Europe. Hopefully since I bought my ticket in cash, the same day, I would be fine. I slept in the airport and made a phone call to one of my oldest friends. I had a promise to keep.

When I finally got back to my apartment after robbing the bank, Austin and I had a talk. One of the things he told me was that if I was going to do anything crazy ever again, I would need to tell him beforehand. I was already in the airport and getting ready to leave. I called him up and told him the plan. His response was priceless. *Deep breath* "OOOOOKKKKKKKK. Wow. At least you kept your promise, thank you for calling me man."

We talked for a few minutes and since Austin was always reading and very up to date on current issues we talked about the situation in Spain. Spain had horrible unemployment, 35% even worse than the great depression, arguably the worst in the world and since I did not speak Spanish, it was going to be difficult. I always surrounded my life with challenges because pressure makes diamonds. I was in for quite a surprise. As I learned later in life "you have to dig through dirt to get to a diamond".

It was difficult for me to sleep and I had an early flight anyways. I woke up and waited for the line to form and I checked in, hoping to make it through my first wave of airport security. As I stood in line, waiting, I looked around and noticed a few police officers communicating with airport security. I was beyond scared at this point, paranoid out of my mind was an understatement. "What are the police doing here? I'm caught, Oh my god, it is over!" I thought. I then noticed the two terminals ahead of me and the police blocked one of them off. I was freaking out. I went through the security checks just fine and as I'm putting on my shoes they unblock the terminal and I see about 30-40 police officers walk down to the end of the terminal, some were dressed in Uniform, but most of them were in off duty police gear. Turns out, some of the local police were heading to Vegas for a conference/vacation and it was their holiday. The group ended up being close to a hundred people and the officers were there just to say "good bye". We all walked down the same terminal, I went left and they all went right. What were the odds? At least I was safe.

I waited about an hour until my flight arrived, I boarded the plane and headed to New York. I slept like a baby for a few hours. Stop number two was a transfer flight at JFK. I had never been to New York before and I had a 45 minute layover. I had always heard nightmares about people missing their flight because they could not make it to another terminal in time. I was also starting to realize how badly I needed glasses. I wore glasses the day I robbed the bank, but they were confiscated during the judicial proceedings and I was so stressed that I did not remember to buy another pair, 11 months later.

"I really need glasses, I have to walk within 5 feet to see anything. I only have $250, how am I going to do this?" My mind was all over the place. Coming down off a multi month MDMA binge was not helping. I was a blind walking zombie, fleeing the country with no idea of what to expect, who to talk to, what to do, but I couldn't be happier. I arrived at my terminal and boarded the plane, I talked briefly to an elderly couple that was sitting next to me and I asked what their secret was. They seemed happy. "The more you have to try, the less it is going to work" This was not the key to success in life, but the key to relationships.

Before boarding the plane I remembered hearing a very strange message that came over the intercom. "Those traveling to Spain, you do not need to show your passport to board the plane. You will only be required to show your passport once you land" I may have heard this wrong, but I could only think about getting to Spain. I showed my passport anyways and boarded the plane. I walked down the terminal and as a poor person, I would have to walk through first class and sit at the back of the large passenger plane.

As I walked through First Class, I saw a beautiful Spanish woman, with her children. She was wearing all white, a white fur coat and a diamond bracelet. She was trying to put her heavy bags in the overhead compartment and since she was short and dealing with her young children, I put my hand on her bag and picked it up with ease. I locked it inside the

210

compartment and she looked at me with the sexiest face I had seen in a long time. We locked eyes for a good three seconds, she looked me up and down, then smiled. She was probably in her mid 30's but looked better than any woman I went to University with. The way she looked at me was nothing except PURE lust. I did not see any husband figure around. If I could put a thought bubble above her head it would have said "Take me, right now, and MAKE LOVE TO ME FOREVER". She put her hand on my chest, then moved it up to my beard and stroked my facial hair. She then said "Gracias Guapo." in a strong Spanish accent.

All I could think was "Yep, I made the right decision. I could get use to this" as I walked back to coach and took my seat. My heart was beating like a drum. I tried to sleep on the plane, but because they served drinks, I decided to have a few free ones. I drank a few baileys and coffee and I think even a beer or two. I ate my meal and looked out the window for the sight of land. It was dark and I was going to arrive at 6am in Barcelona. I had a full view of the curvature of the earth and even the moon. I remember flirting with the receptionist at the San Francisco Airport and she gave me all window seats.

After a nap I saw lights and even a little land. We were high enough that I could see a part of the Iberian Peninsula. I saw a lot of lights in the middle and could only think "MADRID" oh my god I'm almost there. We flew a little further and the sun was just starting to rise. I saw the beach as the plane was in final descent. The waves were crashing on the shore and I finally landed at El Prat, Barcelona. The final challenge of my journey was upon me. I had to pass through customs, get my passport stamped and then I was all clear. The plane pulled up to the terminal and I was beyond nervous. I kept imagining that a police officer was going to be standing at the end of the terminal and I would be detained as soon as I got off the plane.

I put on my father's winter coat, picked up my sister's backpack and exited the plane. I followed the crowd as we all went through customs. I looked right and noticed the line for passport entry. I waited in line with just a few people and then I arrived at the window. The woman checking my passport could not have been more than 25 years old. She was cute and we couldn't help but smile at each other. I handed her my passport and she opened it up to scan the inside. It was 6 in the morning and everybody working was just waking up. I guess it was nice to see a decently attractive human being that early. She even blushed as we kept eye contact.

I slid her my passport and she scanned it. She broke eye contact, looked at the monitor and then directly back at me. But then she looked immediately back at the computer with wide open eyes. My heart was racing. Not only was she beautiful, but she STARED at the computer screen. The next three seconds were the longest moments of my existence. Everything slowed down and I recalled a majority of my life. All I could imagine was my face with a big red FUGITIVE banner blinking on the computer screen. Her facial expression was slowing changing from a look of surprise to a look that I was not expecting. She looks at me again with those big eyes every girl has when you impress her. She turned to her colleague and pointed to the monitor, he was roughly the same age and glanced at the computer. He was leaning back in his chair, yawning and stretching his arms, it was early morning. As I waited for his approval my world was slowly coming to an end. Every second that passed was torturous. He looked quickly at the monitor and then directly at me. He whispered something to the girl and then waved me through with his hand. The girl made eye contact with me again for another couple of seconds, stamped my passport and spoke in Catalan. "Benvinguda a Catalunya" She winked at me and I walked through the final gate. We turned to look at each other as I passed and I walked with purpose knowing that I had just made it into Europe.

I will never know what the computer monitor said, It could have said nothing, or brought up a red flag because I had a warrant for my arrest, or even a special message because it was my first time using my passport. Who knows! All I knew was that I had roughly $250, a backpack and a second chance.

Outro Music
"Paper Planes" by M.I.A.

Chapter 15

"Good things come to those who wait, but only things left by those who hustle."

- Abraham Lincoln

I waited a few hours for the currency exchange to open at the airport and I was not looking forward the small amount of money awaiting me. After a few hours I received roughly 180 Euros.

Ouch.

Well, at least I had money. With money, anything is possible. I was confident that I would find a job, working somewhere, doing something and I would be able to start a new life. I changed into my boots and put on some extra clothes, it was a cold November day and I looked out at the grey sky as the sun was rising above the terminal. I made it. I had actually, made it!

I walked for a few hours and headed towards Barcelona. The airport was roughly twenty minutes away by bus. I relied heavily on my Nokia Lumia 920. I bought the phone because it had a really good camera, excellent maps, and I knew that Nokia was the most durable phone on the market. I walked for several hours and eventually make it to Barcelona. My plan was to find the cheapest hostel and stay a few nights and talk to people that worked there, get on the computer and hopefully find some work. Remember, I landed with nothing but a smartphone and a backpack full of clothes. I eventually found a hostel that was a decent price and they had an excellent computer lab. My plan, was to design a basic website and go around and try to offer economic consulting for small businesses along with website creation. I did not have the proper documents to apply for a real job. All of my jobs would need to be under the table. I found several hostels between 6 and 9 euros and figured that my money would last me for a few weeks.

After I spent a few days in the hostel and found no existence of work. I contacted my brother and asked him what I should do. I was going to run out of money in a few days and it was only getting colder outside. My brother hooked me up on couchsurfing.org. I started adding as many people as possible so hopefully I could buy some time and not spend my money on housing. I was still very shy and my brain was going through withdrawals of MDMA, cannabis and I was not eating very well because I was trying to save money. I always had in the back of my mind that I could steal a bicycle or something and make some money. I was a criminal all of 2013, why stop now? I did not want to steal, I honestly wanted to change my life for the better. I kept trying the next couple of days, but was not having any luck finding work or any accommodation on couchsurfing. On the 5th of December I left the hostel to walk the city. I really needed glasses, but it was not feasible for the budget. I looked like a tourist with my backpack and little did I know, I was being followed.

In the afternoon, I walked around a part of Barcelona that I had not been to before. Earlier that week I was able to buy some cannabis for 20€. It was a really big bag and I wanted to take my mind off things because the situation was not looking good. I rolled up a joint and smoked half, put the other half in my stash jar, which I acquired in college from Gibrarian. I walked for another few hours and took off my backpack and sat it beside me. As I leaned against the wall, I was looking on my phone and taking a casual break. Walking around with a full backpack was exhausting. All of a sudden, I felt a swift rush of air. A man had grabbed my backpack and started to run away. As I looked up, he turned a corner and vanished. I had just been robbed. Not even one week into my "new life" and I was without a change of clothes, all of my resources, EVERYTHING was inside of that backpack.

I was wearing a pair of jeans, a shirt, a green sweater and my military boots. Thankfully I kept my passport, wallet, phone and charger in my jacket, which I was wearing. A special thanks to Leandro from the Omega program for telling me to carry my charger in my pocket. He was also robbed his first time in Europe, coincidentally in Barcelona, years prior. The thief took all of my clothes, personal items, my external hard drive with everything from my computer, every personal trinket I kept with me, my sisters backpack, and literally, my entire existence. Vanished. I took a deep breath as locals around me saw what just happened, I let it out, turned left and kept on walking. The first thought that came to mind was. "Well, I guess this makes it even. I robbed a bank and now life, robbed me."

You cannot imagine how happy I was. Call me crazy, but I had no weight to carry, literally no burdens on my back. I still had some money, my phone which was worth hopefully a few hundred euros more and my passport. I felt free as a bird. I was shocked, amazed, scared out of my mind and for the second time in my life, I felt 100% free. It was at this point that I walked immediately back to the hostel I stayed at the previous night, to tell them what happened. Remember, I just went through months of MDMA abuse and my socials skills were not the best, but I was still able to maintain a polite and respectful attitude.

I went to the hostel and explained what happened and they gave me a free night and a free breakfast. I was also able to use the computer lab to try and find the best way to make the most of my money. I had roughly 80 euros left. It was that night at the hostel that I met a couple from the United States, Dan and his girlfriend. Both of them were studying in Seville and before they finished their semester abroad they took a trip to Barcelona. I told them what happened to me and Dan gave me some clothes from his suitcase. They even went so far as to buy some alcohol and we drank that night, even though we were searching for cannabis. They gave me some money so I could stay a few nights more in the hostel. Very good people. Dan and I caught up years later because of facebook.

Dan and his girlfriend left and I was beginning to feel quite hopeless. The job situation in Spain was worse than anything you could read about in the newspaper. 2013 was the worst year on record and for people under age 30 the unemployment rate was nearly 55%. Unfathomable, the economy and the world, stops turning at this point. I was a social hermit recovering off an MDMA abusive period, it was almost impossible for me to muster up the courage to talk to anyone. I had no confidence and all I could think about was how I was going to end up on the street. The stress was mounting.

I ran out of money staying in hostels after a few more nights. As I checked out of the hostel, I had no idea what to expect. I started looking for places to sleep. Late at night a man finally responded from couchsurfing that I could come stay with him. I would need to take the train to the first stop outside of the city, heading into the mountains. It was over 10km away and it was already 9 at night.

I had some change in my pocket but not enough for a metro ticket. As I asked for change to buy a ticket, everyone ignored me. I even spoke to several people in English and had brief conversations. I guess since I had not shaved in a few days and did not have clean clothes I was probably smelling homeless. Europe was turning out to be a nightmare. I could have easily jumped the rail and gotten on the metro. Inside my head all I kept thinking was "You have come all this way to live a new life, DO NOT STEAL, you cannot afford the karma". I decided to walk, 10km, up the mountain, with a dying cell phone through mountain trails, in the dark, to a destination unknown. It was adventure time.

The walk was literally uphill all the way. Half of the roads did not have street signs and half of the "streets" on the map, were dirt paths with lights every 100m leading up different sides of the mountain. The higher I climbed the colder it was. I was sweating and I needed to find a water source as I had just run out. If it was not for my experiences in the USMC, long distance running and always having strong will power, I don't think most people could have done what I did. I was really low on nutrition and had already lost several pounds since I landed. Coming down off long term drug abuse, I was a hot mental and physical mess. I finally reached the top of Tibidabo mountain and my phone had roughly 5% battery left. I had to find my route, without my glasses, in the dark and hope that I was going the right way.

Wolves or large dogs howled at the moon as I walked through the woods down a dark trail with no houses in sight. I really hoped I was heading the right way. I NEED GLASSES. I turned on my phone again to see if I was headed the right way. My map said 2km more and I would be at the address. It was almost 2am in the morning. I kept walking down the other side of the mountain and I found a large main road. I remembered the map said I should follow the road up the side of another mountain. 2% battery. It had no street sign, but looked like what the map described. I shot a message to the man (Samuel) who was letting me stay at his house. I said I would be there in 20 minutes. I walked up another small road with barely any houses and I started walking towards the address. As I approached the gate a man came up and opened it. Samuel welcomed me into his home.

I was a little scared that a man who lived halfway up the mountain away from other members of society, was allowing people to stay in his house. Was I about to be murdered? Was this a bad story waiting to happen? Its 3am in the morning! I did not care, I was freezing and his house had heat.

I walked down the stairs of his terrace and it turns out, Samuel was a Surgeon at one of the hospitals in Barcelona. What are the odds? The man who wakes up at 3am to come and help a complete stranger, was a Surgeon who had no family and always enjoyed having people stay with him. He also worked the morning shift. He spoke very little English, but gave me a key and said that I could stay here for one week. Another young man was going to arrive tomorrow, and he told me he was from the United Kingdom. I stripped off all my clothes, and took a shower. Samuel made me coffee, we talked for a few minutes more. Samuel had to work at the hospital and I told him that I was probably going to sleep all day. I put on some pajamas that he gave me, and I went to sleep.

I woke up about 12 hours later the next day in his home, full of light and with a beautiful view of the mountains. I looked back and even saw part of the trail that I had to walk. I guess it only looked scary during night time. I found some food in his cupboard and ate some fruit that he said I could have. I was waiting until the man from the United Kingdom would get here later that evening, maybe he would know what I should do.

Samuel came home later that afternoon with a man named George. George was from Brighton, south England and was one of the most hippie people I had ever seen. He had such a happy personality, a great view on life, carried his guitar on his back and joy in his heart. "It's nice to be nice" George would always say. I told him that I was robbed shortly after arriving and explained that I had no chance of obtaining more money from home. My brother and sister lived paycheck to paycheck and my parents did not support me. After George and I hung out the first night, he invited me to spend time with him the next several days. He was going to meet a few people, friends of friends, but they were local Catalan people, students at the art school. George paid for everything, we bought groceries so we could eat at Samuel's house and he paid for both of us to use the metro. He was a very kind and generous soul.

The day we went into town to meet some of his friends, we went to Plaza Catalunya and we waited by the Zurich hot chocolate bar. I was still completely amazed by Barcelona and it was tough to remember, where and what everything looked like. Abuse of MDMA had really fucked up my brain and I did not have glasses. I was reading things in different languages and for the first time, I actually felt like I was learning again. George said we were waiting for a girl named Dagmar.

Dagmar had long dreadlocks, wore unconventional clothing and was as George said "a dirty hippie". We hung out with Dagmar and she took us to the art school to meet some of her friends. George started playing his guitar and we hung out in the courtyard for a few minutes at the steps of the ancient

218

hospital of Barcelona, which was now an art academy. Dagmar had run upstairs to "let the bags" and she was going to take us to eat. Apparently across from the school was a Sikh Temple that served all you could eat vegetarian food. All you had to do was bow before their temple, follow their brief ritual, clean your dishes and you were welcome to eat there. Dagmar came back downstairs and after a few minutes, her, George and I walked across the street to the temple.

We entered into the temple and they were working construction. Since all I had were the clothes on my back, I was wearing my jacket and all my layers. Thankfully Samuel let me use his washing machine the first day I was there. As I entered, all of the Indian guys at the temple stopped construction, started yelling at the other Indian guys in Punjabi and told me to wait at the entrance. Dagmar said this was not normal, so we waited. A man from the temple came forward that spoke a basic level of English and he searched me from head to toe. On the outside of the temple, there was a sign that said "No weapons, No alcohol, No drugs, No Tobacco and No consuming of Meat" I thought they were searching me for contraband. After a few of the guys looked me over, they looked at Dagmar who was a regular and they decided to let me in.

I learned the next week that everyone at the Temple thought I was the Police. The Temple had many people there without papers and they thought I was going to bring trouble. Little did I know, that a few people without papers was only the tip of the Iceberg. Dagmar showed me their ritual. Before entering the temple you had to remove your shoes, then you were required to wash both your hands, and your feet. Once clean, you covered your hair with a bandanna. I walked into the temple and everyone was staring. I could only imagine what the people from Punjab were thinking. I went and bowed before their temple and went over to a man who was in his 60's with a beard older than I was and accepted a handful of what appeared to be apple pie filling. I ate it, sat in meditation for a few minutes and then I was invited to eat.

The Sikhs separated men on one side and women on the other. George and I sat down and we were served round tortilla like bread known as pashata and then servings of vegetables and a rice pudding. They poured me a glass of water and as we sat on the ground eating our food, I could not help but believe what Dagmar had just shown me. They served three meals a day and all I had to do was the dishes. I had found a place to eat. All I needed now was a place to sleep. We all finished eating and went upstairs to wash the dishes. Everyone was humming and singing in a tantric sense the phrase "Wahe Guru" A phrase that I would soon come to call my own. All of us left the temple after an hour and we headed back over to the art school. George had introduced me to new people and I was beginning to feel less scared with no money, in a foreign country.

Both of us stayed at Samuel's house for a few more days and we needed to find a new place to live. Dagmar was in the process of searching for some clothes and a backpack for me so I would not be as helpless. Both of us were waiting for responses on couchsurfing, Dagmar allowed us to stay at her house for a few days. I began to build my network of Catalans and kept in contact with people via facebook and email. All of Dagmar's friends thought I could get a job teaching English, maybe some private lessons since I did not have papers. When Dagmar said we had to get out of her house. I had not found a place to stay. I packed up the backpack Dagmar gave me and I decided that I was going to sleep outside, and "tough it out" until things got better.

Since Dagmar showed me the Temple of the Sikhs, I went there almost everyday for lunch and even sometimes for dinner. Nearby the temple there was also a computer lab for young people that was free of charge. Dagmar introduced me to the people that worked there. I was allowed 30 minutes in the morning and 30 minutes in the afternoon. It was the best I could get for free. I had internet, food, all I needed now was a place to sleep.

My first philosophy was to sleep during the day and then keep moving at night to stay warm. I then realized that if I was asleep during the day I would almost certainly miss my chances to eat at the temple, or use the free computer lab. I decided to sleep outside at night and found places secluded so

220

I would not be robbed. The weather was only getting colder as the days progressed and I had limited clothing. For 5 nights in December, I slept outside in roughly 40 degree weather. One of the nights it rained and It was very difficult to sleep and find somewhere that was not wet.

I was going to the temple regularly and everyone started to recognize my face. They served hundreds of meals a day sometimes and there were always dishes that needed cleaning. I usually went and ate for about 20 minutes and then did the dishes for several hours. The reason I did the dishes for hours, was to show my thanks and also keep me out of the cold. I was a machine at cleaning and everyone in the temple noticed how hard I was working. After the second day, one of the children at the temple spoke decent English and asked what I was doing there. I told him I was robbed when I came to Barcelona and that I had no way of getting money from back home. The child went and started explaining my story to all the people inside the temple.

I was still doing the dishes as many people gathered around and I told my story to the child, he then translated into Punjabi. I finished washing all the dishes and everyone was amazed at how I was homeless, robbed when I first arrived and had no money. It was past the lunch period and I left the temple to go and use the computer lab. After using the computer lab, I went to Plaza Catalunya, sat down and pondered my life. All of a sudden a man named Yonithan, from Sweden, came up to me and asked if I wanted to go to a coffeeshop and smoke weed. I had read about the cannabis associations in Barcelona and since he spoke English, we began a conversation.

We talked briefly about the association and I explained that I was robbed and currently had no money or a place to stay. I asked if he could get me a job promoting and he said we should go and ask the owner. I picked up my backpack and we walked to 420 cannabis association. I went inside and it was full of people with tattoos and gold teeth. He introduced me to the manager and I asked for a job and they were quite excited to hire me. I spoke English and they thought I would bring "high end" clients to the association.

He gave me a bunch of flyers and I began walking the streets. All I had to do was go up and talk to people, see if they consumed cannabis and then bring them to the association. They had to pay a membership fee of 10 euro, but once inside, they could choose from many different strains. I would get to keep 8 euro for every person that came to the club.

I JUST FOUND A JOB.

Easier said, than done. I was a social hermit that does very well in a professional business setting but not well with talking to people on the street. I was still coming down off a long binge of MDMA, depression and poor social skills. I was literally afraid to talk to people. Business settings were fine, but social settings could not be more terrifying.

The club was open everyday from 11am to 2am. I had a place to go until early morning and then I could sleep outside the rest of the night. It was not a dream come true, but at least improving my current situation. For the next 3 days I went and walked the streets afraid to talk to people. I think I approached maybe 6 people over those 3 days. As an introvert, I was out of my element and talking to people socially in a foreign country was the most terrifying thing for me to comprehend. I had no glasses! It was impossible for me to read facial expressions, even tell if they were male or female. How on earth was I supposed to convince someone to drop what they were doing and come smoke weed with me?

I continued to eat at the temple, use the computer lab and I even met up with George the day before he left. I invited George to the Cannabis Club and told him that if he paid 10 euro to go inside I would get 8 back. The first 5 people I brought to the club I would get 8 euro in return and then after that the full 10 euro. George agreed to go with me. When I brought in George, I talked with the guy who was in charge and said, "Hey man, this guy is my friend, can he just pay the 2 Euro that you would keep, instead of paying me later?" The guy in charge looked at me with a very genuine and honest

222

look and I could tell that he was puzzled, but happy. He knew that I had a good heart and I was not trying to rip anybody off. He turned to George and said "Do you have that magical coin?" George handed him a 2 Euro coin and we both went inside and shared a few joints of Moroccan hash.

Later that day, George caught the train to Granada and as we said goodbye at Plaza Catalunya I told him that I owed him a hat. George searched for a hat the entire time he was in Barcelona and never found one. When we were hanging out he was always going into shops and trying on hats. He must have tried on 100 hats, but nothing fit just right. He vanished into the metro and that was the last time I ever saw George.

"Its nice to be nice" - George

I had a job, but had yet to earn any money. There were very few people in Barcelona for the tourist season but Christmas was coming and I was told that the city would fill up with people. I noticed that the cannabis association did not have a website and I thought I would spend my time in the computer lab building a simple website. I built the website using Wix, a monkey could do it. It was a very simple/elegant website that linked the Instagram, Twitter and Facebook accounts, I then showed it to the boss. They were super excited and called the owner who was from Sweden. The owner wanted to meet me when he was in town over new years. I gave them my contact information and I was beginning to feel like I had found a family in Barcelona. Thank you Mary Jane, you have always been the best girlfriend.

After my 5th night of sleeping outside I worked hard all day and at the end of the day I earned, nothing. FUCK. I was still without any euros to my name. After a tough day on the street I spoke with one of the guys closing up 420. As I grabbed my bag to leave, he asked me where I was staying. I told him that I've been sleeping outside for the past 5 nights. He looked at me with his eyes wide open, pulled out a 10 euro bill and said "find a hostel man, you will make that money back tomorrow, I am sure of it". I took the money and searched my phone for the cheapest hostel, costing only 6 euro. I walked all the way there for over an hour and when I got there, it was closed for repairs.

I was really tired, hungry, and it just turned December 24th. I had money, but it was already too late at night for me to stay in a hostel. What I decided to do was use that 10 Euro to buy a metro ticket, go visit Dagmar and ask to do a load of laundry and sleep at her place all afternoon. I was awake almost 20 hours at this point and dozing on and off. The train would open in 2 hours, all I had to do was wait. When the train opened I bought my ticket and I figured that I could sleep on the train for a few hours, ride it all the way to the end and then by that time, Dagmar might actually be awake and I could do some laundry and hopefully sleep at her place all day. I needed a recharge.

When I got on the train I was half asleep/half awake. The train took off towards the next stop and this is where my memory started to fade. I remembered that I was the ONLY person on the train at 5:30 that morning. The only other people were two Police Officers still dressed in their Uniforms and carrying their firearms. What happened next was either the worst dream I ever had, or the truth. While I was on my phone, a brand new Nokia Lumia 920, worth several hundred euros, and the only asset to my name, the two police officers came over to me and said "Movíl" and pointed at my phone. I looked up at them, half awake/asleep and also puzzled. One of them said it even louder "Movíl" I looked at them and said that I do not speak Spanish. One of them put his hand on his firearm and said "¡MOVIL!"

I was scared/confused/asleep/awake at this point and I had no idea what was going on. One of the officers reached forward and grabbed my mobile out of my hand. I said something like "What the fuck!?!?" while they both look at me and said nothing. The officer opened his chest pocket and put the phone inside. He turned to the other one and said "Tourista" calling me a tourist. The train arrived at the next stop and both officers exited the train, leaving me completely alone in the train car.

The next thing I remember, was waking up at the last stop on the train, alone and my phone was not in my pocket. Was I just robbed by the police? Are you kidding me? Did that really happen? I was planning on selling my phone to buy a pair of glasses so I could improve my performance on talking to people on the street. I was able to see about 3 meters without my glasses, after that, everything became very fuzzy. It was almost impossible for me to approach people because I could not see their facial expressions, let alone determine if they were male or female. But now, I no longer had a phone. I just spent my euros on a train ticket and I was feeling so depressed and suicidal I could not even think.

I rode the train to Dagmar's station. The directions to her place were in my phone I had to use my memory, (without glasses) to try and find her place. I walked for about an hour through Sant Cugat and I finally arrived. I rang the bell and she was not home. I decided to sleep in her stairwell for a few hours. I woke up a few hours later, rang her door again and she was still not home. I was rested by this point and decided to head back to Barcelona to try walking the streets and find people for the cannabis association.

What a turn of events! Within a 6 hour period I was given 10 euro to find a hostel, not able to find a place to sleep, robbed of my phone and still not able to shower or wash my clothes. I am both equally stupid and unfortunate. I could not find it within myself to complain, I was making progress. Luthor however, was in prison.

I went back to 420 cannabis association and I spoke to the guy that loaned me the money and I told him what happened. He was disappointed in me and said that I should not come back until I had his 10 euro repaid. I decided to go and collect my thoughts at the temple and grab a bite to eat. I finished eating at the temple and started washing the dishes. I explained my story to many people who barely understood English. I was homeless, I was robbed, etc, etc. It was Christmas eve at this time and I did not want to sleep outside. After I had some chai tea, some of the men at the temple approached me and said "We have found you a place to stay!" At first I was a bit uneasy and a little cautious but I did not want to sleep outside in the cold. I listened and they had me meet with a few other people that spoke better English. The meeting was not in the temple, but the street.

This was the first time, I felt a bit uneasy with all of the people at the temple. We went outside on the street and a few younger Sikhs came up to me and started asking me questions. They were a bit different from the guys I met at the temple. Some of them had tattoo's which was against their belief system. A few others were smoking cigarettes which was also against their ethics. After a half hour of talking, they took me into an apartment next to the temple. The apartment was run down, over crowded and I was sleeping in a room that was full of bugs and extra people. The location of the temple was in the poorest part of town and I was not surprised to find that the flats nearby were in just as poor condition. I could only assume that most of the people living in this establishment were illegal immigrants, or people that had made their way from the developing world to Barcelona in hopes of a better life.

As I was given my place to sleep, next to another man from Punjab, we communicated that the lights had to remain on, otherwise the bugs were going to come. I took a cold shower in the bathroom and laid down next to the other man and I fell asleep with the lights on. I woke up the next morning to sounds of people arguing within the flat and I decided to take my bag and head to the computer lab and keep searching for jobs. After the computer lab, I went to the temple again for lunch and after doing the dishes again for over an hour, I decided to do what most people do in the temple. Meditate.

I sat there and listened to traditional sikh mantra repeated over and over again for several hours and fell into a trance. When I finally woke up after breathing and meditating, several people were looking at me. I stood up, went and took some Chai tea and it was at this time, that the oldest man from the Temple, Babu, (father, or papa) came and sat next to me. He spoke a very basic level of English, but the way he communicated was not through his words, but through his silence. Babu had a beard that was older than I was, scars on his hands and face and was in his mid 60's. When you looked into his eyes, you could tell that he had experienced many things and obtained levels of consciousness that most people never will. He spent most of his time in meditation and words cannot do justice to describe the aura around him. He was by all means the definition of a monk, elder, or in the specific case of Sikhism, a guru.

Babu spoke with me briefly and I told him that I have no place to stay. Babu responded and said "...you do" I was not sure what he meant. He then continued talking and said "You will stay with us... here." I was blown away. In most cultures, seniority is a critical factor when it comes to making decisions and the oldest most bearded man at the temple just told me I was going to stay. I was a little shocked and he called over someone who spoke better English to serve as a translator.

Chapter 16

"Speak only that which will bring you honor"

- Guru Nanak Dev Ji

What Babu had concluded, was that I was a sign from God and that the temple was here to help me. They welcomed me in with open arms and all of the men from India were very excited. Only men were allowed to sleep in the Temple. After they had their evening service and all of the other people left, we sat around and drank a milk called Samundar. It was hot milk with lots of salt and sugar. Samundar means "ocean" in Punjabi and in broken English, they explained to me that this particular sect of Sikhs were known as the warrior clan and to show that they were tough, they drank this salty milk every night before bed. It was very different, but after a few nights I was use to it. All of us slept in the same room in the Temple and it was very funny to watch all of them look at me while I performed my evening routine. All of them watched me with intensive eyes as I brushed my teeth, how I slept in my blanket as if I literally was a "sign from God".

Babu was my personal favorite, he would watch me complete my entire routine and then nod in acknowledgment if he thought if something was worth copying. It was a scene from a movie by all means, I was the new spectacle in the life of the Temple. When I brushed my teeth, Babu watched me until I finished and then copied exactly as I did. I then decided to do pull ups on the stairs before bed. Everyone started yelling at me saying that you cannot do exercise in the temple. Babu however, was laughing hysterically and kindly asked me to not workout in the temple. I think it even made him tear from laughter. I finished getting ready for bed and could not believe where I was, who I was, and the strange turn of events that had saved my life.

As we were all lying down, the doorbell to the temple rang. The water truck with hundreds of 8L jugs were waiting for us. I watched first as they loaded them off the truck and then I noticed that the guys would only pick up one in each hand and bring them into the temple. The jugs had large plastic handles so you could easily hold two. I picked up 4, two in each hand and carried them into the Temple. Babu was ecstatic and instructed everyone else to do the same. We unloaded all of the water into the temple in half the time because everyone was now carrying more than 2 jugs. I guess I truly was a sign from god.

We went to sleep and I remembered waking up at 4am because Babu was vacuuming. Apparently Babu slept only 4-5 hours every day. He would wake up and study their holy book every day at 1am by candle light and some days, he would not even sleep, only meditate. Wahe Guru. The first night that I spent in the temple was Christmas day. Black friday I bought my freedom from the United States and by Christmas in that same year, I had a roof over my head. Sleeping outside for a total of 5 nights in the cold was life changing enough, I cannot imagine those that struggle on a day to day basis.

I never felt 100% welcome at the temple and I was definitely creating tension among those that were regulars. One day while sitting with Babu drinking tea, I asked what he did for fun. He looked at me with a curious face and said "This is my life... Babies, children, family... and me, it is all here.". I then asked "Do you ever become bored? Or need a change of environment?" He looked at me and we made eye contact. In this moment I noticed a rather large scar on his face, it started from his forehead and went through his right eye continuing down to his cheek. The muscles around his green eyes contracted and I was able to see eyes glisten as he responded "Here better than India... better than prison". Babu finished drinking his tea and as he got up, a part of his bana retracted and I noticed that he also had a tattoo.

I will not go all in depth while living at the temple because the daily routine was pretty much the same. During

229

my time at the temple I tried to learn the language of Punjabi but failed miserably. The elders told me that as long as I followed their rules I could stay as long as I needed. It was not so much the religion of Sikhism that taught me life lessons, but more so through the people that I met while staying at the temple.

I will provide a brief summary of my daily schedule.

04:00 Wake up
04:30 Opening Ceremony of the Holy book
06:00 Breakfast
06:30 Prepare food and perform chores for the Day
10:30 Computer Lab (30 Minutes)
11:30 Afternoon worship Service
13:00 Afternoon meal
14:00 Meditate
15:00 Chores/Dishes/Temple procedures
17:00 Computer Lab (30 Minutes)
18:00 Evening Worship Service (closing of the book)
20:00 Dinner
21:00 Samundar
21:30 Temple Locked (Lights Out)

I was always encouraged to go out and look for work which I did to the best of my ability. I was still coming down off a very long abuse of MDMA and thankfully the temple was a substance free environment. For nearly a month, I was fed authentic Indian vegetarian food, placed on a regular sleeping schedule and free from all forms of intoxicants. I did not necessarily feel signs of withdrawal, but I was always quite tired and slept as often as I could. After a few weeks of living in the temple a young woman appeared and started to teach some of the people Catalan. Her name was Marta and I would never forget it.

Marta was a bit chubby and quite socially awkward. She had almost no sense of self esteem and at times displayed signs of autism. After living in a temple with men for a few weeks my testosterone levels were quite high and I decided that I should go and speak with Marta. Marta spoke English, but not the best English. We talked briefly inside the temple and then we ended up walking to a different part of the city, where Marta attended school. When we arrived at the building, I noticed all of the machines were apple computers. Marta was in design school for cinematography.

*Brief Disclaimer. I am not here to hate on people that attend cinematography school, but usually people that enter into this field, come from privileged families. Finding a job in the area of cinema is quite difficult and often not well paid. This goes the same, for digital design, music, art, theater, fashion and all other forms of "jobs" in these areas. People that enter into these fields usually attend VERY private and or expensive schools. These people also, already have a substantial amount of wealth coming from their family so they do not need to worry about paying for their studies, let alone their costs of living compared to most other students. What I am trying to say is "If you go to some expensive school and do not pay for your tuition, let alone, housing, food, gasoline, other expenses and you live off your wealthy parents, and you study something that most people would consider as a hobby and don't have to worry about getting a real job. GO FUCK YOURSELF."

I feel better.

I arrived at Marta's "school" and she sat down and started working on some project about 'tap dancing' and adding subtitles to one of her films. I used the computer next to her and we talked for a little bit. I asked her where she works and she replied that she was unemployed. I asked her how old she was, she sighed then replied "29". I could only help but think "29? Are you serious? you are still attending "school" at twenty fucking nine years of age?!?" I just kept smiling. We talked for a little while longer and I said goodbye and made my way back over to the temple.

Spanish and unfortunately Catalan culture is quite different from how I was raised and what I would consider, normal. Students in Spain, usually attend University from age 18-22, but a majority of them, live at home, or within an hour's drive. Elite Private Universities do not drive the academic standard, as found in the USA. Going to college is simply a continuation of High School. Competition does not exist. The last time Spain won a nobel Prize was in 1989 and it was for literature. They have however won a nobel prize in Medicine, but the most recent was over 50 years ago, in 1959. Compared to their German, French, Dutch, Swedish, or other European accolades, the Spanish are quite lazy and unmotivated. Spain always receives the participation ribbon, never a medal.

On the walk home I could only think that she would make a perfect girlfriend. I bet she had loads of money and her parents were not even keeping track of what they were spending. I could use her for a brief time and possibly find a way out my current predicament. One of the days she invited me to her home and gave me an old cell phone. She lived with her parents and brother. Her father was a doctor and her mother, a dentist. Her older brother who was 33 and did not have to work either. They were a truly rich and dysfunctional family. This made me both happy and sad, but it made me appreciate how hard my parents made me work and what it made me into. To quote the film Fight Club "A guy came to fight club the first time, his ass was a wad of cookie dough, after a few weeks, he was carved out of wood." I would hang out with Marta for the next several days, but little did I know, I was soon being followed, again. This time not by a thief, but by the Sikhs.

As it turns out, only the elders of the temple were okay with me staying there. Once word broke out that a white man from the United States was staying inside the temple, people began to hate me and disrespect the elders in charge. About three weeks into the temple a few men from Birmingham came to visit their fellow Sikhs. If you do not know Birmingham, UK,

232

it is epicenter for the Sikhs in the United Kingdom. The Sikhs own everything, the malls, shopping centers, tram stations and yes, even the Universities.

I explained my situation to these two guys who were about my age and spoke perfect English. They were shocked at the fact that I was robbed and left for dead and even more shocked that I came into the Temple and was now living the life of a Guru. One quote that I will take with me for the rest of my life "You have to dig through dirt, to get to a diamond" came from a man named Jagshar. Jagshar gave me 60 euros and said, go and get yourself some glasses. It was not enough to get glasses, but a good saving point. I finally had some money. The plan was to buy a sim card for the phone Marta gave me. I applied for English teaching positions, but was unable to attach a working phone number to my resume. Starting from 0 was not easy. I went later that afternoon and got a prepaid Sim Card.

The next day, as I made my way back towards the temple, I received a call from one of the guys from Birmingham. It was his last night in town and he said we should meet up before he left for Valencia the next morning. It was getting late and I had to be at the temple soon, but I decided to go and meet up with him regardless. I met with Jagshar or JAG (irony) and another Sikh named Major whom I knew from the temple who spoke a basic level of English. We had coffee and talked a little bit about what was going on. Jag and I talked mainly in English and he served as the translator between Major and I.

The only time I remembered Major, was one night in the temple around 21:00, a few weeks earlier. He entered into a brief argument with the elders of the temple and they started to yell and scream at each other. Major left the temple and did not return for about 10 days. All three of us kept talking and in the middle of hanging out I was able to see Major's passport. At the time, Major was wearing a turban and had a beard that would take several years to grow. When I opened his passport, he had a shaved head, no facial hair, a few piercings and looked like a gangster. Jag turned to the last page in his passport and it read in all capitals "ORIGINAL PASSPORT

233

LOST OR STOLEN" Jag handed the passport back to Major. When major got up to go use the bathroom, Jag turned to me and said "that's all you need to know".

By this time it was about 11pm and we walked across Plaza Catalunya to the bus that Major needed to catch. Jagshar and I broke into a discussion about mind altering substances and how nothing is really illegal or legal. It was at this point we broke the superficial wall and leveled with each other. Jagsher asked me "Do you know how much money the temple brings in?" I said I had no idea. As we both spoke in English and waited for Majors bus, Jagsher turned to me and said "In his backpack is almost 30k euros. Major will take that money to India to help Punjab," I was in shock. As Majors bus arrived, he turned to both of us and said good bye. Jagsher turned to me and said "everything is not as it seems". Apparently Major flew to India once, sometimes twice, per month.

From there our conversation became exponentially more interesting. He had dropped acid several times and was not a "by the book" Sikh. It was at this time, that I felt the need to be honest with Jag since he was being honest with me. I told him about why I was here and that I robbed Banco Americo. I showed him a few articles on his iPhone as we stood outside the apple store in Plaza Catalunya. He looked at the phone and thought out loud and was in shock "Oh wow, you are not lying, that's pretty amazing". We talked for a little bit more and then he needed to catch the last metro home so he could get back to his house that was just outside Barcelona.

He then told me that I should never trust an Indian person. He also told me that as I walked home, I should notice all of the guys on the street selling beer, and see if they too, were wearing a kara. Jagsher then told me something that would forever change my life. "These Sikhs, are not what you think they are. They are a mafia, and the religion is the cover. Almost all of the coke and other drugs coming into Barcelona are controlled by us. I would get out of that temple as soon as you can because it is not a safe place to be. You met 'Bobby' he is the one in charge of the street operation, take a good look at his face, you will see that he looks just like Baba Ji (an elder at the temple) they do not think you are a threat, but if they find out what you did, it will be a horrible situation." My mind was completely blown at this point and the train had just arrived. Jagsher jumped inside and as the doors closed, he said "Best of luck, Avtar Singh" (My name given to me by the Elders. Meaning "one who is good with money" or "the incarnation of god". I find it even more strange that my big brother in the fraternity chose "the christ" as my nickname.) Babu had given me this name, and Baba Ji gave me a kara just a few days earlier.

Fragile and completely awestruck, I walked up the stairs as the guard closed the metro gate and headed back towards the temple. It was roughly 12:30 am at this point and I could not believe what I had just heard. The temple? Baba Ji? Drugs? Mafia? What? My head exploded. I began walking home and since it was already late at night, I noticed men standing on street corners holding 6 packs of beer. I also noticed that each one was wearing a kara. As I approached one of them, he uttered the words quickly "Cerveca, Beer". I denied the offer with a slight head nod and hand gesture. As I came closer he spoke in a different tone, "Hash, coke, weed, Marijuana, Ecstasy".

At this point I was starting to put the pieces of the puzzle together. I walked another block towards the temple and sure enough another group of guys holding six packs of beer. Again, they both said "Cerveca, Beer" and then as I came closer, they said "Hash, coke, weed, charley, mdma" all street names for different drugs. Was I truly sleeping every night, in the belly of the Beast? I turned the final corner, less than one street away from the temple. I saw a man holding another 6 pack, but I recognized his face, and he of course, recognized mine. "Avtar Singh! how R U? You want beer?" He extended his beer to me. At this point I truly felt as though I was in a movie. I saw this man come into the temple almost every single day and I even taught him a bit of English. How fucking crazy is my life right now?!?!?!

I spoke with him for a minute and a prostitute walked by, apparently they knew each other. While drinking a beer, the

235

man made a notion to me that I should go and have a "good time" with her. I denied the offer and we talked a bit more and I headed towards the temple. By this time it was almost 2 in the morning and the temple was locked. I decided to go for a walk and waited until the temple opened closer to 4:30am. I walked around and noticed all of the street vendors, wearing Kara's, offering me drugs and alcohol. I could not believe it, Jagsher was right.

I waited outside the temple for another few minutes until 4:30 and Babu came to unlock the door. "AVTAR SINGH, you did not come home last night! We cannot trust you." I tried my best to explain, who I was with and the scenario, but Babu, was not having a word of it. He explained to me that I could not stay in the Temple anymore and that I needed to leave that next day. I was allowed to come and eat food, worship, do dishes, but I could no longer sleep in the Temple. After nearly a month of learning the ways of a guru, I was back on the street... So close, yet so far.

What I did next, was visit a hostel that I had learned about in the city center. Apparently this hostel allowed you to work during the day and then you could spend the night for free. I packed up all of my things, which were only a few changes of clothes and a backpack and I headed through the Gotic quarter into the Borne district. When I arrived, the hostel was completely empty, it was late January at this point and Barcelona was a ghost town. Not a single tourist was there.

I walked up to the front desk and spoke with a woman and lied to her. "My embassy told me to come here." I showed my American passport. The receptionist went and quickly got her boss. I spoke with the boss for a minute and she said that there was no work at the moment so I had to find another place to stay. I lied again and said "This is where my embassy told me to go am I in the wrong location?" (I had paperwork from the embassy because I declared all of my baggage stolen) I quickly said "I'm from the United States..." I believe her name was Veronica, she went and called her boss and then they said I could stay and work for one week.

236

After Jag gave me the 60 euros I spent about 20 of them on a sim card leaving me with roughly 40 and some coins I found on the street. I then found a thrift clothing store and bought a suit for only 2 euros. I also took a tie from the store and put it inside one of the pockets. I found a pair of used leather shoes for 7 euros and decided it was time that I visited the Embassy to see if they could help me. I still had my train ticket from visiting Dagmar and I took the train wearing my suit and carrying my passport. I was scared when they took my passport at the embassy, not knowing if I would be arrested on the spot. After going inside I filed a report noting that my bag was stolen from me. The embassy offered no help. I explained that I was sleeping outside and asked what I should do. Again, the embassy said they could not help. A man in the lobby overheard what was going on and gave me 13 euros. He felt sorry for me. I then took my paperwork from the Embassy and left to return to the temple. That same paperwork allowed me to work/sleep at this hostel for nearly two weeks.

I worked during the day and made friends with the team. Marta came to visit several times and I was still hunting for a place to sleep. Barcelona was a ghost town and it was over a month since I had tried to work for the cannabis association. I considered that job, lost, and I needed to hunt for another one. I only a few Euro's left over from Jagsher because I had to pay a small fee for staying every night at the hostel. (tourist tax) I also needed to buy a personal items to keep clean and not look homeless.

Everyone at the hostel was really amazed by my work ethic, I did things in record time and performed many tasks that other could not, such as heavy lifting. They let me stay an extra week. It was at this point I had developed a little bit better relationship with Marta. I told her that I was going to become homeless again, and she went and spoke to her parents. Marta was 29 years old and her brother was 33. Yet, both of them, had no job and still lived with their parents. I will be completely honest, it was strange, depressing and almost like watching the Will Ferrel Movie, Stepbrothers. Guess who moved in for almost two weeks? Me. Let's just say I was the cherry on top of an already dysfunctional home.

While looking for work and spending time with Marta, I came across a job in sales. They called me in for an interview and there were only a few people working in the office. Almost everyone was British. It was all phone sales and at the end of the month I would earn 800 Euro. After the first month, it was up to me to make sales and earn my own commission. Soon as I landed the job, I moved out of Marta's house and into a squat that was about 15 minute walk, away from where I worked. Marta served mainly as the translator between myself and the squatters. The squatters explained that the squat was going to be occupied by the police quite soon so I only had a few weeks to live there. I moved in, because I wanted to keep a good image with Marta's parents. Marta was rich and losing her meant I would lose an important connection in Catalunya. I moved into the squat amongst the motley crew and some people had lived there for upwards of 3 years. Hippies by all means, it was a very different life. Better than being homeless, but not comfortable like I had imagined. The building was dilapidated and a few pipes broke leaving the inside to ruin. Imagine an entire apartment building without doors. We all shared one kitchen on the bottom floor which featured recycled food collected from businesses, or waste bins. Most of the people were hoarders, and lived day to day off the scraps of capitalism.

By this time, it was the first week of February and I was going to get paid at the end of the month. I could still eat at the Sikh temple, which was a 10 minute walk away from my work office. The strangest part about the job was that they had no problem paying in cash. I started training, always dressed for work, showing up early and eager to learn. Another man from Morocco started the same time as me, he was late twice to work by only a few minutes and they fired him. I took that as a lesson, I was always at work early. The office situation was a bit weird, there were 4 rooms. One was a big conference room, that was hardly ever used. Another was an office for the secretaries, another was an office for the boss, and the final room for all of the salesmen. The boss was only a few years older than me and said he had been with the company for a while and was in charge of this new office in Barcelona.

You could tell it was a new operation, because everything was really clean and it was not messy like an office usually was. It was also strange the investments that we were selling. They had very high returns and almost sounded too good to be true. I came to work every day and learned from the guys that had more experience. There was one guy at work who was always struggling. He was a bit different and a really nice guy. His name was Liam. Liam and I talked about how work was hard to find and that I needed a job that paid right now. Liam told me that he worked for another Cannabis Association, named Kush and could probably get me a job. That afternoon, we went to Kush and I was given the low down. I met my boss, Baba and he said that I could collect my money the same day. It was the same job as before with street promotion except I could make 20 euros per person.

I experienced a bit of a struggle promoting on my own and was desperate for money. Liam was a bit of a character himself that suffered from drug and alcohol abuse at an earlier age. You could also tell that he was very genuinely trying to change. We tried promoting together a few times, but I was always a bit embarrassed to have him at my side. He was a bit older and was almost nervous when talking to people or just over excited. I decided to recruit on my own.

I worked until 5pm every day and I decided that I could work for the cannabis club after cold calling people on the phone. I worked everyday and was super motivated to make money. I was still dating Marta at this time, but living in the squat in the city center. We shared one cold shower, bugs were everywhere, holes in the wall, no heat and it was winter time. It looked like something from a horror movie. On the bright side, I was not living with the dysfunctional family that was crippling Marta.

My daily routine for about three weeks consisted of the following. I would wake up at 7:30 to the sound of the alarm on the phone Marta gave me. I would get dressed in western business clothes that did not fit and match, and walk for 20 minutes to get to work. I would work until 1pm then have an hour for lunch. Thankfully the temple was within ten minutes walk and I was able to have lunch every day for free. I would then work until about 5pm and either come home and sleep, or hit the streets and try promoting for Kush. On weekends all I did was promote for Kush. The clock was ticking down and I had about three weeks until I no longer had a place to sleep. I was a few days away from being paid and I had a strange feeling that something fishy was going on at work. Some of the guys were making sales, but overall as a team, we were not doing that well. I got dressed for work Friday morning and I went to work as usual. I arrived at the front door and rang the buzzer to the office building, except this Friday morning, no one answered.

I looked at my watch, I was a little bit early, but the boss was always there to let people in. I was already a bit worried and I had that feeling in my stomach that something was awry. A man delivering a package came out of the office building and I slid in through the door. I immediately went upstairs to my floor. I was not able to go inside, the door was locked, but I could see through the small window. All the lights were turned off, half the computers were gone and almost all the files and stationery were missing.

WHAT THE FUCK?

I was just a few days away from being paid and now the company vanished like a magic trick? I must be crazy. As I sat in the stairwell and tried to comprehend what was happening, one of the secretaries, Abena, walked up the stairwell. She said "Ace, sweetie, what are you doing here?" I said "I'm here to work, what the hell is going on?". Abena replied "Didn't you hear, our boss got arrested," My mind was completely torn apart at this point. (Arrested? for what? am I arrested? what? what? WHAT?) "Yeah, apparently the whole thing was an operation for selling fake investments. Thankfully I have the keys. I'm going to take a laptop and see if there is anything else worth of value". Abena and I instantly

240

connected. "Let's tear the place apart and see if there is anything valuable, let's hurry though, the police might be on their way." I was freaking out, I started wiping my fingerprints off everything. I was already a fugitive, the last thing I needed was being arrested for international investment fraud. Just my luck.

All Abena was able to find was a laptop and besides some telephones and office supplies there was nothing else valuable in the office. We left after a few minutes and headed downstairs. Abena and I decided to have a coffee and she explained everything that was going on. She showed me the article on her phone, from the BBC. There was also a video. I was part of one of the largest scams in the history of Europe. Remarkable.

http://www.bbc.com/news/uk-26367166

I hope you enjoyed that video. It still uses flash so it might take a minute to load, but it is definitely worth it.

As I tried to drink my coffee my mind began to race. I was worried about where I was going to sleep in a few days and completely devastated by the fact that I was not going to get paid. I felt thoroughly mind fucked that I potentially could have been arrested for an International boiler room scam, along with having all of my legal problems in the United States. I dodged a bullet. Ridiculous. Abena and I exchanged numbers, then she invited me to her home for another coffee. She lived just next to Kush, but in a very nice high rise apartment. It was from here that Abena and I began our friendship, at times I think both of us wanted to take it to a sexual level, but I always hesitated.

I digress.

I went back to the squat and walked up the staircase filled with bugs, graffiti and holes in the wall to gather my belongings. The police were coming any day now and I did not want to be there when they came. February 28, I was homeless once again.

This was one of the first times that I went to Kush and started to introduce myself to those working there. The place was not very friendly. Many people there were gangsters and if you were not part of their circle, you were a tourist. Tourists had to pay more for everything. I explained to Baba and the front door guys what was going on and I had my backpack and bag with me. They let me put my bags in Kush for the day while I went out and promoted. I walked around for about an hour and in front of the Catedral de Barcelona I acquired my first group. One of the guys was holding his camera (tourist) and he was wearing a "Cannabis University" shirt from Amsterdam. I went up and talked to him and his friends and explained that we have a cannabis club just a few minutes walk away. They were super excited, everyone paid 20 euro and I had finally made 60 euros, in under an hour. I now had almost 100 euros saved and as I was looking for apartments online, rooms were going for about 200-250€. I was one step closer to finding a home.

Chapter 17

It was at this point and time I was beginning to really hate my relationship with Marta. The only reason I was with her, was because she was rich. She had no conceptual thinking of how to make/spend/save money and it drove me crazy. All she would ever do is bitch about how hungry she was. She would refuse to do simple things, such as make a sandwich and take it with her because it was what the "poor people" did. Also, she was for some reason afraid to have sex. 29 years old and afraid to have sex. Catalans. She was not a virgin either. Yet, I was still trying to be nice to her and I completely took advantage of her spending habits. She treated me to restaurants all the time. She would go see a movie after eating at a restaurant, all while spending her parents money. With the same amount of money she spent every month she could have moved out and gotten a room and started her life. She would spend hundreds a month on food yet, eat at the temple for free, crazy.

I did not want to be homeless. I went to Abena and I asked for a place to stay. In her spare room/office however, there was enough space for me to put a yoga mat and blanket. I was safe. I continued to work for a few more days but I barely made any money. Selling people "drugs" or "drug memberships" on the streets in a foreign country, with language barriers is not exactly the easiest task. It was around 2 weeks time that I bounced back and forth between hostels and Abena's place until I finally had enough money saved to find a room. I called up a few apartments and went to go see them. I entered into one apartment in El Clot, Barcelona and it was there that I met Wesley.

To this day, I am amazed at big and how small, the world truly is. Wesley was born in Haiti, raised in Guadeloupe, then lived in France, Spain and now resides in Catalonia. He went to school and studied languages. Wesley spoke Catalan,

Spanish, French, Haitian Creole and English perfectly. He also knows some Japanese and Chinese. He works as a translator for corporate projects. After talking for a few minutes, he showed me the apartment and when we were sitting in the living room he asked where I was from. I always say Los Angeles, because everyone knows where that is. Instead I said my hometown which was close by and he said his aunt lived there. He had visited a few years ago.

No fucking way. I came all the way across the world and it felt like I never left home. Amazing. We instantly connected and I said "do you consume cannabis?" hoping that I would not offend him. He responded "Yes." Boom, instant connectivity. The room was 220 euro with a 100 euro deposit. After working for a few days I had enough saved but it was literally all my money. I moved in at the end of March and I could not believe what happening. I had a place to sleep, a job, free food at the temple and after months of struggle and sleeping outside I was gaining my sanity. Hard work and a bit of luck, pays off. I should have been dead in the streets. It only took 4 months to gain a sense of stability.

I moved in all my bags and I was 45 minute walk, or a (stolen) metro ride, away from the city center. I went every day to the center, the season was just beginning and numbers were low. Recruiting was going to be difficult because I only spoke one language and there were countless other street promoters in Barcelona selling their products. I did not have nice clothing, but I did speak English, and after a few weeks of trying, I finally found a groove.

Marta came and spent the night a few times, she did not fool around, she did not want to have sex and Sant Jordi day was coming up. Cuddling, hugging, kissing, everything, was always quite awkward but I kept on being patient and nice to her. She was probably depressed and it was difficult to communicate. I really tried Marta. Sant Jordi is the Catalan version of Valentines Day. If you visit Barcelona on Sant Jordi Day, the entire city is filled with street vendors selling roses, it is beautiful. Marta planned to visit the house of her dead grandfather in Tossa De Mar for Sant Jordi. She said she would be more comfortable and maybe we could pursue something sexually. After months and months of a horrible relationship, I decided to give it one last try. She went ahead by bus a few days earlier and I was out street promoting, trying to get that money. I really debated on going to see her. It would cost me about 25 Euro for bus tickets there and back. I would have to spend money on food and knowing her, it was not going to be cheap. Also, I would spend a few days with her, meaning that I would not be working and Sant Jordi was on the 23rd and I did not want to be late on my rent payment, or have the chance of not making it. I gambled on the decision, but I figured that I deserved a chance to see a beautiful beach city in the off season and finally get out of Barcelona. I bought my ticket and took what little money I had with me and went to go see her on Sant Jordi Day.

I arrived in the little town and it was completely empty. It was still off season, quite cold and no one was there. Marta said that when I arrived she was completely surprised that I decided to come. This was not attractive, she almost sounded disappointed. What a bitch. Thanks for helping me in the beginning, but my god, what a waste of resources. I spent a few days with her, walked around the city, looked at the castles, and admired the crystal clear water. It was a beautiful place and I totally recommend going there. Tossa De Mar, Catalonia.

The entire experience was beyond awkward. At first she did not want to sleep in the same bed as me. The first night we did nothing I don't even think we kissed each other. The second night after sitting at home and watching television all day, we cooked dinner. It was Sant Jordi Day and maybe this would be the time and the place where we might actually have a sexual encounter. I lit some candles. We agreed to sleep in her parents massive king size bed with all the luxuries a doctor could have. From there, we both got naked and I felt literally no attraction to her at this point. She rolled over to me and asked in horrible English "You want to do the sex?" I stroked her hair while looking her in the eyes and said "only if you are ready" she replied "I don't know" and it was from there that I tried to cuddle with her and fall asleep. Both of us had to catch the bus home that next day and I was already planning my escape to end the relationship. I left something too close to the burning candle, it melted, fell over, and burned a horrible hole in some family heirloom. It startled both of us and I woke up naked trying to put out a small fire all while damaging her parents master suite. Never be with an indecisive person. What a waste. 29 years old, parents pay for everything and she chose to take classes in photoshop and film. Rich people wasting their opportunities.

I went to Barcelona, worked, and made some more money. I paid my rent and felt great. I had a job where I could work whenever I wanted and it paid quite well. Moving on up, as they say. After paying rent my main goal was to save as much money as possible because all good things come to an end. The police were constantly shutting down the cannabis associations. I worked everyday from 11am until 3am and hardly took a break. I was still with Marta at this point and I was holding on, because my birthday was in a few days and maybe I would get a present from her. Who knew what could happen with her spending habits. We were supposed to meet up somewhere and it required me taking the metro to see her. I traveled outside the city center to meet her. I arrived outside her place when we said we were going to meet and she was not there. Spanish time.

I called her, no response. OF COURSE. I waited a few minutes and I called her again and she said "Oh, I am sorry I am with so and so, we were talking and then we went and saw these guys at their place..." At this point, I snapped. I cursed her out on the phone and said get here, you are wasting my time. I waited another 45 minutes for her to get there. She kept saying "You are not okay, why are you so angry?" Rich people have no fucking idea what it is like to have an empty stomach.

I yelled like a child and explained to her, that she cannot waste my time anymore. I had to make money to survive. I gave her the phone she gave me and said "I don't want to be with you anymore". She makes me never want to have a relationship ever again. I could not afford to waste my time anymore, life gave me a second chance and I needed to take it. The next day was my birthday and I could not be happier. Besides, just a few days earlier, out promoting, I met a

246

man, whose character will stick with me for the rest of my life. I will not mention his real name, but Jordan Belfort came from the Wolf Pack criminal syndicate of Vancouver, Canada.

The 1st of May, I was out street promoting near midnight and I stumbled across a beautiful couple walking down Las Ramblas. She was pregnant and both were dressed in high quality street attire. I told them about the cannabis club, and with a closer glance, I noticed many diamonds around his neck infused into a dog tag and a diamond Breitling Watch around his wrist. I gave them a card, and thought nothing of it, maybe they would contact me later. Later on in the night it was maybe 1am at this time, I was walking the same path and I stumbled across them again, he said they had dinner and were interested in going tonight. They did not have their passports so they would have to go home, they invited me by taxi to the hotel. I waited in the cab with his wife, she was in her second trimester and we talked for a few minutes. Jordan came back downstairs and we proceeded to the club.

I took them to Kush, I was able to see both of their passports and identities, it took a few minutes to register, but then we went inside. I took them into the "office" and introduced them to Mark, a fellow gangster at Kush. Mark had lots of tattoos and was from Germany. He was a tough guy by any means necessary. He looked at me, looked at Jordan and all diamonds he had on and nodded back at me. Jordan however, was like a little kid in a candy store, he was looking at all the strains, waxes, pollens, etc. He was quite excited. Mark looked at me and said "shut the door", which was not normal behavior. Jordan and Mark locked eyes and Mark said "you can ask me anything you want..."

A preamble to Mark. One of the first days I worked for Kush, the receptionists introduced me to Mark and he found out I was from the United States. The first thing out of his mouth "Can you get us Guns?!? I want a rifle! They look fucking awesome" All the receptionists (sexy women from Morroco and Brazil and the Dominican Republic) said "MARK! STOP IT" he quickly apologized and we talked about guns for few minutes. I even told them I was in the Marines, from there I earned some respect.

Back to Jordan, he made his selection, then him and the wife went to enjoy the club and I recommend that the wife not consume any cannabis. Jordan was super excited at what he just found and asked me if there were more of these. He gave me an email and said we should meet up tomorrow. I agreed and we met up the next day. We linked up in the afternoon and he was all decked out in street gear, looking rich as fuck. He had a Louis Vuitton carry all and it was stuffed to the brim with 50's. Jordan probably had 15k in his bag. As we were walking to one of the associations, he took out a ten crumbled it and tossed it to a homeless man. He told me he was rich, worked construction with his family and started making good money at age 18. I took him to a sandwich shop and he explained that he had lyme disease. Different diet restrictions, no red meat, etc. We got our sandwiches, headed to an association, got him signed up, then headed towards another one. It was crazy, he paid for everything, tipped me at every place we went and we bonded quite quickly.

It was a bit later in the day and he needed to get back to his wife. He said lets meet up later, grab dinner and check out the last association. I took him to another association, then down to Port Olympic where all the fancy nightclubs were. We were walking by all the fancy waterfront seafood restaurants with all the fish available for selection and he said "You hungry? My treat." How could I say no. What an awesome person. We sat down, everything was elegant and Jordan took off his bag and coat. He said quickly, "I'm gonna go use the washroom" as he walked away from the table leaving his bag in the chair and I said "Hey man, don't you want your bag?" and he said "yeah, you never know". I could have walked away with tens of thousands of Euros, but I did not. Jordan took a very long time in the bathroom and when he came back I noticed all of the tattoos on his arms, of wolves.

Jordan did not even open the Menu. I was looking at everything and it was so expensive. Jordan said "I'll have the lobster, what do you want man? Get the lobster, it looks good." (I have never had lobster before in my life. I figured now was the time to try.) The waiter poured our drinks, water and a beer and then came back in a few minutes with a cart full of live lobsters. There were two different kinds, dark shells and rubber bands around their claws, or exotic live lobsters freshly captured. Jordan quickly told me which ones were farmed, never get the farm ones. The waiter picked up one, twirled it around and it started to flap its tail in fear of being devoured. He did the same for me and then Jordan and I continued our conversation. I honestly forget what we talked about, but it was mainly about business and I was starting to put together the pieces that Jordan was more than likely a gangster. Unbelievably genuine human being, but you could tell that there was a presence inside of him that you should not toy with.

To date, that the was best meal I ever had in my life. Hours later, the nutrients and euphoria I was feeling were almost similar to the hours after experiencing quality sex. Breathtaking.

"Lobster, now that is BRAIN food!" - Jordan

It was about midnight at this time and I had a call from some people I met earlier, while out promoting. I told Jordan I needed to get to Kush, we were done eating, just talking, shooting the shit, so we decided to leave. The bill came. The waiter left it on the table. I saw it and to date, the most expensive meal I have never paid for. Two salads, Two lobsters, Two drinks, two coffee's.

318.00 Euro

My rent at the time was 220.00 Euro. Jeezus

Jordan pulled out a roll of 50's, peeled off 350 and left them on the table. I sincerely thanked him for the meal and he said "Yeah man, no problem! I'm happy you got to try lobster". We hopped in a cab, and headed towards Kush. We decide to meet the next day. I met 3 people and made 60 euro instantly, worked a little bit more that night and made 40 more, jumped the metro and went home early.

I hung out with Jordan the next few days and he took me out for dinner for my birthday. He was 28 at the time and said "23, your Jordan year" I'm not sure if puns were intended, but Michael Jordan, nor Jordan Belfort are bad idols. I asked if we could meet up the next morning, have coffee because I wanted to explain to him the real reason why I was here. He looked at me a little funny, agreed and we met the next morning at a Starbucks next to the Catedral. I thought the entire night that Jordan was not going to show up and our relationship was over. I am not sure why I had this strange feeling, but I have always been pessimistic.

We met at Starbucks, he paid for everything and we sat down for our coffee, I asked to borrow his phone to show some articles. Jordan carried several phones (gangster) and gave me his galaxy s4. I explained my story and how I was in Barcelona looking for a way to escape, start over and begin my life. Jordan's look got a lot more aggressive and much more serious after hearing my story. The first thing he asked is "What happened to the other guy?" I told him he was in prison and would get out in over a year. Jordan said, "Let's walk and talk, I don't want to be in here". Both of us left Starbucks and we started walking down the busy streets of the Gotic quarter. Jordan came clean and told me all about his time with the Wolfpack. He was one of the biggest suppliers of Cocaine to Canada. Showed me a few articles about his gang, how they had to split up and were all over the world avoiding the police. Some guys in Europe, others South America, some Southeast Asia. His network was all over the world.

One of the things we talked about was "the game" and for those of you who do not know what "the game" is, it means the underworld. A common phrase is "I did not choose the game, the game chose me" which I believe to be true. If life gives you lemons, make lemonade. For those that are risk averse, this does not apply, but for others, nothing gets us going more than the rush of doing something new, exciting, highly profitable and illegal.

Jordan was in Europe trying to make connections and see if he could get his blow game going here. The only problem was that it was expensive and opening a business was always difficult. In the back of my mind I thought about the Sikhs, but I did not want to have any part of that type of business. He needed someone who had a business with shipping containers. Long story short, Jordan had a lot of international experience, understood port security and literally had a global network to be reckoned with. He was a deca-millionaire gangster.

Jordan explained that a majority of cocaine was entering countries not in the shipping containers themselves, but underneath the boats. Guys would come in on a submarine with welding equipment and follow cargo vessel as it left the port. They would have the cocaine stored in huge containers and as the ship was moving they would go up underneath and weld the containers onto the hull of the ship. When the ship was arriving to another to another port, in another part of the world, a second submarine would come up to the ship. They would again use welding equipment to reheat the welds which broke off and fell to the bottom a few miles offshore. Later in the week a fishing vessel with the proper gear would drag lines along the bottom and pick up the container. Large shipping companies were distributing coke all over the world and they had no idea.

He said that his crew had Russian connections and they along with other mobsters around the world had their own satellite. This enabled them communicate off the grid. He pulled out his blackberry and it was modified with a battery pack and some type of antenna. Apparently, his crew along with others in Pakistan and some cartels in South America, paid the Russians to launch a satellite and each of them had their own frequency. To build and launch a satellite was apparently around $35 million dollars. But if you are actually aware of how much criminal syndicates make, this is nothing. If you add up all the cartels in South America alone, they earn more than Google does, annually.

We hung out later that night and while we walked up La Rambla towards Plaza Catalunya talking about guns. I explained my military experience and he just casually dropped the line, "Yeah man, one time I had to kill this guy... blah blah blah, what about you? You ever get to snipe anybody? I'm sure you are better with a gun than I am" I froze and missed my step and almost tripped and said "nah man, I've never killed anybody" he replies "It's really not a big deal man, as long as you don't know the person, it's just like playing a video game". We talked about his plan for the next few days, but he said if he did not find the connect he needed, he would leave and try another part of the world.

One of the last mornings before he took off with his wife to Asia, we met up for breakfast and he said "Good morning man, how are you?" I said "I'm fine, a little tired, I did not sleep, can't stop thinking about money" His face lit up and he smiled and said "yeah man, me neither, I did not sleep at all, I"m hungry! One of my guys came through and I just made 80,000 canadian yesterday" I was amazed. I know he stressed and worked for it. OG.

It was about May 10th by now and Jordan decided that him and the wife were off to Asia to try their luck over there. Places like New Zealand were super wealthy and everything was really expensive, he thought he would have better chances. He made a promise to the wife that as soon as the baby was born, he would stop doing everything illegal and would have to settle down. These last few months were part of his final crusade. The last day before he took off, Jordan invited me to his hotel to meet with him and his wife. He called me up and said "Hey man, I bought too much stuff, we can't pack it all, I want to give you a phone, some clothes, see if some things fit, come on over."

What a generous man. Jordan gave me a samsung galaxy s4, a bag full of clothes and a few other things. He also gave me some steroids, that he had acquired and said would help me if I wanted to try em out. He left for the airport that night, we kept in contact through email and blackberry messenger for a few weeks and then I never heard from him again. What a generous man. I thank you until this day Jordan. Gangsters are not real criminals, authority is the real criminal.

"It's a numbers game, you gotta ask."
- Jordan Belfort

I never heard from Jordan again. I hope you and your new family are safe. Stay outta trouble, maybe I will see you again someday.

"Fast and Furious" by Wu-Tang Clan

Chapter 18

"The best way out, is through"

- Robert Frost

It was probably about May 10th at this time and it was at this point that I started to grind. For the past couple of months, while dating Marta, I became lazy and apathetic. She would wake up at noon every day, not have to work, dibble dabble and then go to sleep at 2am and repeat the entire process. Nothing infuriates me more than those who refuse to work. I gave Marta the opportunity, multiple times to come and work at Kush, but she said she deserves better than a job on the street. She was fat, wealthy, lazy and would never understand. She was all the motivation I needed to never have a wealthy and lazy girlfriend ever again. Wealthy yes, lazy, no.

Working and striving to achieve success is much better than having it handed to you. I look at many members of the fraternity I joined and I am truly glad that I had to earn and pay my for my life. Granted my parents helped me in a time of trouble, but they did not help me when they knew I could survive and do it on my own.

Back to work.

May, June, July, I woke up and worked almost every single day, wearing the same pair of jeans, my old military boots and a casual dress shirt. I would walk anywhere from 8 to 20km per day on the streets of Barcelona. I was determined to make my fortune, I had a new phone, barely any savings, but I was thinking if I could make at least 500 euro a month, I could cover all my expenses of living in Barcelona. May was a rough month, there were plenty of tourists, but not the right type attracted to a cannabis association. A majority of "college age" travelers were still in school. The groups that were already on vacation were the Italians and the French. Since I did not speak a word of either of those languages I suffered a great loss. I would walk the streets all day and hopefully make 20€.

There was also lots of competition in the city center. I would say between 16 and 20 associations existed within a 3km diameter in downtown Barcelona. I was working mainly with Kush adjacent to La Catedral. Yet, if i was walking around on a different side of town, perhaps more than a kilometer away from Kush, I would have a tough time convincing someone to follow me for 15 minutes across town. At night time this was exceptionally difficult because people always felt afraid after dark. All the shops on a very busy street closed at 10pm, leaving them desolate during the evening time. I would walk people down a road for 5 minutes and because the buildings in the Gotic Quarter of Barcelona were 400 years old, people would think something bad was going to happen.

As an idiot, whenever I earned money, I always saved a little, but spent a lot of money on things I did not need. I should have invested a little money in clothing, but I decided against it. I should have saved my money and not intoxicated myself, but I didn't. I did not need to go to concerts, but I did. Do I regret it. Yes. 2014 was a very dark year.

Money is literally the only tool besides human capital that humans possess. I was squandering away my funds, because I had a pessimistic outlook on life. I was homeless before, who was to say it would never happen again? I abused drugs before, were the habits going to stop now? Personal control is something that goes in waves. I am either up or I am down. I think those in the medical community call me "bi-polar". I had my thyroid checked continually all throughout university and I never showed any sign or result of a thyroid "problem". Bi-polar was the least of my worries coupled with poor nutrition, personal stress, societal stress, lack of a sex life and my current situation. I was bound to be pessimistic. It is hard to think when you have not eaten properly for months. Chemicals and their reactions comprise who we are. An imbalance of chemicals can lead to serious if not, fatal, results. I was in a situation where I did not have a support network, I had myself, that was it. Stress is the most harmful virus that we inflict upon ourselves. Tortoise or the Hare?

Nothing makes you feel more worthless than not being able to go somewhere you want to. Flights in Europe are ridiculously cheap. I could bomb over to London for 20 euro, skip to Berlin, Amsterdam, Budapest, all for less than 50 euro round trip, if only I wasn't a fuck up. It is not easy being a fuckup, walking the streets asking people to come smoke weed with you. I lived in a foreign city where you do not speak the local dialect and the job economy was one of the worst in the developed world.

Yet, at least I was not living at home off of someone else. The mentality that I found in Catalonia, was that "I have worked hard, my family has worked hard, I deserve a good job". When the reality is, "I have worked hard, my family has worked hard, there are almost no jobs available, I will live at home off of my parents and wait for the situation to become better, I do not want to go out and find a better way for myself, leaching is just fine." Disgusting.

In early September 2015 I went to a Reggae festival in the Northern Mountains of Catalonia. When I hopped on the train, I encountered a couple roughly my age, from Sant Cugat, the same wealthy village that Dagmar was from. We talked for a brief moment and then they went back about their business. We were roughly the same age, but shared some very distinct differences. First off, they were dressed as hippies, but not actually hippies. The boy had on shoes costing well over 200 Euro, hippies style clothing made from very high quality fabric, sporting a couple of instruments and had an iphone. His girlfriend was also wearing nice clothing, but it was in the "style" that hippies would wear. They were clean, they had on cologne and had a ridiculous amount of equipment for a 2 night festival. The boy said he would be performing on stage, Saturday night.

After arriving at the festival, I discovered that many of the people there, were poor hippies, this made me very happy. However, the people performing at the festival, were all rich spoiled brats from the city of Sant Cugat! They had macbooks and expensive instruments, let alone the time and initial start up money to begin producing music. I guess with all the resources gained from their parents, and the apathetic attitude to find work, they started producing horrible Catalan Reggae. Most of the performances were cover songs! Hardly any of the music was new, I am not the biggest reggae aficionado, but I had already heard more than 50% of the songs at the festival before.

Also, you would hear a "cover band" sing a song and then 2 hours later when another "cover band" was on stage, they would sing the exact same song! Ridiculous. Overall, the festival was very small not even clearing 500 people. I really enjoyed it though, especially with Wesley, he came up the second night and even got lucky with a beautiful German woman. Wesley and I were at the mainstage, vibing, enjoying the show, then the guy from the train came on stage to perform a song. He had no instruments with him, just a microphone.

He started to "sing" over a reggae beat, along with some added voice synthesizers. After about 20 seconds, Wesley and I looked at each other in disgust and started laughing. HE WAS HORRIBLE, off beat, out of tune, no amount of technology could save this man. I said "we should stay, maybe it gets better". Nope. The crowd started walking away towards the other stage. By the time his ONLY song was over, there were less than 20 people in front of the stage. He got down off the stage with a look of accomplishment, met his girlfriend and they shared a kiss. It was one of the worst things I had ever heard in my life, let alone, the worst live performance outside of children's choir. I really wanted to go and tell him that he did a horrible job, but I decided that nobody wants bad energy at a festival. No need to hate. Yet, I am very against promoting bad habits, and his musical career is something that hopefully he can overcome in this lifetime.

Because of poor spending habits, I was close to not making rent for the month of June. To try and make some extra cash, I decided to sell MDMA to tourists. Half of the tourists that came to the association were asking me for it anyways so I decided to go for it. I had about 500 euro saved up and because of the Sikhs, I knew I could get everything for cheap. I bought ten grams for 250 Euro but did a few of them myself because of my lack of foresight. MDMA also has a wicked hangover, so if I did MDMA on Friday night, I would not be able to work until Monday morning, coupled with the abuse of the previous year, I was on a highway to hell.

I went through a binge and on one of the come downs with less than 200 euro in my pocket and rent (220) due soon, I contemplated suicide. Looking back on it, it was definitely the drugs talking. I was at home thinking of ways to kill myself when I noticed a small pouch on the bookshelf of Wesleys Flat. Curious as to what was inside I opened the pouch and inside I found an identity card and a bunch of credit cards of a man from the Netherlands, it also contained a motorcycle license. I quickly snapped out of my suicidal thoughts and realized that owning a motorcycle will probably be one of the greatest thrills of my life and I should work towards that freedom. Since then, I have never abused drugs or alcohol. I have gotten drunk, and used other drugs, but never abused them to the point that I would ever inflict harm on myself or another person. I grew up, at least a little bit. January 2016 I became completely sober.

I pulled myself together and went out that day and asked my boss Baba, for a loan of 200 Euro to help pay my rent, I was always good money to him and he did it without hesitation. I felt comfortable, I went out that day and made 300 Euro or so, paid back my debt the same day and had a new level of motivation for the rest of the summer. July I killed it, I saved over 500 euro.

After Jordan gave me a smartphone, I had it for about a month and then went in debt with the Sikhs to try and make some extra money, eventually I gave up the smartphone Jordan gave me to settle my debt with the Sikhs. As Jagsher once said "Never trust an Indian person". The month of June holds the music festival SONAR. SONAR attracts dozens of different artists from around the world and is also a technology expo. I was offered a very good price by the sikhs for mdma and blow. I was short on money and decided that I should sell during the festival and potentially get people to come to Kush afterwards. Over the course of the weekend, I sold nearly 1800 Euro worth of MDMA. Most of it was hardly at a profit because Spain is not the wealthiest of countries. Yet, after all the trouble of going to each and every part of the festival, paying the entrance tickets, food, transportation, consuming drugs myself. I ended up making a whopping 50€ profit. It was a great weekend. But not worth the stress and the hassle. Oh well, at least the festival paid for itself. I did a lot of work to "enjoy" that weekend.

The first day of the festival I ran into Vish, a medical student from the United Kingdom, who happened to be of Indian descent. He ended up coming to Kush, he reminded me a lot of Gibrarian. Kudo's to both of you and I hope that you are both well on your way to becoming "confident, personable (reliable) medical professionals".

I worked for another month into July and then all of a sudden, my life changed forever. I mentioned Wesley earlier, but my other roommate at the time was named Tomi. Tomi was from France, he had lived in Spain for almost 5 years and was more or less a local of Barcelona. I woke up one morning and Tomi had already left for work, as I wandered around the apartment, I noticed that his keys were on the dining room table. (Tomi forgot his keys again, I thought) It was not uncommon for Tomi to forget his keys. I wrote him a message and it was Friday so I knew he would not be home until late. I went about my day and promoted Kush. I made a few sales and by the end of the night I was exhausted. It was probably 2am on Friday night and just as everyone was going out, I wanted to catch some sleep and work a full day tomorrow. Just as I was about to step on the metro, my phone rings. (Hello? ACCCEEEEEE, ITS Tomi, where are you man? Do you have my keys? I forgot them at home!)

I was so close to going home and getting some sleep after a 12 hour day. Tomi was my roommate and not having keys might as well make you homeless. I did not want anyone to feel homeless so I decided to meet up with him and some of his friends. We meet up on La Rambla, outside of the Mcdonalds (American Embassy) and he was noticeably drunk but his eyes were dilated more than usually.

"We took some MDMA!" Tomi greeted me. I could not help but smile, I was sober, but it was nice to enjoy Tomi, he was quite the social butterfly. We start foraging about the night hopping from one bar to another, and eventually it was 5:30 in the morning. Tomi received a call from one of his friends Vincent and we were invited to his house for wine. It was probably 6am and we arrived at Vincent's Flat. Vincent was German, but lived in Barcelona for many years. He shared a flat with a few other people and lived with his girlfriend Vivian. Vivian was from Brazil but lived in Barcelona for 15 years. She loved Europe and in my opinion is very, very attractive.

First things first, I was greeted with cocaine and a nice glass of wine. Both Vincent and Vivian were experts of wine and their wine fridge was bigger than their regular fridge. They gave me my first wine class and explained many things that I had no idea about. It was interesting, and I learned a few party tricks. After a few lines, and a few more drinks, it was 10am and Tomi and I were exhausted. Vivian and I were talking about my situation in Barcelona. I explained that I was here illegally and she said she really liked my personality. Right there on the spot, she offered me a job with a company called HostelCulture. I was going to be a tour guide in Barcelona. I could almost not believe what I was hearing. She asked me "do you have whatsapp?" I held up my simple burner phone. "I have a blackberry, hang on" and then gave me a fully functioning blackberry to use. I would start training in a few weeks.

We decided to leave around 10am and thought it would be best to walk and sweat out the night before. As we approached the house after nearly 45 minutes of walking, I pulled out the copy of Tomi's keys and handed them to him. We drank some water, smoked a joint and slept the rest of the day. Barcelona was slowly turning into a blessing.